Stalking
the Wild
Asparagus

by EUELL GIBBONS

with illustrations by

MARGARET F. SCHROEDER

Including a remembrance
of the author by

JOHN MCPHEE

Alan C. Hood & Company, Inc.
Guilford, Connecticut

To my mother

LAURA BOWERS GIBBONS

who first introduced me to wild food, who gave me the love of nature that has been the chief interest of my life, and who, at seventy-five years of age, is still a good foraging companion, this book is affectionately dedicated.

Stalking the Wild Asparagus
Copyright © 1962 by Euell Gibbons

Distributed by NATIONAL BOOK NETWORK

Library of Congress Cataloging-in-Publication Data

Gibbons, Euell.

    Stalking the wild asparagus. Includes index.
    1. Wild plants, Edible-United States.
2. Wild plants, Edible-Canada. 3. Cookery (Wild foods) I. Schroeder, Margaret.
11. McPhee, John A. 111. Title.
QK98.5.U6G52 1987 581.6'32 87-16933
ISBN 978-0-911469-03-5

Published by Alan C. Hood & Company, Inc., Guilford, CT

PUBLISHER'S NOTE

Euell Gibbons was fifty-one years old when David McKay Company published his first book, *Stalking the Wild Asparagus,* in the spring of 1962.

Gibbons had lived an unsettled life until then. Born in Red River County, Texas, he had made a living in various ways—as a cowboy, hobo, carpenter, surveyor, boat builder, beachcomber, newspaperman, farmer and teacher, living here and there around the country—California, Washington, Hawaii, New Jersey and Indiana, finally settling in rural Pennsylvania. At midlife, Gibbons considered himself a failure.

Gibbons was wrong.

Euell Gibbons had been fascinated with nature all of his life. As a boy he literally saved the lives of his family by providing them with wild foods that he had gathered. *Stalking the Wild Asparagus* was one of the first books to draw to the attention of American readers the importance of natural food and environmental preservation. It was widely acclaimed by book reviewers and food writers. Each year it sold better than the year before. When I arrived at the David McKay Company in 1969, *Stalking the Wild Asparagus* was a crown jewel of the backlist along with its companion volumes, *Stalking the Blue-Eyed Scallop* (1964) and *Stalking the Healthful Herbs* (1966). When I received word that McKay had allowed the "Stalking" books to go out-of-print in 1987, I approached Gibbons' widow, Freda Gibbons, and she graciously acquiesced to my proposal to continue publishing her husband's books. These titles became the backbone of my publishing program.

Those who wish to learn more about Euell Gibbons might begin by reading John McPhee's masterful account of his camping trip with Gibbons in 1967. This was originally published in *The New Yorker* magazine in 1968 and subsequently included in McPhee's book *A Roomful of Hovings* (Farrar, Straus & Giroux). There is considerable information in Wikipedia including several biographies and detailed bibliographies. Euell Gibbons' papers now reside in the Howard Gotlieb Archival Research Center at Boston University.

It is with the greatest pleasure that I observe the fiftieth anniversary of the original publication of *Stalking the Wild Asparagus.*

Alan C. Hood

*Stalking
the Wild
Asparagus*

Acknowledgments

IN the many years that I have been gathering wild food as a hobby, I have consulted numerous books, references, bulletins and articles by many authors. If I refrain from mentioning these by name, it is only because I fear that my faulty memory will cause me to omit some of those to whom I am most deeply indebted. To all these unnamed writings and their authors, I am most grateful.

Among the people who personally helped to gather the material for this book, I wish especially to thank that excellent botanist and wild food expert, Dr. Fred Irvine, presently Professor of Tropical Agriculture at the University of Ghana, who during his year as a Visiting Fellow at Pendle Hill School in Wallingford, Pennsylvania, was often my companion on nature walks and taught me much that I now pass on to you in these pages.

Many others have contributed, for, although a single author's name appears on the title page, a book is nearly always the result of a group effort. Among those who have helped are Mavis McIntosh, literary agent, without whose advice and encouragement this book would never have been started; Joseph Carter, chemist, who made assays and tests on tree saps and other wild food material; Dr. Edward J. Alexander, of Brooklyn Botanical Gardens, who checked the first draft of the manuscript for botanical accuracy. (There has been much added and changed since his examination of the material, and any mistakes you may find are mine, not his.) Margaret Schroeder deserves mention not only for the beautiful line drawings of plants which illustrate this book, but also because she helped me in collecting and trying as food many of the plants mentioned. Richard White drew the picture and diagram of the drip still on page 286.

Then there is Eleanor Rawson, the associate editor at the David McKay Company, whose advice and suggestions eliminated much awkward writing from these pages; Steve and Kay Lee, dear friends and good foraging companions, who helped with the field and kitchen research, and with the proofreading, and there are also their three charming young daughters, Eileen, Toni and Carol who are the most enthusiastic and trusting tasters of wild food dishes that I know.

I feel indebted to Wanda Slayton and Betty Pennock, both of whom corrected and typed parts of the manuscript; and to Laurie Andersen and Richard Downham, good friends who ate many wild food dishes at my table and helped me with frank criticism and encouraging compliments.

Finally there is my wife, Freda Gibbons, who had to put up with having strange roots, bulbs, stems, fruits, seeds and leaves all over her house. She willingly sampled many a nauseous mess as I experimented with new plants and new dishes. It was only because she was willing to work to supplement our income that I could find the time and leisure I needed to compile and write this book. To her and to all others, mentioned and unmentioned, who helped make this book a reality, I am profoundly grateful.

Contents

A Remembrance of Euell Gibbons *by John McPhee*   xi

Some Thoughts on Wild Food   1
The Acorn: ANCIENT FOOD OF MAN   10
The Green Amaranth: INVADER FROM THE TROPICS   14
Wild Apples and Crab Apples   17
Arrowhead or Wapatoo: FAVORITE FOOD PLANT OF AMERICAN
    INDIANS   21
The Jerusalem Artichoke   25
Stalking the Wild Asparagus   28
The Sweet Birch   32
Blackberries and Dewberries   36
The Huckleberry and Blueberry Tribes   39
Great Burdock or Wild Gobo   46
Calamus: CONFECTION, CURE-ALL AND SALAD PLANT   50
Supermarket of the Swamps: THE COMMON CATTAIL   55
Wild Cherries   61
Eat Your Chickory and Drink It Too   69
Wild Cranberries   73
The Official Remedy for Disorders   77
New Food from a Familiar Flower   83
A Salute to the Elderberry: WITH A NOD TO SCARLET SUMAC 87
Using Wild Grapes   96

ix

Ground Cherries for Pies and Preserves   102
The Groundnut or Indian Potato   106
Japanese Knotweed: A COMBINATION FRUIT-VEGETABLE   109
Juneberries, Shadberries or Serviceberries   114
Sweets from Trees   117
May Apple, or American Mandrake   126
The Common Milkweed   130
Mulberries: RED AND WHITE   134
The Cult of the Mycophagists   139
Wild Mustard: NATURE'S FINEST HEALTH FOOD   152
The Wild Onion Family   157
The Pawpaw: A TROPICAL FRUIT COME NORTH   161
The Sugar-Plum Tree: PERSIMMON   164
Beating the Pigs to the Pigweeds   170
Poke: WILD POTHERB PAR EXCELLENCE   174
Purslane: INDIA'S GIFT TO THE WORLD   178
Raspberries and Wineberries   183
The Sassafras for Food and Drink   187
Economics of Wild Strawberries   194
The Spring Beauty or Fairy Spuds   201
The Common Sunflower   204
Wildwood Teas   208
Walnuts and Hickory Nuts   213
The Nose Twister: KING OF WILD SALAD PLANTS   219
Wild Rice: EPICUREAN DELIGHT   223
Winter Cress: THE FIRST WITH THE MOST   226
A Wild Winter Garden in Your Cellar   231
Wild Honey   235
How About the Meat Course   242
Spinning for Bluegills   249
How to Cook a Carp   256
The Crayfish: A REAL LUXURY FOOD   260
On Eating Frog's Legs   265
Turtles and Terrapins   268
Herbal Medicine from Wild Plants   272
The Proof of the Pudding   289
Index   297

A Remembrance of
Euell Gibbons

BY JOHN McPHEE

In 1967, I made a trip with Euell Gibbons, partly by canoe, partly with backpacks, on the Susquehanna River and the Appalachian Trail. The provisions we started off with included no food, except some black walnuts and some hickory nuts. We were gone a week, and what we lived on was Euell's expertise, his extraordinary knowledge of edible wild plants. We killed neither game nor fish. Instead, we ate the riverbank and drank its teas—dock, burdock, chicory, chickweed, winter cress, sheep sorrel, peppergrass, catnip, oyster mushrooms, groundnuts, spearmint, pennyroyal—none of which I would have recognized or known how to prepare.

Euell had not wanted to travel in such chill weather (it was mid-November), and I, eager to tell the story and counting on luck to restrain the clouds, had all but dragged him to the river. As he warmed to the journey bobbing down rips between the gaps in the mountains, he would repeat, from time to time, with mild surprise, "Well, we're not suffering like the early Christians."

And indeed we were not, for his eyes kept sorting the terrain around us, and when something arrested his attention, as it often did, we would head for the shore to forage. Along the way, he told me about his experiences from childhood onward, with an ungilded honesty, trusting, straightforward. He seemed to be struggling, as he talked, not so much to be candid before me as to be uncompromisingly honest with himself.

Euell had begun learning about wild and edible vegetation when he was a small boy in the Red River Valley. Later, in the Dust-Bowl era, his family moved to central New Mexico. They lived in a semi-dugout and almost starved there. His father left in a desperate search for work. The food supply diminished until all that was left were a few pinto beans and a single egg, which no one would eat. Euell, then teen-aged and one of four children, took a knapsack one morning and left for the horizon mountains. He came back with puffball mushrooms, piñon nuts, and fruits of the yellow prickly pear. For nearly a month, the family lived wholly on what he provided, and he saved their lives. "Wild food has meant different things to me at different times," he said to me once. "Right then it was a means of salvation, a way to keep from dying."

In years that followed, Euell worked as a cowboy. He pulled cotton. He was for a long time a hobo. He worked in a shipyard. He combed beaches. The longest period during which he lived almost exclusively on wild food was five years. All the while, across decades, he wished to be a writer. He produced long pieces of fiction, and he had no luck.

Discouragement seemed to come to him with inordinate frequency, so he was not surprised. He passed the age of fifty with virtually nothing published. He saw himself as a total failure, and he had no difficulty discerning that others tended to agree. Finally, after listening to the advice of a literary agent, he sat down to try to combine his interests. He knew his subject first- and second-hand; he knew it backward to the botanies of the tribes. And now he told everybody else how to gather and prepare wild food. From the Red River Valley to the mountains of Pennsylvania (where he would spend his last years) he took us all over North America to places few people knew in the way he saw them, and he showed what provender was there. He called his first book "Stalking the Wild Asparagus." It became a part of the beginnings of the ecological uplift, and it sold well enough to get onto the best-seller lists. In each succeeding year, it sold more copies than it had the year before.

While adults read his books, he reached out to children. By the schoolroomful, he would literally lasso them—exhibiting a once-necessary skill—and he would drag them off to a stream valley to learn to fish and to forage. He was a magnet, for a time, to my children. On Cumberland Island, off the coast of Georgia, he once dug a great pit in the sand, filled it with seaweed and fire-hot bricks, set in there a feral hog (which he had dressed and wrapped in burlap), and covered it over with sand. Drawing on his many years in the Hawaiian Islands, he was attempting a transplanted luau. Up from the earth came scents of fresh ham. People gathered. Ignoring timber rattlers, Euell hacked his way through a palmetto stand to garnish the feast with hearts of palm. The results were all he wanted. The children will never forget it. Nor will certain natives of Cumberland Island, who remember Euell Gibbons as "the one who ruined the pig."

Be that as it may, Euell Gibbons was alone in the extent to which he advanced a special skill. He was a man who knew the wild in a way that no one else in this time has even marginally approached. Having brought his knowledge to print, he died the writer he wished to be.

John McPhee's book "A Roomful of Hovings" (Farrar, Straus & Giroux) contains his profile of Euell Gibbons, which was first published in The New Yorker *magazine in 1968.*

*Stalking
the Wild
Asparagus*

Some Thoughts on Wild Food

WHY bother with wild food plants in a country which produces a surplus of many domestic food products? With as much reason, one might ask, why go fishing for mountain trout when codfish fillets are for sale in any supermarket? Or why bother with hunting and game cookery when unlimited quantities of fine meat can be purchased at every butcher counter?

Why do millions of Americans desert their comfortable and convenient apartments and split-level houses for a time each year to go camping under comparatively primitive conditions in our forests and national parks? For that matter, why does anyone go for a walk on a woodland trail when one could be speeding along a superhighway in a high-powered automobile?

We live in a vastly complex society which has been able to provide us with a multitude of material things, and this is good, but people are beginning to suspect that we have paid a high spiritual price for our plenty. Each person would like to feel that he is an entity, a separate individual capable of independent existence, and this is hard to believe when everything that we eat, wear, live in, drive, use or handle has required the cooperative effort of literally millions of people to produce, process, transport, and, eventually, distribute to our hands. Man simply must feel that he is more than a mere mechanical part in this intricately interdependent industrial system. We enjoy the comfort and plenty which this highly organized production and distribution has brought us, but don't we sometimes feel that we are living a secondhand sort of existence, and that we are in danger of losing all contact with the origins of life and the nature which nourishes it?

Fortunately, there is a saving streak of the primitive in all of us. Every man secretly believes that if he were an Adam, set down in a virgin world, he would not only be able to survive but could also provide well for his Eve and any number of little Cains and Abels. Who has not dreamed of escaping the increasing complexities and frustrations of modern life by running off to some South Sea isle and living on coconuts, fish and breadfruit?

I have tried the lotus-eating life of a Pacific beachcomber and found it lacking. I'm sure it will surprise many when I assert that it is easier to "go native" in many sections of the United States than in the South Seas. There are thousands of spots in this country where, with the requisite knowledge, a man could live solely on the bounty of nature far more easily than on any Pacific island I know. With the judicious, if incongruous, use of a home freezer, he could stay fat the year around by "reaping where he did not sow."

Probably very few of us will ever be faced with the necessity of living off the country for any extended period of time. The outdoor skills, necessary to the survival of our ancestors, are now utilized in the service of recreation. In recent years there has been a great renewal of interest in hunting, fishing and camping. I do not consider this a deplorable atavism, but a creative protest against the artificiality of our daily lives. A knowledge of wild food gathering can contribute greatly to our enjoyment of this back-to-nature movement. It can add new meaning to every camping trip, to every hike or even to a Sunday drive in the country. It involves no dangerous or expensive equipment and is an activity that can be shared by the whole family. Even those too gentle or too squeamish to kill and dress game or fish can enjoy gathering and preparing wild plant food for the camp table. Those who remember when they packed a picnic lunch and went out for a day's berrying or nutting will never deny the possibilities of wild food gathering as a family recreation.

Children, especially, are intrigued with the idea of garnering their food from the fields and byways. The child's unspoiled sense of wonder is excited when he discovers the possibility of living, at least in part, as our more primitive forebears did. His enjoyment and appreciation of nature are vastly increased when he knows her secrets and how she can minister to his needs. I have seen several feeding problems cured merely by interesting the child in the gathering and preparation of wild food plants. Food takes on a new meaning to the child who has participated in this fundamental method of acquiring it. Children who have the opportunity of sharing this fascinating hobby with an interested family for only a single season will learn a great deal more about the basic processes of nature than many years of classroom instruction can teach them.

Another point in favor of foraging as a family hobby is the handiness with which it can be practiced. One doesn't need to go to the mountains or virgin forests to find wild food plants. In fact, mountains and dense forests are among the poorer places to look. Abandoned farmsteads, old fields, fence rows, burned-off areas, roadsides, along streams, woodlots, around farm ponds, swampy areas and even vacant lots are the finest foraging sites.

I have lived at my present address for only a few months and I am not as familiar with the area as I would like to be. But, just for fun and to escape from the typewriter for a while, I interrupted this writing to take my notebook and go for an hour's walk. Without going more than a half mile from the house, I saw, identified and recorded more than sixty species of plants good for human food and several of these had more than one edible part.

A look at this list tells me that I could gather edible fruits, nuts, leaves, buds, blossoms, sprouts, stems, sap, grain, roots, tubers, bulbs and seeds. I could prepare salads, vegetables in all shapes, forms and colors, root vegetables, starchy vegetables, high-protein vegetables, cereals, breadstuffs, beverages, condiments, sugar, desserts, pickles, jams, jellies and preserves from the plants growing in the small area I covered on my walk. Many of these raw materials were present in great quantities. One could forage all the vegetable food a family could use in a season from these few acres and never have the same menu twice.

Of course, not all the plants I saw were in the edible stage when I observed them in early June. However, about half of them were offering nutritious and palatable food right then, and all the rest were fairly shouting promises of plenty to come to anyone who understood their language.

Some might contend that I live in an especially favored locality, but this is not true. Come with me for an hour's walk in almost any rural or suburban area in the eastern half of our country, and I will point out as many edible wild plants to you, though not necessarily the same ones. I have collected fifteen species that could be used for food on a vacant lot right in Chicago. Eighteen different kinds were pointed out in the circuit of a two-acre pond near Philadelphia. We actually gathered—and later ate—eleven different kinds of wild food, in an afternoon spent strolling along Chesapeake Bay. The hunter or fisherman may often come home empty-handed, but the forager, although he may fail to find the particular plant he is seeking, can always load his knapsack with wholesome and palatable food. The species of plants which the forager finds will change as the seasons advance, but the fields and forests can always furnish something good to eat.

The fact that this food costs nothing but the labor of gathering and preparing it will appeal to many. There is seldom a day in the year when wild food, in one form or another, does not grace our table, and I must admit that it helps to keep our budget within the bounds imposed by the income of a free-lance writer, but that is not the primary reason I seek it. Foraging to me, is a sport, a hobby and my chief source of recreation. One must approach wild food with the right attitude, both in the woods and on the table. Don't try it solely as a means of economizing on food bills, when you hate the necessity for being economical. Unless you approach wild food with genuine interest and love, you will never become a skilled forager. If you dislike the activity of gathering and preparing these natural dainties, you will end up with an unpleasant-tasting mess that will satisfy only half your hunger.

There are a number of wild plants that are cooked and served like asparagus, some starchy roots and tubers that are cooked like potatoes, and many green vegetables that are prepared in the same manner as spinach. Don't make the error of thinking of these foods as *substitutes* for asparagus, potatoes and spinach, or you will fail to appreciate them for their own very real merits. Each species has a flavor, aroma and texture all its own, and is a good food in and of itself and doesn't have to pose as a substitute for something else.

Learn to appreciate new flavors. Relegating good food to the category of "an acquired taste" and refusing to eat it for this reason is reactionary. All tastes are acquired tastes, as is easily seen when one examines the bills of fare of populations in different parts of the world. We are not born with a preference for any food except human milk, and, since this product hardly figures in the diet of adults, we have had to learn to like all that we eat. When one says, in effect, that he will refuse to touch any food for which he did not acquire a taste in early childhood, he is showing symptoms of mental and emotional hardening of the arteries.

I consider the mango and the papaya two of the most delectable fruits with which God graced an already bountiful world. Yet, when I was in the tropics, I saw tourists from temperate regions refuse mangoes because they didn't taste like peaches, and show disgust at papayas because they thought they should taste just like muskmelons and didn't. Such people have my pity, but hardly my respect.

Many of the staple foods we eat today, and even some that we consider luxurious dainties, were once refused on the grounds of prejudice. Wild rice was considered very poor fare as long as it was thought of as a substitute for the polished product of cultivated fields and processing plants. Yet today if you tried to buy any sizable amount of wild rice, you would probably have to make some arrangement with a finance company. One of the earliest reports on maple sugar as made by the Indians, written about 1700, says that the sugar "lacks the pleasing, delicate taste of cane sugar." Now we meekly pay many times the price of cane sugar for this finest of sweets.

Some readers will claim that they prefer to buy their fruit and vegetables from a supermarket for reasons of sanitation and cleanliness. This is the most illogical prejudice of all, as is easily demonstrated. The devitalized and days-old produce usually found on your grocer's shelves has been raised in ordinary dirt, manured with God-knows-what, and sprayed with poisons a list of which would read like a textbook on toxicology. They were harvested by migrant workers who could be suffering from any number of obnoxious diseases, handled by processors and salespeople and picked over by hordes of customers before you bought them.

By contrast, wild food grows in the clean, uncultivated fields and woods, and has never been touched by human hands until you come along to claim it. No artificial manures, with their possible sources of pollution, have ever been placed around it. Nature's own methods have maintained the fertility that produced it and no poisonous sprays have ever come near it. Wild food is clean because it has never been dirty. You'll have to find a better argument than the one on sanitation before you persuade me that I shouldn't eat wild foods, for, in the matter of cleanliness, wild products are so far ahead of those that are sold for a profit as not to be within speaking distance.

But doesn't it take a great deal of specialized knowledge in order to recognize the wild plants that are good for food, and isn't that knowledge hard to acquire? Did you ever stop to think how much specialized knowledge and fine discrimination are required in order to tell a head of cabbage from a head of lettuce on a grocer's shelf? How would you describe the difference, so someone who had never seen either could be certain what he is getting? Or how would you go about telling someone the difference between Swiss chard, beet tops, spinach and turnip greens? Yet most of us are not aware of ever having made an effort to learn to discriminate between the common vegetables. We recognize them intuitively, just as we do other familiar things. The same thing becomes true of wild food plants after a short acquaintance.

But isn't there danger of eating a poisonous plant by mistake? A person could get poisoned in his own vegetable garden if he didn't know poison hemlock from parsley. The fields and woods are not nearly so full of poisonous plants as the average city dweller seems to think. True, a person who can't tell the difference between poison ivy and a wild grapevine has no business trying to gather wild food, unless he is accompanied by someone who knows considerably more than he does; just as a person who can't tell one vegetable from another has no business shopping alone, but one is no harder to learn than the other. A forager doesn't have to be a graduate botanist. You don't have to be able to call every plant in the woods by its Latin name before you are ready to begin. As soon as you can be sure that you recognize a single edible specimen, you are ready to start gathering food.

Right here, let me allay any fear that an increase in interest in wild food would result in the depletion or extinction of any of our valuable wild plant life. This mistaken idea arises from the outmoded conception of conservation as nonuse. In the past half century we have witnessed a great upsurge of interest in hunting, but far from leading to a depletion of wild life, this has resulted in the adoption of conservation measures which have led to tremendously increased supplies of available game. Similarly, a genuine interest in wild food plants would lead to conservation measures and extension of areas where these plants grow, while protection and propagation would lead to increased supplies.

Adventurous epicures can expect to find flavors and textures in wild foods that can't be obtained elsewhere. Here are new gustatory thrills that can't be purchased at a restaurant or food market. Some will think that wild food just can't be as good as I say it is. I don't expect everyone to be delighted with every dish I describe; tastes differ, and *de gustibus non est disputandum,* but give each plant an honest trial before passing judgment.

There are many wild plants reported in the literature to be edible that I don't like at all. In research for this book I tried several hundred different kinds of plants, and disliked most of them. But a number proved to furnish superior food, worthy of inclusion in the most refined diet. These are the plants included in this book with methods of preparing them that I have either evolved or tested in my own kitchen. Many of the recipes presented here were preceded by uncounted failures before I came up with a dish that I thought worthy to pass on to my readers. The reason I say that these dishes are delicious is because I have found them so.

However, the goodness of many of these plants is not so intrinsic as to be independent of the cook's skill. As you will see in the articles on certain individual plants, some require special treatment and skillful preparation to make them acceptable to a discriminating taste. If you are unwilling to take the extra time and trouble required to make these plants into something really edible, then I would advise that you pass on to the more easily prepared kinds.

Wild food is used at our house in a unique method of entertaining. Our "wild parties," which are dinners where the chief component of every dish is some foraged food, have achieved a local fame. Many different meals can be prepared almost wholly from wild food without serving anything that will be refused by the most finicky guest. Such dinners are remembered and talked about long after the most delicious of conventional dinners have been forgotten.

Guests are invariably surprised to discover that wild plants can be transformed into such agreeable fare. There is no difficulty about maintaining interesting discussion at a meal where every dish is a conversation piece. The guests always want a list of the strange foods they have enjoyed so they can tell their friends about this unusual experience, so I now make up souvenir menus which they can take home. Here are some examples of dinners that have been served to guests in our house.

One, served in April, started off with a Wild Leek Soup served in individual ramekins. Our salad was made of blanched crowns of chicory, young sprouts of day lilies and the tender, inner portions of calamus stalks, served with a French dressing, to which a bare hint of wild garlic had been added. The main dish was Crayfish Tails Tempura, with a sour-cream sauce containing the tenderest, inner portions of green wild onions. For vegetables we had Buttered Poke Sprouts and Boiled Dandelion Crowns. Hot biscuits, made of Cattail Root Flour, were served with Chokecherry Jelly from our jam cupboard. Dessert was Japanese Knotweed Pie and for a beverage we had Sassafras Tea. The meal was ended by nibbling on bits of Preserved Wild Ginger.

Another meal, served in July, started off with a glass of mixed wild fruit juices and Snapping-Turtle Soup. Then came Chicken-fried Frog's Legs and a Water Cress Salad. The vegetables were Boiled Day-Lily Buds and Cattail Bloom Spikes in melted butter. There were golden muffins of cattail pollen spread with Wild Strawberry Jam. For dessert, we ate Blackberry Cobbler from fresh-picked fruit, drank Dandelion Coffee, then finished with little slices of Candied Calamus Root.

An autumn menu started off with Wild Grape Juice and Wild Mushroom (Shaggy-Mane) Soup. This was followed by Bluegill Fillets, battered and fried, and a salad made of sliced wild Jerusalem artichoke tubers and ripe ground cherries, served with a garlic-bleu-cheese dressing. There were Baked Arrowhead Tubers and wild apples, sliced and cooked with butter and brown sugar until they were nearly caramelized. We had dark muffins of lamb's-quarters seed, freshly ground, and amber May-Apple Marmalade. For dessert there was a mile-high Persimmon-Hickory-Nut Chiffon Pie and Chicory Coffee, followed by a bowl of mixed wild nuts for any who still had a vacant cranny to fill.

I know of no other outdoor sport which can furnish me with as much pleasure as foraging wild food which can be made into exquisite dishes to share with family and friends. If your interest has been aroused, then let me welcome you into the growing army of neoprimitive food gatherers who are finding new fascination and meaning in America's great outdoors.

This book makes no pretense of being an exhaustive treatise on this subject. Among the quarter million described species of plants in the world there are thousands that would be a possible source of human food. I have purposely excluded many of these because of their rarity or limited range, or because they were so unpalatable that one would only eat them as an alternative to starvation. However, there are many perfectly good foods to be found in the wilds that you will not find mentioned here, simply because I have had no experience with them and therefore did not feel that I could add anything significant to the excellent literature that already exists in this field. If your favorite wild food has been ignored in these pages, forgive me. Maybe we can meet some day and exchange information and recipes to the mutual benefit of both of us.

The Acorn: ANCIENT FOOD OF MAN

(*Quercus* species)

MANY of the sweet acorns borne by the White Oak group are not at all unpleasant eaten raw. Roasted acorns easily compete with roasted chestnuts in some parts of Spain, Portugal and North Africa. To primitive man in Europe, Asia and America, acorns were often the "staff of life." If we consider the whole sweep of his existence on earth, it seems likely that mankind has consumed many millions of tons more of acorns than he has of the cereal grains, which made their appearance only during the comparatively recent development of agriculture. It seems a pity that the food which nourished the childhood of our race is today nearly everywhere neglected and despised.

America is blessed with a great many species of oak, and many kinds of acorns were highly appreciated by our Indian predecessors. Our oaks can be very roughly divided into two kinds: (1) those with bristles at the tips and lobes of the leaves, taking two years to mature a crop of acorns, and (2) those without bristly terminal points on the leaves and maturing a crop of more or less edible acorns in a single year. Examples of the former class are the Red, Black and Willow oaks, and of the latter, White, Post and Chestnut oaks.

Primitive man everywhere preferred the sweet acorns when he could get them, but he never refused to gather and use even the bitterest kinds. The bitter and astringent qualities, when present, are due to tannin, which is a substance readily soluble in water, and therefore easily leached out by any one of several simple processes, leaving a sweet, nut-flavored product which can be prepared in a number of palatable ways.

I was a member of a party of six in the mountains of central Pennsylvania one autumn when the chestnut oaks, *Quercus Muhlenbergii*, had borne an extra heavy crop of acorns. We easily gathered a bushel in an hour. All of us tried them raw, and three members of

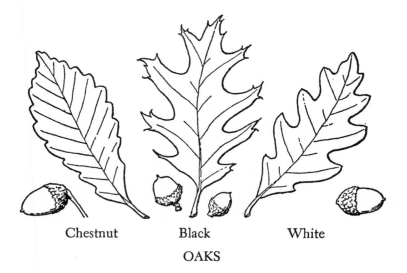

Chestnut   Black   White

OAKS

the party liked them well enough to eat several. I thought them considerably improved when we roasted some in the oven of the wood stove that heated the cabin in which we were staying. This experience convinced me that even unleached acorns of some species are worth the attention of anyone who is really hungry.

We shelled out a number of the acorns and boiled the kernels whole for two hours, changing the water every time it became tea-colored. We kept a large kettle of fresh water boiling on the stove and used this for replacements, so the boiling was hardly interrupted by the water changes. The acorn meats turned a dark chocolate brown and were without a trace of their former bitterness and astringency

When they were roasted, or, more accurately, dried out, in a slow oven, they were enjoyed by every member of the group. I dipped some of the boiled and dried acorns in clarified sugar, in the same manner that the French prepare *marrons glacés* from chestnuts, and after that the job of getting the party to eat acorns was replaced with the task of keeping enough candied acorns on hand. The extra sugar in the sirup was welcome, for much of the natural sugar in the acorn dissolves out during the leaching process.

I have since developed two standard materials from acorns to use in cooking. I call these Acorn Grits and Acorn Meal, and neither is very difficult to prepare.

Acorn Grits are made of shelled-out acorn kernels, boiled for two hours, with several changes of water, as described above, then thoroughly dried in a slow oven and ground rather coarsely. I often use Acorn Grits when a recipe calls for chopped nuts and find them very satisfactory.

Acorn Meal is made by grinding dry, raw acorn kernels, mixing the meal with boiling water and pressing out the liquid through a jelly bag. This process might have to be repeated several times with very bitter acorns. Then the meal is spread thinly in shallow pans and dried in the sun or in a very slow oven. It ordinarily becomes partly caked during this process so it must be reground, this time using the finest plate on your food chopper, or a hand gristmill, set very closely. Both the meal and the grits can be stored in sealed glass jars, where they seem to keep indefinitely.

Both Acorn Grits and Meal are very dark-colored with a sweet, nutlike flavor that nearly everyone enjoys. A lighter colored meal can be made with cold-water leaching. Use a tall can, such as those in which fruit juice is ordinarily sold, and punch the bottom full of holes with a nail. Fit a piece of filter paper or a pad of folded cheesecloth in the bottom and fill the can with coarsely ground meal made of well-dried, raw acorn meats. Fasten a wire bail to the top of the can and hang it over the sink faucet. Open the faucet just enough so the running water will stand above the meal and let the cold water filter through it all night. Dry and regrind as with the hot-water-leached Acorn Meal.

To make Acorn Glacé, put 2 cups of sugar, 1 cup of water, ⅛ teaspoon of cream of tartar and a pinch of salt in a small saucepan and boil until you see the very first hint of browning. Set the small saucepan in a kettle of boiling water to keep the contents liquid and dip in whole acorn kernels, which have been boiled and dried as described above, using a pair of tweezers; then place them on wax paper to harden. This improves the appearance as well as the taste of the acorns and they can be served either as a confection or with a meal, as a good hearty food.

For Acorn Bread sift together 1 cup of Acorn Meal, 1 cup of white flour, 3 teaspoons of baking powder, 1 teaspoon of salt and 3 tablespoons of sugar. Beat 1 egg, add 1 cup of milk and 3 tablespoons of salad oil. Add this to the dry ingredients and stir just enough to moisten everything. Pour into a greased pan, and bake in a 400° oven for 30 minutes. Or you can fill greased muffin tins two-thirds full of the same batter and bake only about 20 minutes for some excellent Acorn Muffins. These breads make a fine accompaniment to wild vegetables or wild fruit jams and marmalades, and taste as if they had already been buttered.

To make Acorn Griddle Cakes follow the recipe for Acorn Bread, but use instead 2 eggs and 1¼ cups of milk. Spoon the batter onto a hot griddle and spread thin. Brown both sides, turning only once. Serve with homemade maple sirup or wild fruit jellies.

For something special in acorn cookery, try Steamed Acorn Black Bread. Mix 1½ cups of Acorn Meal with ½ cup of Acorn Grits, 1 cup of white flour, ½ cup of sugar, 1 teaspoon of salt and 1 teaspoon of baking soda. When these ingredients are well mixed, add ½ cup of dark molasses, 1½ cups of sour milk and 2 tablespoons of salad oil. Wring out a pudding cloth in boiling water, spread it in a round-bottomed bowl and turn the batter into it. Tie up the corners and suspend the bag over boiling water in a closed kettle for 4 hours. This should be served hot from the bag, and a steaming slab of this rich, dark, moist bread is just right with a plate of baked beans.

Nowadays, when people are again coming to appreciate the dark, wholesome breads of our ancestors, maybe the acorn will come back into its own.

The Green Amaranth:
INVADER FROM THE TROPICS

(*Amaranthus retroflexus*)

THE Amaranth, commonly called Redroot, Rough-Weed, Pigweed or Wild Beet, is another of the very wide-ranging food plants. Originally a native of tropical America, it has become a common weed in cultivated grounds from coast to coast as far north as southern Canada. In rich soils, the stout hairy stem, which seldom branches, ranges from a height of three inches to six feet. At the top, it bears long panicled spikes of greenish flowers, followed by an abundance of shiny black seeds. The leaves, which are borne on stems nearly as long as themselves, are rough to the touch, long-pointed and have wavy margins. The root is a bright red.

When picked very young, only a few inches high, the amaranth makes a quite passable potherb with a mild flavor. Some connoisseurs, who like their wild greens to have a more definite flavor, consider the amaranth too tasteless. Even this quality has value, for many other wild greens have an overstrong flavor which can be diluted to your taste by adding the right quantity of green amaranth to the pot. An experienced greens gatherer can tailor a mess of greens to his own taste, by picking a bit of this, some of that and more of the other, right in the field.

I think the green amaranth is very good cooked alone, if one seasons it up a bit. Boil the tender young leaves and tips for twenty

GREEN AMARANTH

minutes, then drain. Meanwhile fry 1 slice of bacon for each person being served. Remove the bacon and leave about 2 tablespoons of bacon fat in the frying pan. Dump in the drained greens, add a little salt, and toss the greens around until they are evenly coated with fat. Cover and allow to steam 5 to 10 minutes. When you remove them from the fire, pour in about 1 tablespoon of cider vinegar and toss the greens again. Serve in individual dishes, garnishing each dish with a slice of bacon and some thin slices of hard-cooked egg.

In cultivated fields, young growing amaranthus, just right for the pot, can be found from spring until fall. Don't pass it by.

The shiny black seeds of amaranth were formerly much used by the Indians to make bread and gruel. Some ethnobotanists claim that this plant was cultivated as a grain crop by some of the Southwestern tribes. It does bear large enough quantities to have made this worthwhile.

Gather the seed when the spikes first get dry in the fall, for they soon shatter out. The best way to do this is to cut off the seed spikes with pruning snips and toss them on a large plastic sheet. When you have gathered a quantity, tuck up the corners of the sheet and carry it to a smooth floor. Thresh out the seed by walking on it with clean shoes, and winnow out the trash. This will sometimes yield a surprising quantity of tiny and shiny black seeds.

Finely ground and mixed with wheat flour, these seeds make acceptable dark pancakes, muffins and biscuits. The baked products have a slight "mousey" odor and taste, which is not entirely to my liking. This would not, however, prevent me from eating amaranthus products if I were at all hungry.

By experiment I found that the flavor of Amaranthus Meal could be greatly improved by roasting the seed before grinding. I poured the seed an inch deep in a pan and roasted it about an hour in a medium oven, stirring occasionally so it would cook evenly. As these roasted seeds were ground, they gave off a very appetizing aroma. The baked products of this roasted meal are well worth a trial.

Why not experiment with green amaranth as a food plant and see how you like it? I'm sure no farmer will object to your taking all you want from his field or garden.

Wild Apples and Crab Apples

(*Malus* species)

WE are so used to thinking of the apple as a cultivated and commercial fruit that we seldom realize that it is also an abundant wild fruit over the whole of northeastern United States. The apple was introduced into Massachusetts only a few years after the landing of the Pilgrims, and promptly established itself as a wild tree. Birds and animals scattered the seeds, and, when pioneers pushed slightly farther into the wilderness, they often found that the apple had preceded them. These were all seedling trees and consequently most of them had hard and sour fruit; but gradually, from the myriads of variations of seedlings, were selected many of the named varieties which we still value.

When you plant an apple seed, you seldom get fruit that resembles the variety of apple planted. Wild apples are of every color, shape, size and quality. One could spend a lifetime sampling the fruit from wild trees and still not find more than one or two worth propagating as a cultivated fruit. Wild apples are seldom very good to eat out of hand and, if eaten green, they are apt to give you a bad colic, but sometimes on a frosty November day, when your appetite has been whetted by a walk in the cold wind, if you come on wild apples that have been softened and sweetened by the frost, they taste delicious.

The very qualities that make wild apples a poor fruit to eat raw make them superior as cooking apples. Their firmness and wild sour taste, with a hint of bitter, makes them cook up into some of the best apple dishes you ever ate. Never mind if some of them are worm-eaten. You can cut away all the parts that insects have damaged and still accumulate fruit faster than from almost any other wild source. The presence of insect damage is your guarantee that these apples have been sprayed with no poisons.

So firmly established is the apple in our culture that one could easily fill a book of this size with apple recipes. Wild apples can be substituted for the cultivated ones in most of these recipes and will usually improve the final product. We can only skim the surface of the wealth of ways in which this feral fruit could be used.

To make a really grand Apple Pie, you will need 5 cups of pared and sliced wild apples, and an oil pastry for a two-crust pie (see pages 112-13). In a large mixing bowl, combine 1 cup of sugar, 2 table-spoons of flour, ½ teaspoon of salt and 1 teaspoon of pumpkin pie spice. This last is a commercial blend of nutmeg, cinnamon, ginger, allspice and cloves, and I find it just right for apple products as well as pumpkin pies. Pour the apples into the mixing bowl and stir it all together. Line a 9-inch pie plate with oil pastry, fill with the apple mixture and dot the top with butter. Adjust the top crust, perforate an escape hatch for the steam and sprinkle with sugar so it will sparkle. Bake in a 400° oven for 50 minutes. Serve warm, topped with cornu-copias made of slices of yellow processed cheese, rolled into funnel shapes and pinned with whole cloves.

Apple Jelly is an old stand-by, and the extracted juice from slightly underripe wild apples is so rich in pectin that it can either be used alone, or combined with other flavorful juices not so endowed. To make this jelly-juice, quarter the apples but do not remove the skins and cores except where they have been damaged by insects. Put the prepared apples in a kettle and barely cover with water. Simmer for 20 minutes without stirring, then strain off the juice. Use this juice as is, or combine half and half with elderberry, blueberry, mulberry or cherry juice. To 4 cups of juice, plain or mixed, add 4 cups of sugar and boil until you get a jelly test (see page 90). Don't try to make it in larger batches than suggested. One of the greatest secrets of home jellymaking is to keep the quantity small enough so it will come to a boil at the proper speed. Store the jelly in half-pint jars, sealed with sterilized lids.

The cooked, quartered apples that are left after the juice is extracted still have plenty of food and flavor left in them. Put through a food mill or ricer to remove the skins and seeds. The resulting pulp makes a wonderful Jellied Apple Butter. To 2 quarts of the pulp add 6 cups of sugar and 1 teaspoon of pumpkin pie spice. Heat it gently until the sugar melts, then boil, stirring constantly, until it gets thick and starts "plopping." Store in straight-sided, shoulderless jars, like freezer jars, so it can be unmolded when served. This Wild Apple Butter jells after being stored a short while, and can be sliced, scooped, diced or spooned, and an ice-cream scoop of this tangy, spicy sauce, added to a cold-plate luncheon, can change it from a drab affair into a memorable occasion.

Besides the naturalized wild apples, America has several kinds of native crab apples. One species or another of this valuable wild fruit is found growing from southern Canada to Florida and west to the Plains, with another species on the West Coast reaching from Alaska to California. All the native crabs produce hard and sour fruit, but few wild materials make better jelly or jellied apple butter. Insects seldom damage these native varieties, and they are too small to bother to cut them in quarters, so they are cooked whole. Just wash the crab apples, discard any blemished ones, cover them with water and boil for twenty minutes or more; then proceed with the Jelly and Apple Butter exactly as described for wild apples.

I cannot leave the subject of apples without mentioning a kind of foraging that is best done in the residential sections of our cities and suburbs. The Hopa Ornamental Crab Apple is a beautiful flowering tree that is literally covered with gorgeous pink apple blossoms each spring and is often planted on lawns and in parks. It has reddish foliage and invariably puts on a tremendous crop of tiny, bright-red apples. Most of these Hopa crabs go to waste, for few people know their value. They, like the native crabs, are usually free of insect damage and can be cooked whole. The Hopa crab is red all the way through and makes a beautifully colored jelly that is a delight to the eyes and a joy to taste. The jelly is made just like the other apple jellies, but this is the aristocrat of them all. The pulp, which is made by putting the cooked Hopas through a ricer or food mill, makes the very finest Jellied Apple Butter.

Spiced Hopa Crabs make a condiment or garnish that everyone likes. Boil together 5 cups of sugar, 3 cups of wine vinegar and 1 cup of water. Tie 1 sliced lemon, 3 sticks of cinnamon and 1 tablespoon of whole cloves in a cheesecloth bag and add to the sirup. Boil all for 10 minutes, let the sirup partially cool, then add 4 quarts of Hopa crabs with the blossom ends removed, but with the stems left on. Heat very slowly to 180° and maintain that heat for 10 minutes. Pour into sterilized jars, seal with sterilized lids and process the jars in water heated to 180° for another 10 minutes. Store in a dark place so the crabs will not lose their bright-red color. Serve with meat, cold lunches or almost any other meal, and you will find them highly appreciated. If you don't have a Hopa crab tree on your own lawn, start getting friendly with a neighbor who does!

Arrowhead or Wapatoo:

FAVORITE FOOD PLANT
OF AMERICAN INDIANS

(*Sagittaria* species)

THIS common aquatic plant is also known as Arrowleaf or Duck Potatoes. The botanical name of the genus is *Sagittaria*, which also means arrowhead. The various species now recognized were formerly included in a sort of catch-all classification called *Sagittaria variabilis*. Since all the species bear edible tubers, there is no need for us to enter the arguments about classification which this plant has raised in botanical circles.

Very common and extremely widespread, *Sagittaria* is found at the borders of ponds, streams and swamps, from coast to coast and from well up in Canada to far down in Mexico. The root fibers spring directly from the base of the cluster of arrowhead-shaped leaves, and the tubers are often borne several feet from the parent plant. *Sagittaria* is easily recognized when in flower, having filmy, white, three-petaled flowers, in circles of three near the summit of the flower stalk. After flowering, rounded fruit heads appear bearing flat seeds.

Sagittaria was eaten by American Indian tribes from coast to coast, sometimes forming their chief vegetable food. Related species grow in Europe and Asia, where they are highly appreciated. It is a cultivated vegetable in China, and some of the Chinese immigrants to this country have learned to use our wild *Sagittaria*.

Some of the early settlers in the eastern part of our country learned about this food from the Indians and used it to supplement their scanty diets until crop production became dependable. As food from other sources became more plentiful, few people were willing to wade into cold mud and water in order to collect these tasty little tubers.

The Indian method of harvesting wapatoo was to wade in the mud and pull off the tubers with their bare toes. At the time of year when the tubers are mature, this is apt to be a chilly business.

Outside the members of the Polar Bear Club, very few people could be persuaded to wade several hours in icy water in order to collect a bushel of starchy tubers which many find no better than the common potato. Fortunately, such Spartan exercise is not necessary in order to gather enough *Sagittaria* for a trial. The favorite habitat of these beautiful plants is the deep, oozy mud near the borders of shallow ponds. After the leaves fall in autumn, the dense colonies in which this plant grows are still marked by the brown leafstalks protruding above the water. Get a potato hook, one of those four-tined garden rakes which looks like a pitchfork bent at a right angle, put on your fishing boots and wade into such a colony. Rake back and forth through the mud, stirring it vigorously, for one must not only free the tubers from the connecting roots, but also wash away the clinging mud, allowing the tubers to float to the surface where they can be secured.

Using this method, I have several times collected enough for a meal in a few minutes. In the pond which is my favorite *Sagittaria* field, the tubers are a bit smaller than those reported from the Pacific Coast. They range in size from small as peas to large as eggs, but the average tuber is little over an inch in diameter.

Don't be afraid your collecting activities will injure or destroy a colony of these decorative pond plants. Rather, the reverse is true. *Sagittaria*, left to itself, tends to grow too thickly. Your rake will never dislodge all of the tubers in a colony, and you will find a better yield next year where you have thinned and cultivated the plants while taking your toll. The tiny tubers which you find too small to bother about will float away and sink into the mud in some new place and thereby start another colony which you may raid in future years.

Raw *Sagittaria* tubers have an unpleasant taste which is dissipated in cooking. You will find them as versatile as the potato. I have eaten these tubers boiled, creamed, fried and roasted, and have appreciated them all these ways. In taste and texture they resemble potatoes, but

ARROWHEAD

don't expect them to be identical. Arrowhead tubers have a distinctive flavor which many prefer to that of the potato. While on a camping trip, you will find these tubers a delightful accompaniment to fresh fish caught from the same pond. After eating a plate of fried wapatoo, or enjoying it cooked like new potatoes with peas or green beans, you will look with new interest and respect at those clusters of arrowhead-shaped leaves and delicate small blossoms which beautify the shores of ponds and streams everywhere.

The finest arrowhead dish that I have ever eaten was a Sagittaria Salad. A quart of arrowhead tubers was boiled, then peeled, and to them were added four hard-boiled eggs, diced, one onion and one dill pickle, both chopped fine, and a cup of mayonnaise. It tasted much like a potato salad but the wild tubers lent a special flavor that blended well with the other ingredients.

The Jerusalem Artichoke

(*Helianthus tuberosus*)

THE Jerusalem Artichoke is a sunflower, unrelated to the French artichoke, and has no connection with Jerusalem. Otherwise, it is well named. It is a native American plant, cultivated and highly valued by our Indian predecessors, from whence it was introduced into Europe. The Spanish call it *girasol*, their word for sunflower, and this word was corrupted into Jerusalem. I can't imagine why they called a tuber-bearing sunflower an artichoke.

This perennial sunflower grows from six to ten feet tall, and bears many yellow flowers that are two to three inches across and are borne on thin stems which appear in the axils of the upper leaves. The botanical manuals say they have from twelve to twenty rays, but I have counted the rays on hundreds this fall and found only eight to twelve rays on the flowers that are left on the plant late in the season. The whole plant closely resembles the Wild Sunflower, but it grows in thicker clusters and has more slender stalks. The leaves are narrower and more pointed, looking like a slender lance head, the larger ones eight to ten inches long and three to four inches broad, with the widest part near the base. The flowers are a lighter yellow than most species of wild sunflower and they lack the large brown disk which bears the edible seed of the sunflower. The center of an artichoke flower is much smaller, yellow in color and hemispherical in shape.

This excellent food plant is native to the central part of our country but was cultivated in the East both by Indians and, later, by whites. It long ago escaped from cultivation in this area and has become thoroughly naturalized, being fairly common in old fields, waste places and along roadsides. I seldom travel in September or early October without seeing many clumps of Jerusalem artichokes growing along the roads or on the railroad right of ways.

The plant is most easily located when in flower, and that is the time to select your foraging ground for later in the fall. One should not dig artichokes until after frost; they will keep perfectly well in the ground until the following spring, so they can be collected any time in the winter when the ground is not frozen. Strangely, they will not keep nearly so well in a cellar as they will when left in the ground where they grow.

I know an abandoned garden where there is an almost solid stand of artichokes. They bear tremendous yields, and I can get all the tubers I can use from a few square yards of ground. The tubers are as large as medium-sized potatoes, but more slender and slightly flattened. They have as much food value as the potato, but most of the starch is in the form of inulin, making this tuber valuable for diabetics and others who need a low-starch diet.

One of the best ways to eat artichokes is to peel and slice the raw tubers into a tossed salad. I find that they combine very well with water cress and thinly sliced cloves of wild leek, all served with a French dressing. Sliced raw artichokes are very crisp, with a sweet, nutty flavor.

They also make an excellent pickle if the peeled tubers are boiled only a few minutes, then covered with wine vinegar and stored for a few weeks.

I like to put the peeled tubers around a roast of beef and let them cook in the gravy. Or they can be peeled and oiled and just roasted alone in the oven.

Fried artichokes are edible but they do not become crisp and crusty, like fried potatoes.

Many like them just boiled and mashed and eaten with plenty of butter. They taste quite good this way, but they do not become smooth and creamy like mashed potatoes, but appear somewhat clear and watery.

A hearty casserole dish can be made by mixing 4 cups of boiled and mashed artichokes, 2 cups of fine bread crumbs, ½ cup of melted butter, 2 beaten eggs and a little black pepper. Bake for 30 minutes in a medium oven and serve hot.

If you would like to serve the very ultimate in artichoke products, try making an Artichoke Chiffon Pie. In a saucepan, combine ¾ cup of brown sugar, 1 envelope of unflavored gelatin and 1 teaspoon of pumpkin pie spice. Slightly beat 3 egg yolks, add ½ cup of rich milk and stir this into the brown sugar mixture. Cook and stir until it reaches a boil, then remove from the heat and stir in 1¼ cups of cooked and mashed artichokes. Chill until the mixture mounds slightly when spooned; this will take the better part of an hour. Beat the whites of 3 eggs until soft peaks form, then gradually add ⅓ cup of sugar, beating until stiff peaks form. Fold the slightly stiffened artichoke mixture into the egg whites and pile it all into a 9-inch graham cracker crust. Chill until firm and serve in huge wedges.

Stalking the Wild Asparagus

(*Asparagus officinalis*)

WHEN I was about twelve years old we lived near the Rio Grande in New Mexico. At that age, I didn't mind school so badly when winter weather made it disagreeable to be outdoors, but, when the first warm days of spring arrived, I only existed through the five school days each week in order to really live on Saturdays. I would be off early every Saturday morning to the river, the woods or the surrounding hills to see what nature was doing about bringing the earth back to life, and to revel in all the changes that had taken place since the week before.

One such bright Saturday in spring, I was walking along the bank of an irrigation ditch, headed for a reservoir where I hoped to catch some fish. Happening to look down, I spied a clump of asparagus growing on the ditch bank, with half a dozen fat, little spears that were just the right size to be at their best. The idea of "reaping where I did not sow" has fascinated me all my life. I took out my pocket-knife, cut the tender tips and dropped them into the pail in which I had intended to carry home any fish I might catch. Even while I was cutting this cluster, I saw another with several more perfect little sprouts. Alerted, I kept my eyes open and soon found another clump, and then another.

About this time I noticed that an old, dry, last-year's stalk stood above every clump of new asparagus tips. If I could learn to distinguish these old asparagus stalks from the surrounding dried debris, then I would be able to locate the hidden clusters of green spears from a distance. Despite my impatience to be off seeking more of these tender spears, I sat down on the ditch bank and for five minutes I did nothing but just *look* at one old dry asparagus stalk. It looked very much like the dead weeds and plants that surrounded it, and yet there were differences. The old asparagus plant stood about three

WILD ASPARAGUS

feet high and had a central stem or "trunk" about a half inch in diameter which easily distinguished it from weeds with forking stems. Wind and winter weather had long since robbed the plant of its soft, threadlike foliage, but the horizontal branches were still there, though badly broken about the outer ends. These side branches, evenly spaced along the old stem, were larger near the ground and tapered to very small near the top, giving the whole plant a slender Christmas tree outline, although it was a very thin scraggly tree so late in the year. The color was different, too. Like all the rest of the dead plants it was straw-colored, but on the old asparagus the shade was lighter and the color somewhat brighter.

After getting the size, color and form thoroughly in my mind, I stood up and looked back along the ditch bank. Instantly, I saw a dozen old dead asparagus stalks that I had missed. I went back to where I had found the first clump and worked my way down the ditch again, and this time I really reaped a harvest. My pail was soon full, so I took off my undershirt, tied up the sleeves and neck opening, and filled it, too, full of fresh asparagus. I didn't bother to go fishing at all. Fresh, tender asparagus tips were far better food than the bony suckers I could catch in the reservoir.

During the next week we ate fresh asparagus every day. We had boiled and buttered asparagus, creamed asparagus, asparagus on toast and asparagus soup. I doubt that young people today can realize how good the first green vegetables of spring tasted in those days before quick freezing and fast transportation began furnishing us with fresh green vegetables all winter.

The next Saturday I was back out along the ditch bank gathering asparagus. Until school was out in June, I made a weekly visit to what I had come to think of as *my* asparagus patch. By this time, all the wild asparagus that had not been kept closely cut was waving its fernlike foliage in the breeze, but where I had taken each spear as soon as it had appeared, the perennial roots kept sending up more new shoots to replace those I had stolen. My family grew tired of asparagus, but they never complained. Only recently my mother told me that she was actually giving a large portion of the bounty I was bringing home to the neighbors secretly, for she did not want to dampen my enthusiasm or dull my enjoyment of the task.

Before another spring, my parents had moved to a high, dry plateau farther west, and I was a middle-aged man before I saw wild asparagus again. The next time I saw those familiar dead stalks that had beckoned for me to come and pick the green treasure at their bases was one spring when I was driving along a country road in Pennsylvania, shortly after moving to the Commonwealth where I now make my home. At first I wondered why those bright, straw-colored dead weeds by the roadside gave me such a feeling of nostalgia. Then the memory of those long-past spring days on the ditch bank came rolling back. I stopped the car and examined the nearest stalk. Sure enough, near its base the little green tips were just peeping through the ground. Although I was a stranger in the East, this was like a welcome home. I was back in wild asparagus country again.

Since then, each spring I go out along the field borders and byways and gather wild asparagus, not only enough for current use, but some to store in the freezer, so I can bring back the joyous spring days any time of the year merely by cooking a dish of wild asparagus. That five minutes I spent so long ago, concentrating on one dead asparagus plant, has led me to many pounds of this most delicious of early vegetables. The eyetraining it gave me has lasted until now. Whenever I drive, in late winter or early spring, my eye automatically picks up the dead asparagus stalks by the roadside, and I make an almost unconscious mental note of the places where the green spears will be plentiful when warm weather arrives.

I suppose this wild vegetable is really no better than the cultivated kind, but, because of the memories it evokes, it always tastes better to me. It is exactly the same species as the cultivated varieties. Birds long ago scattered the seeds from domestic plants, and now, all over the eastern states and in irrigated sections of the West, wild asparagus grows in fence corners and hedgerows. The mature plant is familiar to everyone who takes any notice at all of wayside plants, for its lacy green foliage decorates the roadsides from early summer until the first freeze. A frond or two from this graceful plant will never fail to improve the appearance of a wild-flower bouquet. In the fall, some plants are covered with bright red berries a quarter-inch in diameter, each containing from one to six hard, black seeds, but the birds soon take care of these.

The edible tips and spears, in which we are chiefly interested, appear long before the asparagus puts on its summer finery, and they must be located by that drab, old, last-year's stalk. My neighbors often smile when they see me by the roadside with my asparagus knife and pail. They think it is much simpler to merely buy the asparagus one wants at the supermarket. But I have a secret they don't know about. When I am out along the hedgerows and waysides gathering wild asparagus, I am twelve years old again, and all the world is new and wonderful as the spring sun quickens the green things into life after a winter's dormancy. Now do you know why I like wild asparagus?

The Sweet Birch

(Betula lenta)

B LACK BIRCH, Cherry Birch, Sweet Birch—all these are common
names for a delightful tree with fragrant bark and twigs, smelling
and tasting like wintergreen. Found from Maine to Tennessee and
west to Iowa, it is usually a tall slender tree, often reaching eighty
feet in height, with a trunk diameter that seldom exceeds two feet.
The dark-colored bark, much resembling that of the cherry tree, is
smooth on young trees, becoming checked and flaky on old ones. The
erect, cylindrical, fruiting catkins, about an inch long and half an
inch in diameter, borne on the tips of the fine branches, usually persist
over winter and help to identify the tree in early spring before the
foliage appears, which is the time at which we are chiefly interested
in this natural woodland fountain.

Fountain? Yes, the sweet birch produces a copious flow of sap which
is at its height about a month later than in the maples. This is an
advantage as one's sap-gathering equipment is not otherwise engaged
at this time, and the weather is usually more pleasant. A camping trip
in the sweet birch country during the sap flow can be a lot of fun
if these valuable trees don't happen to grow near your home. Other
foragables are beginning to make their appearance at this time, to
add variety and interest to the camp diet. The nights might still be
cold, but with warm sleeping bags in a tent or station wagon you

will be comfortable enough. Bothersome insects have not yet appeared to plague the camper, as they will in hot summer weather, and getting out in the fields and forests after being cooped up inside all winter is sheer joy.

Birches are tapped exactly as maples are, so see the maple section for the necessary equipment and techniques. The sap of the sweet birch is the pleasantest of the tree saps to drink, straight from the collecting pail. Don't expect it to be strong-flavored; it tastes more like pure spring water than anything else, but it has a faint sweetness and a bare hint of wintergreen flavor and aroma.

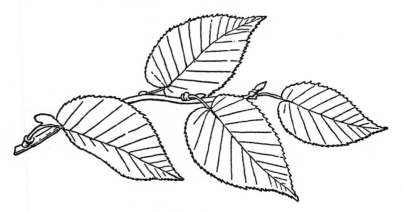

BLACK BIRCH

To make a wintergreen-flavored tea, cut some sweet birch twigs in small pieces and cover them with boiling birch sap. Let it steep for a minute or two, then strain out the twigs and sweeten the tea to taste. Some like to add cream or hot milk. Children are usually very fond of this beverage and it's perfectly harmless and wholesome.

Birch Tea can also be made of the red, inner bark of sweet birches, but removing this bark from standing timber disfigures and injures the trees. If sweet birches are being cut down anyway, as in land clearing or lumbering, one can gather a supply of this fragrant bark without feeling like a vandal. The bark from the stumps and roots is considered the best. Use a knife or a carpenter's wood scraper to remove the outer, dry layer and then peel off the red inner bark. It peels best in spring or early summer. If this is cut in small pieces and dried at ordinary room temperature, then sealed in fruit jars, one can have the makings of Birch Tea throughout the year. Use boiling water when birch sap is not available. Never boil the twigs or bark in making this tea and never dry the bark in too warm a place, for the wintergreen flavor is very volatile, and is easily driven off by too much heat.

Commercial wintergreen flavoring is not made from the wintergreen plant (*Gaultheria*). When not synthetic, it is distilled from these same sweet birch twigs and bits of bark. For some reason, known only to Mother Nature, these two unrelated plants yield an essential oil which is identical in both species. If you would like to make your own Essence of Wintergreen, turn to the section on medicinal herbs and see how this can be done with a jury-rigged apparatus.

A better-known beverage that can be made from this tree is Birch Beer. Measure 4 quarts of finely cut twigs of sweet birch into a bottom of a 5-gallon crock. In a large kettle, stir 1 gallon of honey into 4 gallons of birch sap and boil this mixture for 10 minutes, then pour over the chopped twigs. When cool, strain to remove the now-expended twigs and return the liquid to the crock. Spread 1 cake of soft yeast on a slice of toasted rye bread and float this on top of the beer. Cover with a cloth and let it ferment until the cloudiness just starts to settle. This will usually take about a week, but it depends somewhat on the temperature. Bottle the beer and cap it tightly. Store in a dark place, and serve it ice cold before meals after the weather gets hot. It has a reputation for stimulating the appetite. More than a glass or two at a time is likely to stimulate other things, for this beer has a kick like a mule. This is one birch beverage that is definitely not suitable for children.

The sap from this species is only about half as sweet as that from the sugar maple, but the sweet birch makes up for this defect by growing closer together and producing a more copious flow. I have collected a gallon of sap from a single tap on a sweet birch in only an hour, and so closely do these slender trees sometimes grow that it is often possible to collect fifty gallons of sap in one day from an area no larger than would be occupied by one large sugar maple.

Birch Sirup is good, with a flavor resembling that of sorghum molasses. It takes about ten gallons of sap to make one pint of sirup, so go heavy on evaporating equipment if you intend to make any quantity of this woodland product. Fuel from fallen branches and dead trees is usually plentiful wherever sweet birches are found, and at this time of year a fire often feels good, so the tedious task of evaporating can be part of the fun. When one is camping, time is not usually at such a premium that one cannot spare enough to make some Birch Sirup.

I am writing this after recently returning from a camping trip in central Pennsylvania. A friend gave my wife and me permission to camp and tap the birches on a patch of woodland he owns there. A beautiful stream crosses the place and its banks are lined with sweet birches. The trees right around our camp furnished all the sap we could use, even with four 5-gallon evaporators boiling continuously.

In a grassy, abandoned field on a nearby sunny slope, the chicory and dandelions were just putting up their first leafy crowns, furnishing us with delicious fresh vegetables. A patch of wild day lilies in this same field contributed tasty little tubers which we roasted and ate like peanuts, as well as tender shoots for our salads. A mile downstream, the creek flattened out and became marshy, and there I gathered a bundle of cattail roots and washed out the flour as we needed it for pancakes or biscuits. On the floor of the surrounding forest grew an abundance of wild leeks and pepper root, giving savor to our salads and condiments for our meats and sandwiches.

On the fourth day of our stay trout season opened, bringing an influx of fishermen. We had already spied out the pools where trout were lurking and on the first day of the season we caught our limit before midmorning. Freshly caught trout, pan-fried over the open fire, were added to our menu.

The stream was clear and cold, but there were hunting lodges and fishing camps upstream, making the water of doubtful purity. We drank birch sap, boiled our food in it and even used it to brush our teeth. We ate Birch Sirup with Cattail Root Pancakes for breakfast, and drank Birch Tea as we sat around the fire at night, swapping lies with the visiting fishermen and boiling off the day's haul of sap. It was work, but this kind of outdoor activity was just what I needed after a sedentary winter. Can you wonder that I am enthusiastic about the sweet birch?

Blackberries and Dewberries
(*Rubus* species)

THE Blackberry and Dewberry species are so numerous and so technical in their differences that we will leave all such arguments to the botanists, and simply call all those borne on upright canes blackberries, and all those borne on trailing vines dewberries. Considered together, these berries are easily the most valuable wild fruit crop in America. Many millions of dollars worth of these berries are gathered from the wild each year, and either sold in the markets or used at home. One species or another occurs over nearly the whole of the United States. Everyone recognizes and appreciates the blackberry when the ripe fruit is discovered in midsummer, but not enough has been said about the beauty of the large white blossoms in early spring. Especially with dewberries, this is the time to select your future picking grounds, for they become inconspicuous after the flowers fall. Blackberries and dewberries can be used interchangeably in the recipes we will consider.

Blackberries can be eaten as fresh fruit with sugar and cream, or cooked in dozens of ways. Blackberry Jelly can be made using the old-fashioned, long-boil method, if you have gathered some partially ripe fruit to mix with the fully ripe berries. Add 1 cup of water to each quart of berries and boil for 10 minutes, then squeeze out the juice through a jelly bag. To each cup of juice, add 1 cup of sugar and boil until you get a jelly test. Don't try to use more than 4 cups of juice to each boiling if you want the best possible jelly.

I think a better Blackberry Jelly is made if one uses only ripe fruit and never boils it with the seeds still in, but then one must add commercial pectin to make it jell. Just crush or grind 2 quarts of fully ripe berries and squeeze out the juice through a jelly bag. You should get about 3½ cups of thick juice. To this add 1 package of powdered pectin and bring it to a boil. Then add 5 cups of sugar, bring to a boil again and boil hard for one minute, pour into half-pint jars and seal.

To make the best Blackberry Jam, crush 2 quarts of fully ripe berries and put at least half of the pulp through a sieve, so the finished product won't be too seedy. You should have about 5 cups of pulp when you are finished. To this add 1 package of powdered pectin and bring it to a boil. Then add 7 cups of sugar, bring it to a boil again and boil hard for 1 minute, pour into half-pint jars and seal.

Dewberry Pie is a great favorite in the South, but one just as good can be made with any plump and juicy variety of blackberry. Line a 9-inch pie plate with oil pastry and fill it with washed dewberries or blackberries. Mix together 1 cup of sugar, ¼ cup of flour and a dash of salt. Sprinkle this evenly over the top of the berries and dot the top with butter. Adjust the top crust, perforate a steam escape, and bake for 45 minutes in a 400° oven. Serve slightly warm with a big scoop of ice cream on top.

When I was a child, I always looked forward to going blackberrying with my grandmother each summer. When we returned with our pails loaded with the jeweled fruit, Grandma would always make a large bake-pan full of Blackberry Cobbler, covered with biscuit dough. I have worked out a smaller and more modern version of the old-fashioned dessert that is a favorite at our house. Put 4 cups of fresh berries in a casserole. Mix together 3 tablespoons of cornstarch, 1½ cups of brown sugar and a little salt, and sprinkle this over the berries. Now mix 1 cup of commercial biscuit mix with a scant ½ cup of cream and spread this over the berries. Bake in a 350° oven for 30 minutes, or until the biscuit dough is nicely browned. Serve warm with cream.

Blackberry Juice, squeezed from the raw crushed berries or extracted with a juicer, makes a great summer drink when mixed half and half with lemonade. Used as a medicine, Blackberry Juice was once considered the finest remedy for diarrhea or "summer complaint." Blackberry Cordial or Liqueur is made by adding 2 cups of blackberry juice to 2 cups of sugar and bringing it just to a boil. Let it stand until perfectly cool, then carefully decant off the juice so none of the cloudiness in the bottom is stirred up, and add this sweet juice to a fifth of grape brandy. Serve only in tiny liqueur glasses, for this cordial is too sweet and too precious to drink in quantity.

Blackberries and dewberries can be made into wine that is not so bad as some homemade wines, but it takes a lot of sugar. To 6 quarts of berries, add 6 cups of water and boil gently for about 15 minutes. Press out the juice, measure and to each quart of juice add 2 cups of sugar. Pour it into a large jar or crock, spread 1 cake of yeast on a slice of toasted rye bread and float it on top of the juice. Keep the crock covered for 1 week; then carefully pour off the wine into gallon jugs and stop loosely with wads of cotton. Keep in a cool place until the wine clears and shows no sign of further fermentation. It should then be carefully decanted into sterilized bottles and tightly capped. Let it age, at least until the weather gets cold. The best way to serve this vintage is as mulled wine. Pour 1 bottle of Blackberry Wine into a flameproof glass saucepan, add 6 sticks of cinnamon and sugar to taste. Heat until it is as hot as you can drink it, but do not boil. This is a real "warmer-upper" on a cold day.

A friend of mine, who keeps bees, makes a Blackberry Honey Wine that he likes. He adds 4 pounds of honey, 6 sticks of cinnamon and 2 tablespoons of whole cloves to 1 gallon of blackberry juice and boils it all for 10 minutes. When almost cool he pours it into a crock and adds ½ package of activated dry yeast dissolved in 1 cup of the juice, and then proceeds exactly as in the former recipe.

Finally, in the spring when next year's canes are sprouting from the base of the blackberry plant, one can gather these tender sprouts before the prickles harden, peel them and slice them into a tossed salad. Surely we can spare some time this year to gather a fruit of so many uses.

The Huckleberry and Blueberry Tribes

(*Vaccinium* and *Gaylussacia* species)

THERE is much confusion about the names "blueberry" and "huckleberry." East of the Appalachians, both high and low varieties of *Vaccinium* are called Blueberries, and the name Huckleberry is apt to be reserved for some of the darker-colored *Gaylussacia* species, but even in this section there is some confusion. I once asked an old hand in New Jersey to explain the difference between huckleberries and blueberries. He pointed out a bush of light-blue berries which he called blueberries, and another nearby bush with smaller and darker berries which he said were huckleberries. On examining the two plants, I discovered that they were both seedling variations of *Vaccinium corymbosum*, and therefore of exactly the same species.

If you really want to know whether the berries you are picking are *Gaylussacia* or *Vaccinium*, examine the seeds. *Gaylussacia* has ten hard, seedlike nutlets inside, while the *Vaccinium* has many softer seeds. In the mountains of Pennsylvania I asked a small boy whether the berries he was picking were huckleberries or blueberries and he answered, "Who cares? They're both good to eat."

That's the right philosophy. Several varieties of both *Gaylussacia* and *Vaccinium* often get mixed in the same pail, but the huckleberry pies and blueberry muffins still taste just as good. There are no poisonous members of this family, so if we come on ripe blueberries or huckleberries we'll spend our time picking rather than trying to identify the exact species. Even the botanists are not agreed about how many species there are, and I would rather eat than argue. For the purposes of this chapter, let's lump them all together and call them blueberries, while remembering that huckleberries will work in the same recipes.

One species or another of this valuable wild fruit grows from above the Arctic Circle to Florida. There are twenty or more species east of the Plains, and a dozen more on the West Coast. They are often very abundant, especially northward, and the berries were a major

HUCKLEBERRY (left) and BLUEBERRY (right)

source of food to many Indian tribes, who ate them fresh, stewed or cooked with meat, and dried great quantities for winter use.

Some species are found only in the mountains, while others grow only in swamps. By driving to various localities and seeking out different species, I have picked them from June until late September. The size of the plants has ranged from the tiny dwarf blueberries (V. *pennsylvanicum*) standing six inches high, to swamp blueberries (V. *corymbosum*) in New Jersey that tower fifteen feet high.

One summer I gathered blueberries along Rancocas Creek in New Jersey from a canoe, pulling myself along by the heavily laden limbs that overhung the edge of the water, and stripping off the fruit into a pail held between my knees.

That was a pleasant way to pick berries, but not so fast as another way I learned from a fellow forager. He showed me how to lay a plastic sheet under the bushes and shake down the berries by the quart. He once gathered sixty-four quarts this way in one day. They were cleaned that evening by running them over a piece of hardware cloth with openings small enough so no decent-sized berry would fall through. This removed the small green berries and fine trash. Then the berries were covered with water, and everything that floated to the top was skimmed off.

Some of the finest blueberry picking I ever had among the upland varieties was where forest fires had burned off the woods several years before. As Robert Frost says in his poem, "Blueberries"

> There may not have been the ghost of a sign
> Of them anywhere under the shade of the pine,
> But get the pine out of the way. You may burn
> The pasture all over until not a fern
> Or grass-blade is left, not to mention a stick
> And presto, they're up all around you as thick
> And hard to explain as a conjuror's trick.*

One year, when picking was poor in my regular foraging areas, I asked at a State Forestry Office where I would likely find some good huckleberrying. An obliging ranger brought a map and showed me where there had been forest fires, three years before. I subsequently went to several of these spots and found excellent picking in them all. A forest fire is always a disaster, but there is no harm in salvaging the little benefit they bring in the way of better berrying.

The use of blueberries as fresh fruit, or in pies and muffins, is too well known to need much comment, but there are other uses of blueberries which are not as much practiced as they should be. The Indian custom of drying blueberries for winter use is one that we could emulate with profit. By spreading them thinly on a tray and putting them in the sun each day and in a warm room at night they will dry in about a week. If the weather is inclement they can be kept in the warm room through the day. I dry blueberries by spreading them only one berry deep over clean paper on the floor of a hot attic. Here they dry perfectly in about ten days with no attention from me. When they are thoroughly dry I pack them in fruit jars, set the jars in a very low oven for twenty minutes, then seal them with sterilized lids. In this way they will keep until blueberries are ripe the next year.

Dried blueberries can be substituted for raisins or currants in many recipes. The Indians often cooked them with meat or soup. This is really much better than it sounds. A cupful of dried blueberries and a chopped onion or two will make an otherwise tasteless stew into an interesting and palatable dish.

As a fresh berry to eat straight from the bush, or to carry into the camp or house to eat with milk or cream, the blueberry has few peers. The richest-tasting blueberries I ever ate were prepared by a mountain woman in Pennsylvania. She whipped 1 pint of cream from their own cow, sweetened it slightly, then folded in as many wild blueberries as it would hold. This was chilled until very stiff, then served, and it was a delectable dream.

Most people think that Huckleberry Pie is the height of the pastrymaker's art, but there are those who think that blueberries are always better raw than cooked. For these people we have developed the Blueberry Fluff Pie, which is never taken near the fire. Crush about 3 dozen vanilla wafers into fine crumbs, using a rolling pin. Combine these with ⅓ cup of melted butter or margarine, and ½ teaspoon of unflavored gelatin. Mix until all the crumbs are evenly dampened, then press into the bottom of a pie plate.

The upright edges of the crust are formed of whole wafers, stood on edge. To make a tight job, trim the wafers on the bottom and joining edges with a pair of scissors. Chill this crust until the bottom is firmly set.

Now cream ½ cup of butter until it is soft, then gradually add 1½ cups of sifted powdered sugar. Add 2 beaten eggs and then beat the whole mixture until it is fluffy. Pour into the vanilla wafer crust and smooth the top. Whip 1 pint of cream until it is stiff, then fold in as many fresh blueberries as it will decently hold. Pile this over the butter-egg mixture and sprinkle the crumbs you have cut from the edging wafers over the top. Chill at least 4 or 5 hours or, better yet, overnight. This dessert is hardly suitable for calory-counters but it is certainly delicious.

If you like the old-fashioned, two-crust Huckleberry Pie (and who doesn't?), line a 9-inch pie plate with uncooked pie crust. Then combine 4 cups of fresh blueberries, 1 cup of sugar, 3 tablespoons of flour, ½ teaspoon of salt, the juice of ½ lemon and a little of the grated rind. If you like spice, add ½ teaspoon of grated nutmeg, which is the spice which combines best with blueberries. Mix well, but gently, and fill the pie shell. Dot the top with butter, then seal on the top crust, perforating it in several places with a fork. Bake in a 400° oven 35 to 40 minutes. This is good, served either warm or cold.

Blueberry Muffins are so popular that several companies have started putting out ready-mix packages so that anyone can make Wild Blueberry Muffins. Unfortunately, all the commercial mixes I have tried have turned out too cakelike for my taste.

Always use wild blueberries in baking if you can get them. Wild blueberries are usually smaller, drier and have a tougher skin than the cultivated varieties. These qualities are all advantages in baking. The large, juicy, tender-skinned cultivated blueberries make an excellent dessert fruit, but they tend to break and run when baked, causing the muffins to stick to the pans, and I believe most cultivated varieties lack the spicy flavor of the wild fruit.

The two great secrets to remember in making good Blueberry Muffins are (1) to flour the berries, and (2) not to overmix the batter. I have been making Blueberry Muffins on the average of once a week for the last seven years. Here is the recipe I finally settled on. Sift into a round-bottomed mixing bowl 2 cups of flour, 2 tablespoons of sugar, ½ teaspoon of salt, 2 teaspoons of baking powder and 1 scant teaspoon of soda. Stirring carefully from the outside of the bowl, mix in 1 cup of well-drained but still damp fresh or canned wild blueberries. Stir gently so as not to crush any of the berries until they are all separated and each one is evenly coated with flour. Then add 1 slightly beaten egg, 2 tablespoons of melted butter and ¾ cup of buttermilk. Stir barely enough to dampen all the ingredients. The mixture will be thick, more like sticky dough than batter. Use a small ice-cream dipper or a tablespoon, and fill greased muffin tins half full. Bake in a 400° oven for about 18 minutes.

Another good way to use this fruit, either in camp or at home, is in Wild Blueberry Fritters. Add 3 tablespoons of sugar to 1 cupful of commercial biscuit mix. Stir in ⅓ cup of milk, 1 beaten egg and 1 cup of blueberries. Drop by spoonfuls into hot fat, and, when they are nicely browned, drain them on paper towels or a paper bag, and sprinkle with powdered sugar.

To make a festive Steamed Blueberry Pudding, cream ½ cup of butter with 1 cup of sugar. Add 2 beaten eggs and ½ cup of buttermilk. In another bowl, sift 2 cups of flour with 1 teaspoon of soda, ½ teaspoon of salt and ½ teaspoon of ground nutmeg. Stir 1 pint of wild blueberries gently into the flour until they are evenly coated. Then combine all ingredients and stir carefully until they are thoroughly mixed.

Dip a square of clean muslin in hot water and wring it out, then spread it in a round-bottomed bowl and pour the batter into it. Tie up the corners to make a bag and suspend over boiling water in a large covered kettle for 4 hours. Serve warm with wine sauce or whipped cream.

One reason I am so fond of blueberries is because of the ease with which they can be preserved for out-of-season use. If blueberries are gathered on a dry day, packed, still dry, in fruit jars and placed in the refrigerator, they will keep perfectly fresh for a month or more. If you pick more than you can consume in a month, they are the easiest fruit in the world to can or freeze, or some of them can be dried as outlined above.

To freeze blueberries, simply pack them dry in containers and set them in the freezer. What could be easier than that? They need no processing whatever. If you like sugar added to your blueberries, put it on when you eat them. Sugar added to blueberries before they are frozen makes them tough and robs them of flavor.

Canning blueberries is almost as simple as freezing them. Pack the berries into jars, cover them with a sirup made of 4 parts water to 1 part sugar, seal and process in boiling water for 20 minutes. Check the seal and store them away.

Frozen blueberries, when defrosted, can be used exactly as you would use the fresh fruit. We find the canned berries are very good in pies and muffins.

If you can ever assemble all the ingredients at one time, try making a Blueberry-Maple-Nut-Loaf. Sift together, 2 cups of flour, 1 teaspoonful of soda and ½ teaspoon salt. To this add 1 cup of well-drained canned blueberries and ½ cup of coarsely chopped hickory nuts. Stir from the outside of the pan, gently, so as not to break the berries, until the blueberries and nuts are all separated and evenly coated with flour. In a separate bowl combine ⅔ cup homemade maple sirup, 2 well-beaten eggs and ¾ cup melted butter or margarine. Mix well and pour into the dry mixture. Carefully stir, only enough to mix everything well and dampen all the ingredients. Line two small oblong loaf pans with wax paper and spoon half the batter into each one. Bake for one hour in a 325° oven. This recipe combines three different kinds of wild food into one of the most delicious fruit-nut breads ever made.

Our favorite pie made with canned wild blueberries is the Glazed Blueberry Cream Cheese Pie. You will need 1 quart jar of blueberries and 1 baked pastry shell. While you are baking the pie crust, cut any leftover crust into daisies, hearts or other little fancy shapes and bake them, too. Watch these small pieces as they bake very quickly. When the pie shell is cooled, work a 3-ounce package of cream cheese until it is soft, then spread on the bottom of the pie shell. Drain the berries and reserve the juice. Pour the drained berries into the pie shell over the creamed cheese. Mix ¾ cup of sugar and 3 tablespoons of cornstarch in a saucepan. Gradually add the drained-off juice from the berries. Cook, stirring constantly, until it is thick and clear. Cool slightly, then stir in 2 tablespoons of lemon juice. Pour this glaze over the berries in the pastry shell. Trim with the fancy pastry shapes. Serve with whipped cream and hear the family rave.

Great Burdock or Wild Gobo

(*Arctium lappa*)

WHO would think that common Burdock, the ordinary coarse weed of back yards and roadsides, was good for food? I first became acquainted with the culinary possibilities of this rank-growing biennial in Hawaii, where Japanese truck farmers grow a domesticated variety called Gobo. The sliced roots of this vegetable are a common ingredient in *sukiyaki*. Domestic burdock is usually better than the wild, but only because it is more apt to be harvested when it is in just the right stage. The garden plant has been little improved over the wild variety which grows everywhere in our northern states and southern Canada. I found the roots of our common Great Burdock being sold in Japanese markets in Chicago under the name of Wild Gobo.

In Hawaii, the island people firmly believe that eating gobo will give one strength and endurance. When faced with an exhausting task, the islander will sometimes say, "I need gobo." Likewise, it has a great reputation as an aphrodisiac. A rather coarse honeymoon joke is to publicly present the bride and groom with a bunch of gobo. If these beliefs about burdock gain enough currency in our own country, maybe this troublesome weed will disappear from neglected dooryards where it is now an aggressive pest.

Whether burdock really has the recuperative powers attributed

BURDOCK

to it, I do not know, but I do know that it is a good vegetable when harvested at the right time and skillfully prepared. Also, this is another of the versatile wild food plants furnishing four different food products.

Once we tore down an old shed on a country place in Pennsylvania. This building had been used at different times to stable a milk goat, a pet deer, a pig and a pony. Between times it had been used as a woodshed. The ground where the shed had stood was covered a foot deep with chips, trash and manure. The next year in July, we went to this same farm for a vacation and found the old shed site covered with a lush growth of burdock. The plants were easily pulled from the chips and trash and were at just the right stage. The long slender roots have a fairly thick rind which peels easily from the edible core. After they were peeled, I had several dozen white roots, a half inch in diameter and about a foot long. These were sliced thinly, crosswise, and cooked for thirty minutes in water to which a pinch of soda had been added. This water was drained off, and the gobo was cooked again for ten minutes in a very little water and seasoned with butter and salt. It was surprisingly good.

Most people are all too familiar with the burdock as a door-yard weed. It is easily recognized by its large, egg-shaped leaves, up to a foot long and more than half that wide. The leaves are borne on long stalks, are deep-green, slightly wavy-edged and many-veined—the small connecting veins giving the upper surface a mosaic-like texture. The larger veins and the leafstalk are striped with purple on the upper surface. The young plant has a superficial resemblance to the Rhubarb plant. The stout seedstalks, up to an inch or more in diameter, spring from the crown of the plant and grow very rapidly, sometimes reaching a height of three feet or more. It has tubular, purple (rarely, white), flowers which are followed by the spherical burrs, about three-fourths inch in diameter, which are the seed pods. These are covered with pliable, bristly stickers that catch easily on your clothes as you walk by.

I sometimes wonder whether the strength this vegetable is reputed to give, doesn't come from the exercise one gets in gathering it, rather than from any intrinsic quality of the food. Unless one finds burdock growing in a chip pile as I did, gathering enough roots for a meal can be a formidable task. When growing in ordinary ground they cannot be pulled, but must be dug out. I finally discovered that a posthole digger was the best implement for this, although a slender spade works pretty well. Dig a hole, a foot or more deep, close beside the root, then pull the root toward the hole. By judiciously choosing the spot to dig, one can sometimes pull the roots of two or three plants into the same hole.

Burdock is a biennial, and the roots should only be collected from first-year plants. These can be recognized because they produce no flower stalk. The roots are at their best in June and early July. After that, they become too hard and woody to be very attractive.

The roots are not the only edible product of the burdock. In early spring, the very young leaves make a passable potherb when cooked in two waters, with a pinch of soda added to the first. The young leafstalks, caught before they begin to lengthen, can be peeled, dressed with oil and vinegar and served raw as a salad, or they can be cooked like asparagus.

I think the best products of the great burdock come from the pith of the rank-growing bloom stalk. These must be gathered just when the flower heads are starting to form. These quick-growing stalks are often more than an inch in diameter and several feet high. Every bit of the bitter green rind must be peeled off. This leaves a white pith, a half inch or more in diameter, which is an excellent vegetable when prepared according to the directions given for cooking the root.

This pith can also be used to make an unusual confection. Cut it in 3-inch lengths and boil for twenty minutes in water to which a pinch of soda has been added. Drain, then put in a sirup made by adding ½ cup of water and the juice and grated peel of 1 lemon to 1 cup of sugar. Boil the pith in this sirup until it looks clear, then drain and roll in granulated sugar.

Why not give burdock a trial? You may find that it really does give you strength, endurance and the vitality of manhood. You might even find it good enough to repay the labor of gathering it. At the very least, you will get some healthful exercise and clear a patch of ground of some very unsightly weeds.

Calamus:

CONFECTION, CURE-ALL AND SALAD PLANT

(*Acorus calamus*)

CALAMUS, or Sweet Flag, is also known as Myrtle Sedge, Wild Iris, Sweet Grass, Sweet Rush and so many other common names that one recognizes that here is a plant that has entered deeply into folklore. It grows in shallow water, pond edges, wet meadows and along sluggish streams throughout the United States and around the world in the North Temperate Zone. This plant spreads by underground rhizomes and is usually found in extensive patches. It should be easy to locate a supply anywhere in the eastern half of the continent.

A patch of calamus, from a distance might be mistaken for either wild iris or young cattails, although it has yellow-green leaves rather than the blue-green of those two plants. Calamus leaves are shaped like very narrow, flimsy, two-edged swords, measure up to three feet or more in length, and all spring from the base of the plant. Where they join the stem, usually just under the surface of the ground, they are of a reddish-purple color and tightly clasp one another. The calamus flower is a dry, finger-like spike which grows off at an angle from a flower stalk that resembles a slightly altered leaf, and is usually found from one to two feet above the ground. As you can see by the illustration, the stem turns at an angle, just under the surface, and there are numerous roots on the bottom of it. Every part of the

CALAMUS

calamus plant, the leaves, stem, roots and rhizome, has a spicy, aromatic aroma, and this pleasant fragrance can be used to distinguish this herb from others that resemble it superficially.

In England, where this plant is called the sweet rush, people used to gather great quantities of it to spread on the floors of their churches for special occasions. Then, as everyone walked over the rush-strewn floor, they bruised the foliage, causing it to give up its pleasant perfume. A friend of mine who was recently in the Isle of Man reports that the Manxmen still use the sweet rush in this way on certain holidays.

Our New England forefathers often used the calamus in this same way on the floors of their homes. I feel that this is a much nicer way to perfume a house than is using the modern room deodorants with a smell that always reminds me of the rest room in a cheap movie.

Candied Calamus Root was a popular confection a few generations ago. It was sold in shops and on street corners and was often made at home. The early Shaker communities made a specialty of this product. Now we have forgotten how to make it, and even how to eat it.

While searching for a recipe for this colonial candy, I came on several sets of directions which said to use the large underground rhizomes and to boil them for two or three *days*. That's enough to scare most people off. By experiment, I learned that the candy made of these large rhizomes was apt to be fibrous and tough regardless of how long it was cooked and that the more tender underground stems of the individual plants made much better candy and this could be made in an hour or less. Also these tender stems are much easier to collect than the large rhizome. By pulling gently on the plant, the underground stem will usually break off where it joins the larger rhizome from which it originates. Cut off the upper plant about where it reached ground level and this will leave you the short underground stem about three to six inches long and about one inch or less in diameter. Cut off the clinging roots, wash and peel the stem and cut it into half-inch lengths. Covered with boiling water and placed on the fire these small pieces will cook perfectly tender in thirty minutes. However, one should change the cooking water several times, always using boiling water to replace that thrown off in order not to slow down the cooking. This is done in order to weaken the calamus flavor down to edible proportions. The spicy pungency of the calamus is a good flavor but there is a bit too much of it for most tastes, unless one changes the cooking water four or five times.

When the pieces seem tender, drain, then boil for twenty minutes in sugar with just enough water to make a rich sirup. Drain and place the candy on wax paper and let it dry for a day or two, then roll in granulated sugar. Store in tight jars if you make more than can be consumed in a few days.

This confection is too pungent and strong-flavored to be consumed in quantity, but it does make a tempting nibble. Besides its spiciness it has a strong flavor that some people dislike, describing it as a soapy taste. However, I have found that if one keeps some around and takes an occasional nibble, the job of learning to like it is soon replaced with the task of keeping enough on hand.

Besides furnishing the makings for a very interesting confection, calamus also contributes one of the tastiest salad materials to be found growing wild. In the spring, when the plants are about a foot high, the tightly compressed, unborn leaves in the center of the young stalk are sweet and tender. I like to peel the young stalks and eat this tender tidbit on the spot, but carried home and sliced into a tossed salad they will never fail to improve it. They carry just enough of the calamus flavor to be interesting, but never enough to repel anyone. Try it. It's really something special.

As a medicinal herb the calamus has a long and venerable history. It was one of the favorite remedies of the Greeks and Romans, and still appears in modern medicine. The American Indians considered it a panacea, using it in various ways for dozens of ills. It is still considered by many to be an excellent remedy for indigestion, sour stomach and heartburn.

For medicinal purposes the yellowish, horizontal rhizomes, an inch or more in diameter and found only a few inches underground, are the part most often used. A sharp trowel or an asparagus knife is the best tool for collecting them. Just grasp the rhizome with one hand and slide the cutting edge of your instrument along under it to sever the numerous roots that hold it down.

The unpeeled rhizome should be washed and thoroughly dried in the sun. On drying it loses part of its biting pungency. It can be taken in several ways, the simplest of which is to merely cut off a half-inch length of the dried rhizome and chew on it, swallowing the juice.

Some find it more pleasant to take as a tea. Put one tablespoon of the grated, dried rhizome in a cup of boiling water. As soon as it is cool enough to drink, strain, sweeten to taste and drink it like ordinary tea. Those who have acquired a taste for calamus candy will not find these remedies hard to take.

Supermarket of the Swamps: THE COMMON CATTAIL

(*Typha latifolia*)

FOR the number of different kinds of food it produces there is no plant, wild or domesticated, which tops the common Cattail. In May and June the green bloom spikes make a superior cooked vegetable. Immediately following this comes the bright yellow pollen, fine as sifted flour, which is produced in great abundance. This makes an unusual and nourishing ingredient for some flavorful and beautifully colored pancakes and muffins. From fall until spring a fine, nutritious white flour can be prepared from the central core of the rootstocks for use as breadstuff or as a food starch. On the leading ends of these rootstocks are found the dormant sprouts which will be next year's cattails. These can be eaten either as a salad or as a cooked vegetable. At the junction of these sprouts and the rootstock there is an enlarged starchy core the size of a finger joint. These can be roasted, boiled or cooked with meat. In the spring, the young shoots can be yanked from the ground and peeled, leaving a tender white part from six to twelve inches long which can be eaten raw or cooked.

Whenever I recite the virtues of the cattail, the first question I encounter is always, "Then why aren't they used?" Why will a European go hungry rather than eat the tender green corn growing in his fields, when we consider it the finest delicacy the garden produces? Why was the tomato raised solely as an ornamental for two hundred years before anyone discovered it was good to eat? Human food prejudices are not related to logic or reason.

Taking the food products of the cattail in the order given, the green bloom spikes, gathered before the yellow pollen shows on the outside, and boiled only a few minutes in salted water, makes one of the finest vegetables that can be collected from the wild. Cut the young spikes just about the time they are ready to break through the papery sheath which encloses them. This sheath must be removed like husking corn, and, like sweet corn, the spikes are best when cooked soon after gathering. The boiled spikes should be liberally doused with melted butter, for they tend to be somewhat dry and granular in texture. The simplest way to eat them is just to pick the slender spikes up in the fingers and nibble the buds from the tough central stalk. This wiry core is inedible, so the "cobs" look like a plate full of plastic knitting needles. Most people like cattail bloom spikes if their carefully taught food prejudices do not get in the way of their enjoyment of them. My own family and several neighboring families always look forward to cattail season even though it comes at a time when garden vegetables are plentiful. Cattails have no strong or disagreeable taste; they smell somewhat like sweet corn while boiling, and there is nothing strange or unusual in the taste. I can only describe the flavor as a good hearty *food* taste. It should always be eaten hot, for it is not nearly so palatable when allowed to cool.

If you dislike nibbling the buds from the spikes at the table, then you can scrape the bud material from the cores, mix 2 cups of buds with 1 cup of bread crumbs, a beaten egg and ½ cup of milk. Then salt and black pepper to taste and bake in a casserole dish in a medium oven for 25 minutes.

Cattails never bloom all at once, so the season in which they can be gathered extends over about six weeks. If you would like some of the spikes for out-of-season use, they can easily be stored in the freezer. Just boil the spikes for five minutes, scrape the buds from the core, package and freeze.

Any bloom spike you leave will, in a few days, show a thick coating of bright yellow pollen. The heads can be bent over into a pail and the pollen rubbed off with the hand. I have gathered several pounds this way in a few minutes. Put through a fine-meshed sieve, this pollen is fine and smooth as talcum powder. Substitute up to one-half pollen for wheat flour in your favorite pancake or muffin recipe and it will give the product a bright golden color and a pleasing flavor. Although the food value of cattail pollen has not been investigated, the chance seems good that these golden pancakes have also been improved nutritionally over those not so fortified. If the analysis of this yellow flour resembles that of other pollens, then it will be high in protein, and should the brilliant yellow color prove to be carotene, then we have discovered a rich, natural source of potential vitamin A.

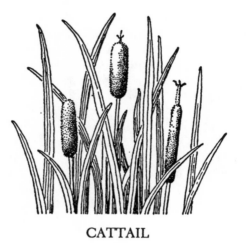

CATTAIL

The starchy roots with their adherent by-products are messy to dig, but could be the source of tremendous quantities of excellent food. These ropelike roots crisscross a few inches below the surface and any square yard of cattail swamp will yield enough to make several pounds of nutritious white flour with an analysis very similar to grain flours. During the First World War, a scientist at Cornell developed a method of making this flour by drying the peeled roots, grinding them and sifting to remove the fiber.* I made a sample of flour by this method, but didn't find it as palatable as I had hoped it would be.

*P. W. Claasen, "A Possible New Source of Food Supply," *Scientific Monthly* (August, 1919).

I remembered studying about how the people of New Guinea refine sago by washing the starch from the fibers in cold water, then allowing it to settle to the bottom of the container and pouring off the water. I worked out a method of preparing a good-tasting flour in this way. As soon as the roots are dug and washed, they should be peeled, for when they are partially dry the outside layer of the root becomes more difficult to remove. As in most swamp plants, there is a spongy layer between the core and the bark of the roots, but, since this facilitates the peeling operation, let's not kick about it. The white cores will be about a half inch in diameter. Fill a large container with cold water. Then wash and crush the cores of the roots with the hands until the fibers are all separated and washed clean. Strain out the fibers and allow the wash water to settle for half an hour. By this time, the starch will have all settled to the bottom. This first water will be very slimy and ropy. It should be carefully poured off, the container filled with cold fresh water, the starch stirred up in this water again and again allowed to settle. Two such washings are usually enough, but you can refine the starch still further by more washings if you wish. On the last washing, allow the starch to settle in a solid layer on the bottom of the container and then pour off all the water you can drain out of it. The resulting "flour" will be a fine white product with no disagreeable taste or odor. I suppose it could be dried and stored, but I have always washed out only what I needed and used it immediately in the wet state. Most people who have tried it agree that the flavor of bread, cookies, biscuits and muffins is improved when cattail flour is substituted for about half the wheat flour usually used in these products. Drop Biscuits made with 100 per cent cattail flour were found to be perfectly edible, and, in fact, quite palatable.

The bulblike sprouts found on the leading ends of the roots have a sweetish taste and can be peeled, boiled and served with butter or they can be cooked with meat. In the spring, when these sprouts begin to elongate but before they break through into the light, they can be peeled, parboiled, covered with hot vinegar and sealed. In a few weeks you will have an excellent pickle.

In the center of these sprouts, at the base, just where they join onto the rootstock, there is a sizable lump of tender starchy material. This can be boiled and seasoned with butter, or a few handfuls can be put in the roaster with your meat, as you do with potatoes.

When the young plants are about two feet high it is time to gather "Cossack asparagus," so-called because the Russians of the Don are so fond of this food. If one grasps the inside leaves and pulls, the tender inside portion will usually break clean from the root and slip out. Peeled down still further, there is revealed a very tender white part, up to a foot long. This can be eaten either raw or cooked. The quality seems to vary from place to place, but gathered anywhere it is a very passable vegetable.

We like it best cooked with meat. Cut some shinbone beef, which can be bought cheaply, from the bone and add the marrow fat from inside the bone. Put this with a little oil in a frying pan and cook until it is done. Meanwhile, cut some Cossack asparagus in small pieces crosswise, and parboil for a few minutes, then throw the water away. Add the vegetable to the meat and cook until the cattail hearts are a light brown. A dash of soya sauce will add a Chinese flavor to the dish, but it is very good just salted to taste and eaten as is.

The usefulness of the cattail is not exhausted by the many foods it produces. Many people gather the heads (or should I call them tails) when they are first grown, before the "cotton" loosens, and dry them indoors to use in winter flower arrangements. A duck decoy with dried cattails tastefully arranged around it makes an unusually attractive autumn decoration.

The cotton, or down, from the ripe heads is very soft, light and fluffy. It was formerly much used to stuff mattresses which were used like feather beds to make for warmer sleeping in unheated bedrooms. It has been used in life rafts and to stuff life preservers. I have stuffed plastic bags with this down for a very effective insulation in a home freezer.

The stems on which the fruiting heads are borne are round, smooth and of uniform size. They can be fastened together with ordinary dress pins and used by the children as "logs" for building toy log cabins, forts and stockades.

The long basal leaves of the cattail furnish the material from which rush seating is made for chairs. For this purpose the leaves are gathered when full-grown but still green, and the midrib is removed and discarded. The four- to five-foot-long leaves are hung in bundles, under cover, to dry in the shade. Before using they are soaked to make them soft and pliable. The strands are twisted together by hand as the seat is woven.

Many substitutes for rush seating have been mass-produced, but none have ever achieved the beauty, strength and durability of the original handcrafted product. As I write this article I am sitting on a beautiful curly-maple chair with a rush seat woven by some now unknown craftsman of the last century. It has been in continuous use for a hundred years and is still in perfect condition.

I hope this article doesn't cause the owners of cattail marshes to surround them with electrified fences and locked gates, but I do hope we start giving this beautiful but neglected plant the notice it deserves. Because of its beauty and potential usefulness in so many ways, there are few plants with a greater claim to our attention.

Wild Cherries

(*Prunus* species)

THE birds that raid the farmer's cherry trees have done the foragers a favor. Although America has some fine native cherries, some of the very best wild cherries to be found came originally from seedlings of cultivated varieties, and the birds have been the chief agents in scattering the seeds.

Known as the Mazzard, or Wild Sweet Cherry (*Prunus avium*), this naturalized immigrant is found from eastern Canada to Georgia and west to the Great Plains. I have gathered and enjoyed the fruit in places as far separated as Quebec and Texas.

Mazzards, like all seedling fruit, vary in size, color and quality from tree to tree. One often finds sweet cherries that rival the named varieties in flavor, although the wild cherries are seldom as large as the cultivated kinds. The color of the ripe fruit ranges from red through brown to black, and the cherries are usually from one-half to three-quarters inch in diameter. I know of one group of seedling trees where all the cherries are yellow with a red blush, like the cultivated Royal Anne or Napoleon varieties. These cherries are almost as large as the cultivated kind, firm of flesh and quite palatable, although slightly bitter. I gather some there each year to make Cherry Olives.

Cherry Olives are unsweetened pickled cherries and taste nothing like olives. They probably acquired their name because they are used somewhat as one would use ripe or green olives. They provide an unusual and welcome addition to the salad plate, the cocktail snack or the picnic lunch. They are very easily made and one can use any firm-fleshed cherry, although my wild Napoleons make the best I ever tasted.

Just wash firm, unblemished cherries in cold water, then pack them fresh into half-pint jars. To each jar add ¼ teaspoon of salt and 1½ tablespoons of cider vinegar. Fill the jars with cold water and seal. Allow at least three weeks before using them.

Mazzard cherries are not nearly so tedious to pick as some of the other wild fruits. One sometimes finds a single tree which will furnish all the cherries a family can use. My son and I once found such a tree in central Pennsylvania growing by the roadside. Never have I seen another tree so loaded with cherries. We drove our station wagon under the tree, climbed to the luggage rack on top and picked half a bushel of cherries. Even then the tree remained so laden with fruit that one could hardly see where we had been.

The Pie Cherry, or Sour Cherry (*Prunus cerasus*), has also escaped from cultivation over the same area where one finds the mazzard. These cherries grow on a smaller tree than the mazzard and the fruit is softer, red or brown when ripe and quite sour. It makes the very best of cherry pies and this and the Pin Cherry are the only cherries I would recommend for jellymaking without the addition of other fruit juices. All cherries lack pectin but commercial pectins always include a recipe for Sour Cherry Jelly on the bottle or in the box. This bright red, tart jelly is very good to eat with fowl or meat.

We have some native American cherries that are not to be despised. The best of these is the Rum Cherry or Sweet Black Cherry, the *Prunus serotina* of the botanists. This grows on a large tree which furnishes a valuable cabinet wood. It is found from Nova Scotia to the Dakotas and south to Florida. In the Southwest its habitat extends into Texas and even into Mexico, and, with a few skips, down into Colombia, South America. In Mexico this cherry often grows twice as large as it does in our northern states. It is the only cherry available in Mexico, as the climate is not suitable for the northern domestic cherry. I was very fond of this cherry when I was a small child in eastern Texas. As I remember it, it seemed much larger than the ones I now pick each year in Pennsylvania and neighboring states, but of course all things look larger to a small child.

In the North, the fruit on this cherry is quite small, from three-eighths to a half-inch in diameter, and shiny black when ripe.

The rum cherries can be distinguished from mazzards by the different way in which they bear their fruit. As you can see from the drawing, the flowers of mazzards spring from scaly buds borne on the branches. These appear in very early spring before the leaves. Rum cherries bear their flowers and fruit on long racemes, which terminate leafy branches, the flowers appearing when the leaves are about half grown. The rum cherry ripens a month or more later than does the mazzard, this extending the wild cherry season over much of the summer.

The rum cherry acquired its name because it was used by early New Englanders to turn the raw rum they imported from the West Indies into a sweet, smooth and beautifully colored Cherry Liqueur. If you would like to try this drink, crush 1 quart of rum cherries, add 1 dozen or so crushed seeds and 1 cup of water, then simmer for about 15 minutes. Strain through a jelly bag, return to the fire and add as much sugar as you have juice. As soon as it boils again, pour it into bottles or jars and seal tightly. This sweet juice can then be added any time to rum, whisky or brandy at the rate of 1 part juice to 2 parts ardent spirits, and my friends who appreciate such things tell me it's very good.

Real old-fashioned Brandied Cherries, or Cherry Bounce, was made with uncooked rum cherries. Fill a quart jar three-fourths full of well-washed rum cherries and add 1 cup of sugar; then fill the jar to the top with commercial brandy. Seal the jar, set it away in a dark place and forget about it for at least three months.

A New Englander, who thought his Brandied Rum Cherries were especially good, decided, after some hesitation, to give a jar of them to his minister. He waited with much trepidation for the preacher's comment. Finally he received a little thank-you note which read:

Dear Parishioner,

You can't imagine how delighted I was to receive your little present. But what I appreciated even more than the gift was the *spirit* in which it was given.

The most common American wild cherry is the Chokecherry, the *Prunus virginiana*. It is found from Newfoundland to Georgia, and west to Nebraska and Texas, and is familiar to nearly everyone

CULTIVATED OR MAZZARD CHERRY (top)
and WILD CHERRY (bottom)

in this wide area. It bears its fruit and flowers on racemes, in the same manner as the rum cherry, but the chokecherry is usually a much smaller tree, seldom being over twenty feet high and is often only a small bush. This tree often puts on really bumper crops of fruit. As I write I can see half a dozen chokecherry trees around the pond where I go fishing. Two months ago these trees were so laden with fruit that I picked two gallons from one tree and still left plenty for the birds. Earlier in the season, while walking along Chesapeake Bay, I saw dozens of chokeberry trees with their branches already bending under the weight of their half-grown fruit.

Since they are so plentiful it is too bad the fruit is not of better quality. The cherries are small, about the size of a pea, and usually quite astringent, although one occasionally finds a tree which bears cherries that are almost edible raw. This species is chiefly valuable as jelly material, and it makes an excellent product, especially when apple juice is added.

When I was a boy in New Mexico, I was once riding horseback across the country in May and came on a shallow canyon with a small stream at the bottom. On each side of the stream, the canyon floor was covered with wild cherry bushes which were in full bloom. A more refreshing contrast to the barren country which surrounded this little oasis would be hard to imagine.

We called this local variety chokecherries, but the botanists now say that it belongs to a separate species, the *Prunus melanocarpa*. The cherries, when ripe, were nearly black and much less astringent than the chokecherries I have tasted elsewhere. We used them for jams, jellies and preserves.

The only early, light-red American cherry is the *Prunus pennsylvanica*, commonly called the Bird Cherry or Pin Cherry. Unlike the rum and chokecherries it bears its blossoms and fruit in tufts or clusters, like the mazzards. It is quite sour, usually has a thin pulp and a large seed, and is considered worthless by most people. However, one occasionally sees a tree with better fruit. Near my sister-in-law's place in New Jersey grow several pin cherry trees which bear cherries that are slightly larger and have very small seeds. She makes a jelly from them that is as good as any I have ever tasted. It has a beautiful color and a pronounced cherry flavor.

This was made by adding 1 cup of water to each quart of fruit and simmering for 30 minutes. The juice is strained through a jelly bag and then she merely follows the recipe for Sour Cherry Jelly, found in the package of pectin.

To make jelly of mazzard, rum or chokecherries, crush the unpitted cherries in a kettle and add 1 cup of water for each quart of fruit. Simmer for 30 minutes, then strain through a jelly bag. Obtain some underripe apples and slice them cores, peels and all, into another kettle. Cover with water and simmer for 30 minutes or until the apples are tender. Don't crush them. Strain off the juice through a jelly bag. Now take 2 cups of cherry juice and 2 cups of apple juice and add 4 cups of sugar. (Don't try to double, or otherwise increase, this recipe. To be certain of success, jelly must always be made in small batches.) Boil the juice and sugar hard until the jelly test (see page 90) tells you the jelly will set. All wild cherries make excellent jellies, that from the rum cherry being especially rich and dark with a delicious winy flavor.

If you want to make maximum use of mazzards and rum cherries, you will need a cherry pitter. This device works on a simple principle and does a surprisingly good job.

Mazzards and rum cherries both make fine pies. To 3 cups of pitted cherries, add 1 cup of sugar, ¼ cup of white flour and ¼ teaspoon of salt. Mix well and pour into a 9-inch uncooked piecrust. Using ½-inch strips of the same pastry the crust is made of, weave a lattice top for the pie. Bake in a hot oven 35 to 45 minutes. Serve faintly warm.

If you find wild sour cherries, you can use the same recipe by adding another ½ cup of sugar, and get an even better pie.

The best way to keep wild cherries for out-of-season use is to freeze them. Pack pitted mazzards or rum cherries in jars and cover them with *cold* sirup made by boiling 3 parts sugar in 4 parts water until it dissolves. Seal the jars and freeze as rapidly as your freezer will do the job. For sour cherries use a sirup made with equal parts (by measure) of water and sugar. These frozen cherries can be used in pies or puddings, or as fresh fruit for desserts.

Did you ever hear of Cherry Soup? Fruit soups are often served in Scandinavia and in Central Europe, but Americans are only now learning how much they can add to a meal. Our own experiments in using mazzards and rum cherries in this way have been very successful.

Wash 1 quart of unpitted cherries, then crush and pound them until the seeds are broken. Add 1 quart of water and a pinch of salt, then simmer for 30 minutes. Put through a sieve to remove the skins and seeds, then return to the kettle and thicken with 2 tablespoons of potato flour. Simmer a few minutes more, then add sugar to taste. This can be served hot at the beginning of the meal or ice cold as dessert. If you want to be fancy when serving it cold, float 1 handful of pitted fresh cherries and 1 spoonful of sour cream on top of each bowl of soup.

An easily made dessert which is popular in our house is what we call a Blushing Betty. To make this with fresh mazzards or rum cherries, add 1 cup of brown sugar and ½ teaspoon each of cinnamon and nutmeg to 3 cups of pitted cherries. Let this stand a few minutes to allow some juice to run out. Then, in a baking dish, spread alternate layers of ordinary cornflakes and the cherry mixture, using 3 cups of cornflakes. Pour the juice from the cherries over the top, then dot with butter or margarine and bake in a moderate oven about 20 minutes. Serve hot with maple sauce. This can also be made with thawed, frozen cherries, using only half the amount of sugar because of the sirup that is already on the frozen fruit.

If there are plenty of mazzards of rum cherries in your neighborhood, you may want to try your hand at making Cherry Wine. A Swiss rancher I knew in New Mexico claimed that good wine could also be made of the local chokecherries, which were probably *Prunus melanocarpa*. The sample he gave me didn't taste like anything to shout about, but then I am no judge of wine. Wine making always seemed like a deplorable waste of good fruit juice to me, but not all my friends agree.

One of these friends gave me the following directions for making wine of mazzard and rum cherries. This recipe is for a small quantity, so you can see how you like this vintage before going into wine making on a larger scale.

Crush 3 quarts of cherries into a 2-gallon crock. Dissolve 6 cups of sugar in 2 quarts of boiling water, add this to the cherries and stir well. As soon as the mixture has cooled to lukewarm, dissolve 1 scant teaspoon of activated dry yeast in a little of the liquid and add this to the brew, stirring well again. Cover with a cloth and leave in a warm room for 8 days. Then strain the new wine into a gallon jug, plugging the neck of the jug with a wad of cotton and capping loosely. Keep the jug in a dark, cool cellar for 30 days, then carefully decant the wine into bottles and cork or cap tightly. Wrap the bottles in thick brown wrapping paper and keep in a dark place until used.

Shall we go out and pick some wild cherries?

Eat Your Chicory and Drink It Too

(*Cichorium intybus*)

CHICORY, although originally naturalized from Europe, is now a common roadside plant from Nova Scotia to Florida and west to the Plains. It is also found up and down the Pacific Coast and locally elsewhere. Succory is another name by which this plant is known, and on account of its pretty-colored but tattered-looking flowers it is called Blue Sailors or Ragged Sailors.

In early spring the first leaves that appear at the top of the perennial taproot greatly resemble those of the closely related dandelion in both size and shape. They are often gathered indiscriminately with dandelion leaves by those seeking spring greens. This is no misfortune, for the taste of the two is almost identical, and both are equally healthful.

In early summer the chicory puts up a loosely branched stalk that reaches two or three feet high, bearing slender, sparingly toothed leaves that are dark green in color with a purple midrib. In the axils of these leaves are the branches that bear the bright blue flowers, which are about two inches across and resemble a dandelion in form, but have ragged-looking edges because of the unevenness in length of the strap-shaped petals. These flowers are very erratic about opening and closing, seldom being found open after noon, except on cool cloudy days.

As cooked greens, and even as raw salad, chicory is the equal of the dandelion, and that means it's tops. However, unless you gather the leaves while they are very young, you will be disappointed, for they soon become too bitter to eat. To get the finest Chicory Salad, you should almost be there to grab the first leaves as they form. The best tool is a weeder or asparagus knife, for the best part of the chicory is found underground. You don't so much *pick* this salad as *dig* it. Slide your tool underground and cut the root near the top. Trim off the root just high enough to keep the crown of leaves together. The white, underground parts of the leaves make an excellent salad, just washed and dressed with oil and vinegar. Or you can cook the whole top as a potherb, boiling it only a few minutes and seasoning with salt and butter. When collected early enough, chicory is unexcelled as a spring green.

Where chicory is plentiful, one can upend a flowerpot over several plants, stopping the hole in the bottom to let them blanch in darkness. It is only when they grow in light that they become excessively bitter. You can even dig up the roots of any unwanted plants, trim off the large leaves, and plunge the roots in a box of wet sand or sawdust in your cellar and get a crop or two of blanched salad greens. To raise this salad in winter, see the directions given in the section on a wild winter garden.

In the literature on this subject one frequently finds reference to the use of chicory roots as a vegetable, cooked like parsnips or salsify. Our own experiments along this line have not been too successful. When the young, first-year roots are peeled of their tough rind, there is little left. These slender, white cores, cut crosswise, cooked and flavored like parsnips, are edible, but they are certainly nothing to rave about. We felt that they fell far short of repaying the labor of digging and preparing them.

It is as a substitute for, and an adulterant of, coffee that the chicory root is most often used. In some sections of our country coffee blended with chicory is overwhelmingly preferred to pure coffee. Each year we import many tons of chicory root for this purpose. This imported root is exactly the kind that you will find under those common blue flowers that decorate our roadsides with homely, unpretentious beauty.

To make your own Chicory Brew, dig some of the long taproots, scrub them thoroughly and roast them slowly in an oven until they are hard and brittle, showing dark brown on the inside. Then grind

CHICORY

and brew exactly as you would coffee, except that chicory is somewhat stronger than coffee, so less of it should be used. When skillfully prepared, chicory is an excellent coffee substitute, more nearly approaching the taste of real coffee than most.

Wild Cranberries

(Vaccinium macrocarpon)

THIS ground-hugging relative of the blueberry is well known as a market fruit, but few people know that the Cranberry is also a widely available wild fruit. Found from North Carolina to Newfoundland, and west to Minnesota, it is only because of its low, inconspicuous growth and its habit of hiding in boggy peat swamps that the wild fruit is not more often found and utilized.

Wild cranberries were a favorite food of many Indian tribes who cooked them with maple sugar or honey before the white man brought cane sugar. Cranberries were probably the first native American fruit to be eaten in Europe. There are plenty of records to show that, in early days, wild cranberries were gathered by the ton, packed in barrels and covered with water, then shipped to Europe. Because of the excellent keeping qualities of these acid berries, they were able to cross the Atlantic in good shape, even in the days of sailing ships.

Of course, like all wild fruits, cranberries are more plentiful in some parts of their range than others. A woman friend writes from Michigan that wild cranberries are very common there, being especially abundant and easily procured in her section of that state. Another friend, who loves Cape Cod in autumn when the "summer people" are gone, reports finding a little bog between some sand hills on that cape where enough wild cranberries were growing to supply several families.

One June, while canoeing on Rancocas Creek in New Jersey, I noticed the small creeping plants, with their tiny leaves and pale, rose-colored flowers, growing in a creekside bog. I noted the location and have returned there each year, in late autumn, to gather as many cranberries as my family can use.

To most people, cranberries are nothing but the main ingredient of a tart sauce to be eaten with the traditional turkey at Thanksgiving or Christmas. This is a good way to use cranberries, but it's far from being the only way.

Did you ever hear of Cranberry Glacé? I made some last Christmas and it was our favorite holiday confection. In a small saucepan put 1 cup of sugar, ½ cup of water, ⅛ teaspoon of cream of tartar and a pinch of salt. Boil until the mixture shows the very first sign of browning, then snatch it from the fire. Set into a pan of boiling water so it will stay liquid, then spear cranberries on toothpicks and dip them in the hot mixture. This makes them beautiful as well as tasty, and a few dozen of them stuck into an apple or a chunk of plastic foam make a very pretty and very edible Christmas decoration.

A lady who was our guest during the holidays tasted a glacéed cranberry, arched her eyebrows and said one word, "Piquant!" Piquant? That's a good word, and I'm going to use it oftener, especially when describing cranberry products. I looked it up in the dictionary and the first two meanings given were: (1) "pleasantly tart" and (2) "having a lively charm." I seriously doubt that there is another word in our language which so perfectly describes glacéed cranberries.

To make the traditional Cranberry Sauce to serve with fowl, boil 1 quart of the wild berries with 2 cups of sugar and 1 cup of water until the berries all pop. This only takes about 10 minutes. If you want to keep part of the sauce for later use, just ladle it, boiling hot, into sterilized jars and seal with sterilized lids. No processing is necessary.

If you prefer a strained Jellied Cranberry Sauce, boil 1 quart of berries with 2 cups of water for half an hour, then strain through a sieve. To the liquid, add 2½ cups of sugar and boil and stir for 5 minutes, then pour into half-pint jars or let it cool in a fancy mold.

To serve with beef, try a Cranberry and Horseradish Relish made with wild cranberries. Grind 1 pint of the berries in a food chopper, using a medium plate. Add ¼ cup of horseradish, ½ cup of sugar and the juice of ½ lemon. Stir this together well and let it stand in the refrigerator for a day or two to allow the flavors to blend.

If you have a knife-type blender, you can make wholesome and delicious Cranberry Whip. Dissolve 1 package of orange-flavored gelatin in 1 cup of hot water or hot Cranberry Cocktail. Put this in the blender with 1 small, unpeeled red apple, cut in small pieces and ½ cup of sugar. With the blender running at high speed, drop in raw wild cranberries, a few at a time, until the mixture gets too thick to continue circulating. Pour immediately into individual dessert dishes and set in the refrigerator to chill. Serve with whipped cream.

Never stop picking wild cranberries because you are afraid you'll get too many. There are so many ways to use cranberries and they keep so well that there is little danger that any will go to waste. To keep them for long periods, wash firm berries repeatedly in cold water, then pack in sterilized jars, cover with sterilized lids and set them in the refrigerator; they will stay plump and fresh for months and months. To freeze cranberries just pack the dry berries into jars or other noncrushable containers and set them in your freezer.

Many people make two-crust "mock cherry" pies of cranberries, but my favorite cranberry pie is of the "chiffon" type. Boil 1 pint of cranberries with ¾ cup of sugar and ½ cup of water for 20 minutes, then rub through a sieve or colander. Dissolve 1 package of lemon-flavored gelatin in ½ cup of boiling water and mix it with the strained cranberries. Let it chill until partly set, then beat the mixture until it forms soft peaks. Beat the whites of 3 eggs until they form soft peaks, then gradually add ¼ cup of sugar and continue to beat until it forms very stiff peaks. Fold the beaten egg whites into the berry-gelatin mixture and pour it into a previously baked and cooled pie shell. It's better than good; it's "piquant"!

A woman friend of mine, on reading the first draft of this chapter, asked, "But couldn't I just make these things with cranberries from the market, without having to crash through poison ivy and wade through peat swamps to get wild berries?" Of course that could be done, and the products would be good. Unlike the strawberry, the wild cranberry is not outstandingly better than the cultivated kind. I feel better eating the wild berries because I know they haven't been sprayed with insecticides and weed killers, but beyond that there is something deeply satisfying about foraging your food directly from nature's larder. A Cranberry Whip or a Cranberry Chiffon Pie might taste the same to your guests, whether it is made of wild or cultivated fruit, but you will find you approach these desserts with a new interest and delight if you located and picked the wild cranberries yourself.

The Official Remedy for Disorders

THE chapter heading above is the approximate translation of *Taraxacum officinale*, the botanical name of the common dandelion. Until quite recently, thousands of people about the earth died each winter and early spring from diseases now known to have been caused by vitamin deficiencies. Ancient herb doctors dug up the perennial roots of the dandelion, which could be obtained even in midwinter. These were washed, then the juice was expressed from them and given to the sufferers. When this was done, the patient always improved. Then, in early spring he was advised to eat raw as many of the first young dandelion leaves as he could consume. This healthful salad soon restored him to health and vigor. I do not think it is an exaggeration to say that this vitamin-filled wild plant has, over the centuries, probably saved a good many lives.

But how the mighty have fallen! This herbal hero, one of the most healthful and genuinely useful plants in the materia medica of the past, is now a despised lawn weed. Now that supermarkets sell green vegetables throughout the winter and the druggists are vending tons of synthetic vitamins, we no longer need to depend on the roots and leaves of this humble plant to ward off sickness and death, so we have turned on the dandelion. Every garden-supply house offers for sale a veritable arsenal of diggers, devices and deadly poisons, all designed to help exterminate this useful and essentially beautiful little plant which has so immensely benefited the human race.

I learned to love dandelions when I was a small child. Not only did I enjoy the delicious dandelion greens my mother gathered and prepared, but the bright yellow flower, with its wonderful composite construction, fascinated me. I never believed that spring had really come until I saw the first dandelion in bloom.

Did you ever see a child who did not enjoy blowing the fuzz-winged seeds from the hoary seed balls of the dandelion? This always tells the child something, though what he learns from it seems to vary from place to place. We used to blow three times, then the number of seeds left indicated how many children we would have. It was sometimes an alarming number. Other children have told me that if one blows three times on a dandelion head, the number of seeds left would tell the time of day, thus making it unnecessary to carry a watch. I sometimes think my own children must use some such system to determine when it is time to stop playing and come in for dinner. Once in southern California a little girl ran up to me and said, "Look. I blew on a dandelion head and there's four seeds left. That means I'll get married four times."

Fortunately the dandelion still has important uses other than as a dispenser of somewhat unreliable information. I believe we would be better off, both financially and nutritionally, if we still procured as many of our vitamins and minerals as possible from wild green plants rather than depending on the synthetic products dispensed by the druggist. This is especially true when the vitamins come in as palatable a form as dandelion greens in early spring.

Nearly everyone has heard that dandelion greens are edible, but the actual gathering and preparation of them seems to be an almost forgotten art. How many people have told me that they have tried dandelion greens and didn't like them? On questioning, it always turns out that these trials consisted of boiling some leaves from old flowering plants. Would you decide that you disliked asparagus because the old stalks and foliage of midsummer are inedible? Our most prized vegetables are only good when gathered at just the right stage, and dandelions are no exception. Don't judge this most wholesome and delicious of all boiling greens until you have tasted them at their best.

DANDELION

The best dandelions are never found in closely mowed lawns but in some place where they and the grass have been allowed to grow freely. Long before the last frost of spring, a slightly reddish tangle of leaves appear at the top of the well-developed perennial roots. At this time the dandelion is a three-storied food plant. Using a narrow spade or bar, dig out the dandelions, roots and all. Occasionally one sees a dandelion root that is single, like a thin parsnip, but most of them have several forks as large as your little finger. In my opinion, these white roots furnish a better vegetable than either parsnips or salsify, although it tastes very little like either of them. The newly grown roots are tender and peel readily with an ordinary potato peeler. Slice them thinly crosswise, boil in two waters, with a pinch of soda added to the first water, then season with salt, pepper and butter.

These roots also furnish what I consider to be the finest coffee substitute to be found in the wild. For this purpose, the roots are roasted slowly in an oven until they will break with a snap and appear very dark brown inside. This roasting will take about four hours. These roots are then ground and used just as one uses coffee, except that you need slightly less of the dandelion root to make a brew of the same strength. Drink it with or without sugar and cream, just as you take your coffee.

On top of the dandelion root, which is usually down two or three inches, there is a crown of blanched leaf stems reaching to the surface. This tender white crown is one of the finest vegetables furnished by the dandelion and can be eaten raw in salads or cooked. Slice the crowns off the roots just low enough so they will stay together and slice again just where the leaves start getting green. Wash them thoroughly to dislodge all grit. Soak in cold salted water until they are ready to be cooked or made into salads.

To make a tasty Dandelion Crown Salad, cut the crowns finely crosswise, add a little salt, a pinch of sugar and 1 small onion chopped fine. Fry 2 or 3 slices of bacon cut in small pieces. When the bacon is crisp, remove it and add 2 tablespoons of cider vinegar to the hot bacon fat; then, as it boils up, pour it over the chopped dandelion crowns and stir. Garnish with the pieces of crisp bacon and slices of hard-boiled egg and serve immediately.

To prepare dandelion crowns as a cooked vegetable simply boil in considerable water for about 5 minutes, then drain and season with butter and salt. Return to the fire just long enough to dry out slightly and allow the seasoning to permeate it throughout. Many people consider this the finest way of all to eat dandelions.

The only food product of the dandelion that is known to most people is furnished by the tangled rosette of leaves above the surface. These are the justly famous Dandelion Greens, and, if gathered early enough, they are really fine and require very little cooking. After the plant blooms they are too bitter and tough to eat. Wash the young, tender greens well, place them in a kettle and pour boiling water over them. Let them boil 5 minutes, then drain and season with salt and butter or bacon fat.

One of the secrets of the dandelion's ability to bloom very early is that it starts producing the beginnings of the blossoms down atop the root in the center of the protecting crown, then only shoves them up on stems when the weather is favorable. The developing blossom material is found inside the crown as a yellowish, closely packed mass. This material, when cut out and cooked, furnishes still another dandelion vegetable. Just covered with boiling water and cooked only about 3 minutes, then drained and seasoned with butter and salt, these little chunks of embryonic blossoms are delicious, with something of the flavor and texture of the finest artichokes. Until this blossom material is fairly well developed, the crowns and greens are still edible, although it would be advisable to cook them in two or more waters toward the end of the season. As soon as the plant starts sending up bloom stalks, the dandelion season is over as far as vegetables are concerned. I have tried cooking the unopened buds of the flowers later, and they make a passable vegetable but are not nearly so delicious as the developing buds that are still hidden inside the crown. Dandelion Coffee can be made of the roots at any time of the year, although I prefer that made in early spring while the roots are still filled with foodstuff intended for the developing plant.

A better-known and more ardent beverage made from this versatile plant is Dandelion Wine. I used to think that this wine was just another of the clever concoctions invented by Americans in the twenties to evade prohibition, but now I find that Dandelion Wine has been made and appreciated in England for many generations.

Gather 1 gallon of dandelion flowers on a dry day. Put these in a 2-gallon crock and pour 1 gallon of boiling water over them. Cover the jar and allow the flowers to steep for 3 days. Strain through a jelly cloth so you can squeeze all the liquid from the flowers. Put the liquid in a kettle, add 1 small ginger root, the thinly pared peels and the juice of 3 oranges and 1 lemon. Stir in 3 pounds of sugar and boil gently for 20 minutes. Return the liquid to the crock and allow it to cool until barely lukewarm. Spread ½ cake of yeast on a piece of toasted rye bread and float it on top. Cover the crock with a cloth and keep in a warm room for 6 days. Then strain off the wine into a gallon jug, corking it loosely with a wad of cotton. Keep in a dark place for 3 weeks, then carefully decant into a bottle and cap or cork tightly. Don't touch it until Christmas or later. My "drinking uncle" says that, even during the worst blizzard in January, a glass of Dandelion Wine will bring summer right into the house.

Once I called the attention of some friends to a report that some of the inhabitants of the Island of Minorca had, during a famine, been forced to subsist on dandelions. This was in March, so we decided to see how much of a meal we could prepare using only dandelion products and added seasonings. We had Dandelion Roots, boiled and buttered, Dandelion Crowns, both cooked and in a salad, Dandelion Greens, and the tender developing blossom material cut from the crowns, cooked and seasoned. All this was washed down with glasses of Dandelion Wine left over from the former season, and we finished with steaming cups of Dandelion Coffee. That meal was so delicious that it completely cured any anguish we were feeling over the plight of the Minorcans.

New Food from a Familiar Flower

THE Day Lily, called *Hemerocallis fulva* by the botanists, has become abundantly naturalized throughout much of America, and
now easily ranks as a wild plant. The orange-colored blossoms are a
familiar sight along roadsides and in abandoned fields during June
and July. The day lily grows easily from seed and a single plant will
spread underground and soon form a large clump. With such repro-
ductive ability it is no wonder that it long ago escaped from flower
gardens and took to the lanes and byways.

Although very widespread and familiar to nearly everyone, very
few people know that the day lily is a valuable food plant. The blooms
and buds are an important vegetable in China and Japan and this
is one Oriental food which is perfectly acceptable to Western palates.
Nearly everyone who tries it likes it.

Gather the unopened flower buds when they are nearly full-sized,
boil only a few minutes, then butter, season and serve like green beans.
They are really delicious, with no bad taste of any kind.

If you want to make a hearty and easily prepared luncheon dish,
just dip the buds, or even the opened blossoms, in a rich egg batter,
then quickly fry in very hot fat to a golden brown.

Buds and flowers can be added during the last few minutes of cooking to soups and stews. Like okra, they impart a desirable gelatinous quality and the flavor is delightful.

The showy orange blossoms are open but a single day. Hence the name day lily. Incidentally, the botanical name of the genus, *Hemerocallis*, could be translated, "one-day beauty." While gathering day lilies you will notice the closed and withered blooms of yesterday, ready to drop to the ground. These are good for food, too. They will give a somewhat different, but equally good, flavor to soups and stews. If you'd like to use an authentic Oriental recipe, try this one:

Fry ½ pound of fresh pork, cut into bite sizes, until it is nicely browned. Add 1 quart of water, 2 tablespoons of soya sauce and 1 teaspoon of salt. Cover and cook slowly for about an hour until the pork is very tender, replenishing the water if it boils away. Then add 1 packed cup of the withered blooms and 1 teaspoon of monosodium glutamate. Cook only a few minutes more until the withered blossoms are tender. If you are a purist you will serve this with rice and tea, eating the solid parts with chopsticks and the soup with a porcelain spoon. With fortune cookies for dessert, this makes a very unusual and economical Sunday night supper.

Although the Oriental uses and appreciates the green buds and the freshly opened flowers, he also dries large quantities for out-of-season use. Many people think the flavor is actually improved by drying. These Dried Lily Buds can be purchased in the Chinese markets of our larger cities. But it is very easy to dry your own supply. Just spread the freshly gathered buds or withered flowers on newspapers in a warm attic room. In a week, more or less, according to weather conditions, they will be dry. You can then seal them in fruit jars and keep them in a cool place the year around. Dry and store the buds and withered flowers separately, for the withered flowers are more quickly finished than the green buds. Also, although these two products can be usually used interchangeably in most recipes, you will find that you will prefer the buds in some dishes and the flowers in others.

To regenerate the dried product, add only enough water to insure complete soaking. This soon makes them soft, pliable and somewhat gelatinous. They can then be added to soups or stews which are already cooked, the whole merely brought to a boil again and the dish is ready to serve. Or cook them separately in a little butter for

DAY LILY

only a few minutes, then use them as a sauce or garnish on meat or vegetable dishes.

The day lily is a double-barreled food producer, not only bearing delicious vegetables on the naked flower stalk, but also producing edible tubers underground. These little tubers, only about a half-inch in diameter by an inch long, are borne abundantly, clustered right under the plant. They are somewhat tedious to prepare, but hardly more so than garden peas and they are fully as worth-while. Freed of the connecting rhizomes and the tiny feeder roots, washed and boiled in salted water for about fifteen minutes, they have the sweetness and texture of whole-grain sweet corn and a mild and delicious flavor all their own. They can be dug any time of the year when the ground is not frozen. The older tubers become soft and inedible, so take only those which are firm. In spring and summer you will find many young tubers still snowy white. These are sweet and crisp, with a nutty flavor when eaten raw, and they make an excellent salad.

Don't feel like a vandal while digging day lily tubers. A spading fork full of plants removed here and there from the clump will only give it a much-needed thinning and cultivation. If you would like to see more of these interesting and useful plants growing, then set out some of the plants in new places after you have removed the tubers. They will live and each one will soon form a new colony about itself.

Once, after gathering day lily tubers, I set out a row of the de-tubered plants in my garden. In about six weeks I dug down and found that everyone of them had put on a new crop of snowy, crisp tubers. Even the rhizomes were white and tender, making them much easier to prepare. These were very fine and we enjoyed them boiled, creamed and raw in salads.

In the spring, long before the bloom stalks appear, the sprouting stalks of day lilies are edible. Cut just above the roots and, the larger leaves removed, the tender inner portions of the stalk can be sliced into a tossed salad or cooked like asparagus. If the well-washed stalks are boiled only a few minutes and seasoned with butter and salt, they make a tender, sweet vegetable that will be pleasing to even the fussiest eater.

Thus we see that the common and familiar day lily furnishes salads; cooked vegetables from its sprouts and developing stalks, buds, freshly opened flowers and withered blossoms which can be used fresh or dried; and sweet tubers which can be eaten raw or cooked. One must admit that this interesting and beautiful roadside flower is also a wild food plant of no mean order, and is even worthy of a place in our vegetable gardens.

A Salute to the Elderberry:

WITH A NOD TO SCARLET SUMAC

THE common Elderberry, known to botanists as *Sambacus canadensis*, is one of the most abundant, most useful, most healthful and yet most neglected of our native wild fruits. It has attractive pinnate leaves with from five to eleven leaflets. The white flowers are borne in large saucer-shaped cymes during June and July, and at this time the elder is a very ornamental shrub. These flowers are followed by great umbels of purple-black berries which weigh down the stems and are just asking to be snapped off and dropped into a pail.

Unlike most wild fruits, the elderberry is neither hard to find nor tedious to gather. Locate your foraging ground while the attractive bloom makes the plant conspicuous, then return in August or early September to harvest the fruit. The whole cluster can be picked off at once, so it only takes a few minutes to fill a large pail.

The elderberry has recently been investigated for its nutritional qualities and it was found that here was one of nature's richest sources of vitamin C. It is far richer in this most-needed vitamin than citrus fruits or tomatoes. Remember, you are dropping health into that pail, as well as flavor and color.

Elderberries lack acid and are not palatable as fresh fruit, having a rank "eldery" taste and odor which is very noticeable when a green stem of elder is broken. But don't let this discourage you, for, when the fruit is properly prepared, all objectionable taste and odor disappears.

Elderberries have been best known as the raw material for a spicy, homemade wine. I don't drink wine myself, but for those who do, this is probably a less pernicious drink than most. Yeast fermentation would add B vitamins to the naturally high C vitamin content, making this wine so vitamin-fortified that it should build you up as it tears you down.

My "drinking uncle" says he takes 20 pounds of elderberries, mashes them into a 5-gallon crock and adds 5 quarts of boiling water, then covers the jar and lets them stand 3 days. Then he strains the juice, returns it to the jar and adds 10 cups of sugar. He lets this stand in the covered crock until all fermentation ceases, then the scum is removed, the wine strained, poured into bottles and tightly capped. My uncle always lets it stand 20 minutes to age, but it's much better if it is not touched for a year.

But it is for unfermented food and drink that I value the elderberry. As jelly timber it has few equals and no superiors if it is mixed with other fruit with a more acid juice. Sure-Jell, a commercial pectin, has a recipe for Elderberry Jelly in each package, using lemon to give it the desired acidity. You may see a wild crab-apple tree or some half-ripe wild grapes while you are gathering your elderberries and, if you do, take them. Either of these fruits combine wonderfully with elderberry to produce some of the prettiest and best jelly you ever saw or tasted.

Just wash the crab apples, put them whole into a kettle and cover with water. Boil until the fruit is tender, about 20 minutes, then strain off the juice. This is really a watery extract instead of a juice, but it is rich in pectin, acid and apple flavor.

Treat the grapes and elderberries alike, filling the kettle not over half full and adding 1 cup of water to each quart of fruit. Simmer gently for 10 minutes, then mash the fruit, simmer 10 minutes more, pour into a jelly bag made of several thicknesses of cheesecloth and squeeze out the juice

To make the jelly take 3 cups of elderberry juice and 3 cups of crab apple or grape juice, or mix them any way that suits your taste, as long as you use at least half pectin-rich juice. Add 6 cups of sugar

LOCUST (top), SUMAC (middle),
ELDERBERRY (bottom)

and boil until the jelly test tells you it will jell when cooled in the glasses.

Do you know how to make the jelly test? It is more easily done than described, but roughly, it goes like this: After the jelly is boiling hard, use the cooking spoon with which you are stirring it. Take up a little of the mix and wave the spoon around over the kettle until the juice cools slightly. Then pour it back into the pot. If it runs off like water, the jelly is nowhere near ready. If it drips off the spoon in two places, it is approaching the jelly point. When the last two drops run together, sheet off the spoon and seem to break at the edge of the spoon when they drop, snatch the jelly from the fire. No amount of instruction can take the place of experience in performing this task well. Go ahead and try it; you will be surprised how quickly you will master this art.

The jellies can be stored in glasses covered with paraffin, but a better way is to use the straight-sided half-pint jars which seal with two-piece lids. They are wider at the top than at the bottom and the jelly unmolds perfectly if you wish to serve it in a fancy dish, and these wild fruit jellies deserve fancy dishes. Properly packed, these jars will travel safely through the mail and you can have confidence they will arrive in good shape, and that is more than I can say about any paraffined glass. Wild fruit jellies make unique, inexpensive and very acceptable gifts, and what a subtle way to brag about your jelly-making ability.

My own favorite Elderberry Jelly utilizes another wild fruit that is almost totally overlooked. This is the Scarlet Sumac, which grows all over the area where the elderberry is found, so it is always available. This is the *Rhus glabra* of the botanists and is a very familiar roadside shrub or small tree, where its feathery leaves with their numerous pointed leaflets lend an almost tropical air to the landscape. In August, when the elderberry is also ripe, the sumac bears large rhomboidal clusters of hard, bright red, berrylike fruit. There is a poisonous species of sumac, but it bears white berries on loose strings, so if you only go for the dense clusters of red berries there is no danger of picking the poisonous kind by mistake. Like the elderberry, these are not tedious to pick. Just break off the whole cluster; I have seen hundreds of places where a bushel basketful could be gathered in a few minutes.

When we go out for elderberries we also gather a bushel or two of sumac. Formerly, we only used it to make a cooling drink very like pink lemonade to ease us through the August "dog days." The hard fruit of the sumac is covered with tiny, acid red hairs. This is malic acid, the same acid found in unripe apples, and it is readily soluble in water. Try to gather your sumac before hard rains wash out most of the acid. The American Indians liked this cool, sour drink so well they used to gather large quantities of the heads when they were in their prime and dry them indoors, so they could make this beverage all winter.

Once, our method of preparing it was to put the heads in a large container, cover them with water, and pound and stir it for ten minutes with a wooden pestle or potato masher. My son, disliking hard work in hot weather, invented a new process. He just dumped a basket of sumac heads into the washing machine, covered them with water and set the washer to run ten minutes, then caught the *Rhus*-ade in our big canning kettle as the washer pumped it out.

Always strain this juice through several thicknesses of cloth to remove all the fine hairs. Sweetened to taste, it is quite as palatable as lemonade.

I used to make my Elderberry Jelly by adding lemon juice, but one day I prepared to run off a batch and found there were no lemons in the house. There were a couple of 1-gallon jugs of unsweetened sumac extract in the refrigerator. So, instead of adding water to the elderberries as I cooked them, I put in sumac juice, quite a lot of it; in fact I covered the berries in the kettle with this acid solution. The jelly turned out very well and I liked the hint of tartness the sumac imparted so well that I wanted more of it. In the next batch I used half elderberry juice and half sumac juice and something wonderful happened. Instead of the purple-black of elderberry, the jelly came out a clear translucent red, and all cloying oversweetness was gone. It had a delightful, clean tartness that invited you to eat more, and then more.

Neither of the fruits employed have enough natural pectin, so this will have to be added. I mix 1 package of Sure-Jell with 2 cups of elderberry juice and 2 cups of sumac extract. As soon as this boils, I add 5 cups of sugar; then, when this comes to a hard boil, I let it roll for 1 minute, take it off the fire, skim it and pour it into half-pint jars and seal immediately. This jelly is economical and easy to make and will be very popular, so make quite a lot of it.

Don't get the idea that the elder is only good for wine or jelly. Elderberry Juice, extracted with sumac, as above, can be canned for winter use. A little of this juice added to other fruit juices will contribute flavor, color and healthfully fortify it with vitamin C. Or, if you would like to can a healthful and palatable juice which is ready to serve, mix 3 parts sumac extract with 1 part elderberry juice and sweeten to taste. Bring it to a boil and immediately pour it into hot, sterilized bottles or jars and cap or seal, as the case may be, with sterilized caps or lids.

For a little fancier drink you can make Elderberry Rob. For this you put the elderberry juice in a kettle and for each quart, add 6 cloves, 1 whole nutmeg and 1 stick of cinnamon. Boil for ½ hour, strain, then for each quart add 1 heaping cup of sugar. Boil a few minutes, skim and seal as above. When serving, dilute this with other fruit juices or sumac-ade.

As fresh-cooked fruit the elderberry has little to recommend it. In the course of my research I tried numerous recipes for pies, sauces and fruit soups, and found them all pretty nauseous mixtures. But dried elderberries are a different matter entirely. Collect the berries when they are fully ripe, separate them from the stems and dry them on flat trays in the sun in a homemade dehydrator or even in the oven of your range (see page 137), and you will have an economical raw material for making some wonderful fruit dishes in the winter. All the rank elder taste is dissipated by drying.

Some people like dried elderberries just stewed with sugar and a little lemon and served as a sauce. I like to boil the dried berries with a little sugar, then drain off the juice and use the berries to make Mock Blueberry Muffins which are not inferior to the original. Or substitute the dried, stewed elderberries for blueberries or huckleberries in a favorite pie recipe. For, after they are dried, elderberries make excellent pies. The drained-off juice will be brightly colored and by all means add it to the fruit juice you serve for breakfast the next morning.

While you have dried elderberries on hand be sure to make some Elderberry Chutney. Take 3 cups of dried elderberries, 1 large onion, chopped fine, 1 clove of garlic, pressed or minced, 1 teaspoon of ground ginger, 1 teaspoon of salt, a tiny pinch of cayenne pepper, mix them all together and cover with a sirup made of 1 cup of water, 1 cup of sugar and 2 cups of cider vinegar. Tie up in a small square of cheesecloth 1 finely sliced lemon and 1 tablespoon of mixed pickling spices. Drop this bag into the kettle with the other ingredients and boil it all until the chutney is quite thick, stirring it often to keep it from scorching. Remove the spice bag and pour the chutney into half-pint jars while boiling hot and seal immediately. This is a real gourmet's condiment and, served with the meat course, it will transform a very ordinary dinner into something your guests will write home about.

The elder is a very versatile plant and the berry is not the only useful product it yields. I start asking the elder to contribute in January, when I make spiles from the stems for collecting maple sap (see page 120). The old stems of the elder have soft pith in the center which is easily punched out with a small iron rod. Children, and adults like me who have never really grown up, find these thick-walled, hollow stems very useful for manufacturing peashooters, blowguns, water pistols, popguns, whistles and flutes.

The broad umbels of creamy-white flowers which the elder bears all during June and July are not only beautiful, but also edible, and, for that matter, drinkable. These blossoms are called Elder Blow, when used in culinary arts, and some of my friends think this is the finest product of the elder. Gather the umbels at the very height of bloom, remove the coarse stems and dip the clusters in a batter made of 1 cup of flour, 1 tablespoon of sugar, 1 teaspoon of baking powder, 2 eggs and ½ cup of milk. Fry the dipped clusters in deep fat, heated to about 375° for approximately 4 minutes, or until they are a golden brown. Place them on a paper towel, squeeze a little orange juice over them, then roll in granulated sugar, serve while they are piping hot and watch them disappear.

Let me digress for a moment to point out that the large clusters of flowers borne by the Black Locust (*Robinia pseudoacacia*) and those of the Wisteria (*Wisteria*, several species, all equally good) can be treated in the same manner. Each kind brings its own distinctive flavor to the table, but all make delicious fritters.

Of course, there will be no elderberries on the stems where the flower cluster has been broken off, so maybe you had better gather your flowers at a distance from where you intend to collect berries. If you catch the blossoms just before they are ready to fall, you can rub your hand gently across the flower head and catch the urn-shaped corollas in a pail as they fall. I have gathered a gallon or more of pure, stemless elder flowers in this way in a short while, and then returned a month or so later and picked the berries from the same stems. To make fritters of these flowers, just use the same batter as for clusters and stir in as many elder flowers as it will dampen. This will make a very stiff batter which can be dropped into the hot fat from a small ice-cream dipper or a tablespoon. Treat them just like the cluster fritters and you will find them equally good.

Use these flowers to make Elder Blow Pancakes and Muffins. Just mix your regular pancake or muffin batter a little thin and stir it full of elder flowers. It makes them wonderfully light and adds a distinctive and delicious flavor.

You can even make face cream from elder flowers, which is reputed to "beautify the complexion." I haven't tried this, for beautifying my complexion would be too great a task to ask of any cosmetic. Those who are better endowed need only buy 8 ounces of cocoa butter and 1 ounce of lanolin from the druggist, melt these in the top of a double boiler and add all the elder flowers the mixture will cover. Cook it gently for an hour, then strain and pour into small jars. This cream is also recommended for use as a healing salve for sores on man or beast.

While we are on the subject of medicinal uses of elderberries, I must pass on the information that a hot poultice of elder leaves is said to relieve the pain, and promote the healing, of sprains and bruises. The dried flowers with the addition of a small quantity of dried mint leaves make a palatable tea which has long been familiar as a diet tea for dyspeptics. A palatable and effective cough sirup can be made by following the recipe for Elderberry Rob, with the exception of substituting 1 cup of honey for the heaping cup of sugar. This cough sirup, again, may be diluted with a half-sumac extract, made this time by covering the berries with water and boiling for 10 minutes, and it then makes a healing gargle for treating sore throat.

Tea is not the only beverage that may be made from elder flowers. Again, I am indebted to my "drinking uncle" for the information that Elder Blow Wine has a delicious taste and a beautiful, pale-yellow color. He says it is too fine a product for the guzzling of his drinking friends, so he keeps his supply for special guests. He puts ½ gallon of elder flowers and 10 cups of sugar in a 3-gallon crock, then fills the crock not quite full with lukewarm water and adds 1 cake of yeast. This is covered with a cloth and allowed to stand 9 days. Then he takes 3 1-gallon jugs and puts 1 pound of raisins in the bottom of each. The wine is then strained into the jugs, capped not too tightly and stored in his cool, dark cellar for 6 months. It is then carefully decanted into bottles and tightly capped. If you can forget it for another year, so much the better.

Now you can see that it is possible for the many products of the elderberry to add to the richness of living throughout the year. In the future, let's show more appreciation for this common shrub which stands at the roadside, freely offering food and drink, medicine and beauty. It would be churlish indeed to refuse such graciously offered gifts.

Using Wild Grapes
(*Vitis* species)

A MERICA is blessed with an abundance of Wild Grapes of many species. It is this wild fruit which gave our country the first name by which it was known among Europeans. There is now little doubt that the Vikings from Norway, Iceland and Greenland made not one but several voyages to what is now the coast of New England, beginning with that of Lief Erikson in the year 1000. Finding a profusion of wild grapes, they named the country Vinland and tried to establish settlements there. But the Atlantic was too wide, the ships too small and the Indians too fierce for this to succeed. So, for nearly five hundred years, the dimly remembered knowledge of this western continent lay buried in Viking sagas, where it was reported as a Land of Wild Grapes.

America is still a vineland, from New Brunswick to Florida, and far to the West. I have picked good wild grapes (*Vitis arizonica*) along canyon bottoms in New Mexico, and I have plucked Fox Grapes (*V. labrusca*) within the sound of the Atlantic surf.

Several species of our northern wild grapes are sweet and pleasant to eat as fresh fruit when they are thoroughly ripe, but none of them are as sweet and tasty as the southern Muscadine (*V. rotundifolia*) for eating out of hand. But all of our wild grapes, large and small, sweet and sour, are valuable for making juice, jellies, conserves and

96

pies. Some of the smaller varieties are actually less tedious to pick than the larger ones, because they grow in tighter clusters and can be picked by the bunch rather than by the grape.

Wild Grape Jelly is even more fragrant and delicious than the well-known product of cultivated vines. To make it the old-fashioned way, use a mixture of ripe and unripe grapes. Wash, stem and crush the fruit and, for each quart of grapes, add ¼ cup of water. Cover and cook for about 15 minutes, then strain the juice out through a jelly bag.

WILD GRAPE

Now, here's the secret to perfect Grape Jelly: let the juice sit overnight in a crock or mixing bowl. The tartrate will crystallize and settle to the bottom of the container or cling to its sides. If this tartrate is allowed to crystallize in the jelly, it will make it gritty.

Next day, carefully dip out, or pour off, the juice. To each quart of juice, add 4 cups of sugar and bring it rapidly to a boil. Boil until you get a jelly test (see page 90), then pour into half-pint jars and seal. Don't try to make Grape Jelly in larger batches, for kitchen ranges just won't heat larger quantities fast enough to make perfect jelly.

If you prefer, you can pour the freshly prepared hot juice into quart jars, seal with sterilized lids and process in a boiling water bath for ten minutes. Check the seal, then store in a dark cabinet, and any time of the year, when you have the time, ambition and empty jars, you can run off a batch of fresh Grape Jelly in a few minutes.

Old-fashioned Wild Grape Conserve was one of the most delicious products to come out of our grandmothers' kitchens. Slip the skins off three pounds of fully ripe grapes. Cook the naked fruit a few minutes, then put through a food mill or a sieve to remove the seeds. Grind the raw skins in a food chopper with ½ pound of raisins and a strip of orange peel. Combine the seeded pulp and the skin-raisin mixture; add the juice of 1 orange and 2½ cups of sugar. Cook very slowly for about an hour until the mixture thickens. Then add 1 cup of finely chopped hickory nuts or pecan meats, stir well, cook for 5 minutes more, then pour into half-pint jars and seal. This recipe may be from "away back" but the delicacy it produces is still "away out."

You follow a similar process in making the best kind of Wild Grape Pie. Slip the skins from 4 cups of fully ripe wild grapes, simmer the pulp a few minutes and put it through a food mill or sieve to remove the seeds. Chop up the skins and return them to the now-seedless pulp. In a mixing bowl, combine 1 cup of sugar, ¼ cup of flour and ¼ teaspoon of salt. Add the juice of 1 lemon, 2 table-spoons of melted butter and the grape pulp. Mix well, then pour into an unbaked Oil Crust and decorate the top with scraps of pastry cut into grape-leaf shapes. Bake in 400° oven for about 40 minutes.

Grape Juice, when prepared for jellymaking as outlined above, makes a very poor beverage. An excellent drinking juice can be made from wild grapes, but you will need a deep, canning kettle and a cooking thermometer to prepare it properly. The secret of delicious homemade Grape Juice is never to boil the grapes.

Wash, stem and crush the grapes in a kettle, then barely cover with water. Heat to 160° and hold that heat for 20 minutes. This will free the juice which can then be strained from the pulp through a square of muslin or a double thickness of cheesecloth. Sweeten the juice to taste, then reheat to 160° and seal in thoroughly sterilized jars, bottles or jugs. Set the containers in a water bath heated to 170° for 20 minutes, check the seal and store in a dark place until ready to use. This juice is delicious to drink alone, mixed with other juices or served half and half with ginger ale. It will not make jelly unless pectin is added to it.

A simple method, which I often use, yields both grapes and juice. Put 1 quart of washed and stemmed grapes into each sterilized ½-gallon jar. Add 1 cup of sugar to each jar, then fill the jars with boiling water. Seal immediately and pasteurize the jars in a hot water bath at 170° for 20 minutes. It will be a month or more before they are ready to use. Drain off the juice as a delightful beverage and use the grapes to make a pie, following the recipe given above, except that one uses only ¾ cup of sugar.

To most people, grapes mean Grape Wine, but, according to professional wine makers and connoisseurs, there are no native American wild grapes which make good wine. This is probably true if one attempts to make wine of wild grapes just as it is made from cultivated wine grapes. I have sampled the results of several attempts to make wine from wild grapes by standard methods and, to me, they were all utterly undrinkable.

I consider myself fairly knowledgeable when it comes to tastes in food, but I am afraid I am no judge of wine. I find most wines nauseating, even those which are so highly praised by the experts. To me, most home wine making is a criminal waste of good fruit juice. However, on two occasions I tasted sweet wines made of wild grapes which I thought the finest drinks that had ever passed my lips. One of these wines was made in Texas from mustang grapes (*Vitis candicans*) and the other was made in Pennsylvania from fox grapes, but the methods used were identical and the results tasted much the same, both being excellent. These wines were sweet but light, with a clean, sparkling flavor and a beautiful color. The method of manufacture must be the secret, and this method seems perfectly suited to wild grapes, and can be used to make any quantity from a gallon to a barrelful. The results might fail to pass a panel of professional wine-tasters, but it tastes perfectly delicious to everyone else. Since there are so many more ordinary people than experts, this wine should prove popular.

Making this sweet wine is simplicity itself. The grapes are washed and stemmed, but never crushed. Make the wine in any large jar, crock or keg. Just put 2 cups of grapes in the container and cover with 1 cup of sugar, then 2 more cups of grapes and another cup of sugar and so on until you run out of room or grapes. Cover the container but do not seal tightly, and set it in a cool, dark place. The temperature should be kept at between 55° and 60°. It takes about

2 months to ferment and settle out, to appear clear. At this time, it should be carefully decanted into bottles and tightly capped. If you catch it at just the right time, it will still be a little sweet and have a bit of a sparkle when opened.

Grape Leaves are also edible. They have a pleasant, acid flavor, even when raw, but they are a little too tough to consider adding them to a tossed salad. They become tender when cooked, and impart a delicious flavor to other food. For cooking purposes, grape leaves should be gathered in June, when they are full-sized but still tender. They can be preserved with salt for use at other times of the year. Lay each grape leaf flat in a covered glass or earthenware dish and sprinkle each leaf liberally with salt. Continue until the jar is full, then cover and keep in a cool place. To use these preserved leaves, wash them gently several times in fresh water and proceed as with fresh leaves.

A really de luxe way of cooking small game birds such as quail, doves, pheasant or grouse is to use vine leaves. Here is my recipe for quail which can be adapted to the others according to size. I rub the cleaned birds inside and out with a little salt and fill them with celery stuffing, then wrap each bird in 2 large vine leaves and pack four of them in a glass baking dish with a tight-fitting cover. I then cream ½ pound of butter with 1 tablespoon of flour, season it with a little salt and pepper and pack this around the birds. This is tightly covered and cooked for about 40 minutes in a 400° oven. The next time you are giving a dinner for people who really appreciate good food, try serving squab or Cornish hen in vine leaves, and watch their eyes light up.

Stuffed Grape Leaves is one of the finest foods to ever come out of the Middle East, yet it is really a very economical main dish and very easy to prepare. To make the stuffing, put 1 cup of rice in a saucepan and cover with 2 cups of cold water. Bring rapidly to a boil, then turn the heat low and cook until the water is absorbed, about 30 to 40 minutes. Mix this partially cooked rice with ½ pound of ground lamb or beef and add 1 package of commercial spaghetti sauce mix. Place one tablespoon of the meat-rice mixture on each grape leaf and roll from the base toward the point, carefully tucking in the ends. Steam the rolled grape leaves in a covered kettle for 1 hour and serve hot.

Nearly a thousand years have passed since the ancient Vikings first reported the abundance of wild grapes growing on our continent. These wild vines are still not the least of our country's assets. One of the privileges of living in Vinland is having access to this excellent wild fruit. Let's exercise this privilege more often, shall we?

Ground Cherries for Pies and Preserves

(*Physalis pubescens*)

THE Ground Cherry is no relation to the cherry, but is a member of the Nightshade Family closely related to the tomato. It is also called Bladder Cherry, Husk Tomato, Strawberry Tomato and Dwarf Cape Gooseberry. The Chinese Lantern Plant, orange-red in color, is a ground cherry that is raised in flower gardens for its decorative husks, which are much used in dried flower arrangements. The exact number of species of *Physalis* is still much debated among botanists. All members of the genus produce edible fruit, but the quality and size of the berries vary greatly from species to species.

Physalis pubescens is one of the commonest and most widespread of this group, and I consider it the best, although other species have their advocates. It is sometimes raised in gardens and often escapes from cultivation, thus introducing "wild" ground cherries into a new area. It is a weed to be encouraged.

Wild ground cherries grow on a sprawling plant that seldom reaches over a foot in height, although it sometimes covers several square feet of ground. The leaves are irregularly notched, pointed, and range in size from minute to three inches long by two inches broad on the specimen that is lying on my desk as I write. The fruit is borne abundantly in little papery, five-sided husks, which closely resemble the familiar Chinese lanterns of dried flower arrangements, except that *pubescens* lacks the orange coloring of the Chinese lantern, being a plain straw color when ripe, and it is also somewhat smaller than the lanterns, being only about one inch in diameter. These husks hang by stems about one inch long that spring from the axils of the leaves. The fruit inside the husk is a single, smooth, yellow-green berry, about a half inch in diameter. The husk containing the fruit often falls from the plant before the berry is ripe enough to eat, but it will ripen and become sweet lying on the ground. When the husks are thoroughly dry, the fruit can be stored, husks and all, in a dry place and it will keep for a month or more, growing sweeter all the time.

GROUND CHERRY

Ground cherries are found growing wild from New York to Florida, and west to Minnesota and Iowa, southwestward across the country and down into the tropics. It is, however, somewhat local and rather rare over much of its range.

The ground cherry is well known in Hawaii, where it is called *Poha* in the native tongue. Once, a group of us was hiking through Haleakala Crater on the island of Maui. We stopped to drink at a spring near the crater wall, and I noticed a dozen or so ground cherry plants growing above the little water hole. I gathered more than a quart of the husked fruit, and, as we climbed out of the crater, we ate them whenever we stopped to rest. They quenched our thirst and gave us badly needed energy on that 3,000-foot climb, and they were pronounced delicious by all the party.

Despite the many luscious tropical fruits with which it must compete, the ground cherry is greatly appreciated in Hawaii. Poha Jam and Poha Preserves are great favorites with the islanders. Since returning from the islands, I have made jam and preserves from wild ground cherries which I picked in Pennsylvania, and found them indistinguishable from the Hawaiian products.

In this country, ground cherries are most often found in cultivated or fallow fields, and sometimes in burned-over areas. On new ground the plants are sometimes a troublesome weed for the first few years of cultivation. They have the ability to spring up in midsummer and make a crop before frost. I have gathered them in cornfields where they had come up and matured fruit after the last cultivation.

Last year I planted a patch of melons and covered the ground between the melon hills with a heavy hay mulch. The ground cherry seemed to be the only wild plant with the ability to find its way up through the mulch, so I reaped a double crop.

I like to eat ground cherries just as they come from the husk. Whenever I come on ripe ones, while tramping the fields, I fill my pockets with the little balloons, then husk and eat the fruit as I hike. When served as a fresh-fruit dessert, they should be husked, washed and sweetened to taste with a little honey, then served with cream. The taste will remind you of strawberries and tomatoes, but ground cherries have their own flavor, too, and it's so good it doesn't have to resemble something else.

To make the unjelled, sticky and perfectly delicious Poha Preserves, as the Hawaiians do, make a thick sirup from 3 cups of sugar and 1 cup of water. Add 1 lemon, cut in very thin slices, and 1 stick of cinnamon. Boil this together 10 minutes, then add 1 quart of husked and washed ground cherries, and boil until the fruit looks clear and the sirup is thick. Allow to stand overnight; next day, heat the preserves to boiling again and pour immediately into half-pint jars and seal.

To make jam, crush 1 quart of husked ground cherries and add the juice of 2 lemons, the grated peel of 1 lemon, ½ cup of water and 1 package of powdered pectin. Boil for five minutes, then add 4 cups of sugar. Boil hard for a minute or two, or until you get a jelly test (see page 90); pour into half pint jars and seal immediately.

Poha Pie is a real taste thrill. Combine ¼ cup of white flour, 1 cup of sugar, ¼ teaspoon of salt and ¼ teaspoon of cinnamon in a mixing bowl. Mix these dry ingredients thoroughly, then add the juice of 1 lemon and just enough water to make a smooth paste, about as thick as the thinnest pancake batter. Stir in 3 cups of husked and washed ground cherries. Line a 9-inch plate with rich pastry, pour in the ground cherry filling and fit another crust on top. Perforate the top crust in a number of places with a fork to keep it from trapping steam and puffing up, then bake for about 45 minutes in a medium oven until nicely browned. Serve slightly warm with cheese, ice cream or plain. The taste is reminiscent of both apples and apricots, and there are few fruit pies which surpass it in flavor.

With these instructions, I'm sure you'll be able to use all the ground cherries you can find. If there are any left over, call me.

The Groundnut or Indian Potato

(*Apios americana*)

WHEN I first heard of Groundnuts as a boy, I was fascinated by the possibilities of this excellent and interesting food plant, and it became the object of a quest that has lasted half a lifetime. My grandmother told how she had gathered "Indian potatoes" during the Civil War to help eke out their scanty food supplies. I finally learned that this was the same plant the history books called groundnuts when they told how the Pilgrim Fathers had depended on them during those first hard winters. I knew that the Indians considered this wilding the very finest of food.

Later I had the opportunity of examining a rare facsimile of a quaint old book by one Thomas Hariot, originally published in 1590, which told of an almost forgotten attempt by Sir Walter Raleigh to found a colony in Virginia in the sixteenth century. This little book, titled A *briefe and true report of the new found land of Virginia*, contains what is probably the first mention of groundnuts in the English language. He says:

Openavk are a kind of roots of round forme, some of the bigness of walnuts, some far greater, which are found in moist and marish grounds growing one by another in ropes, or as thogh they were fastened with a string, being boiled or sodden they are very good meate.

While still a small boy, I read everything I could lay my hands on concerning this plant. I learned that it was found from New Brunswick to Minnesota and south to the Gulf of Mexico and that its southwestern limit extended at least to the Red River Valley where I then lived.

Several people assured me that they had seen the groundnut growing wild in our neighborhood, but, though I searched many a wood and stream valley, I never found a single specimen. Then my parents moved farther west, out of the groundnut's range, and it was thirty years before I again set foot on soil in which this fabulous food was reputed to grow.

When I moved to eastern Pennsylvania, I renewed my quest. I knew that the groundnut had been common there in early days, for there were records that the Swedes and Finns who first settled the Delaware Valley had made much use of them, but even there it was a long time before I saw my first living plant.

Then, one day in August, I was making my way down a wooded stream valley looking for a likely fishing hole, when I noticed a delicious fragrance in the air. Following my nose, I soon saw not one but several groundnut vines trailing over some elderberry bushes. Although they were the first I had ever seen, I recognized them instantly. The soft, thin vines trailing over the brush, the compound leaves with from five to nine leaflets and the purplish-brown, almost chocolate-colored blooms with their heavy, sweet fragrance, had been pictured too often in my imagination for me to mistake them now. Trailing one of the vines to its source, I scratched into the soft ground with my bare hands and unearthed the first string of groundnuts I had ever seen. There were only seven of the tuberlike swellings on the root, and the largest of them was only a little over an inch in diameter, but how thrilled I was to at last be holding this elusive dainty in my hands. I searched and found others, and that night I had my first taste of this long-sought food.

Was I disappointed in the taste of groundnuts after the terrific build-up that more than thirty years' search had given it? That would be hard to say. I was a bit surprised at the smooth, sweet, slightly turniplike flavor, for I had been led to think that it was very like the potato. Had I been served this food without having ever heard of groundnuts, I'm sure I would have thought it passably good, but nothing extra. But to me that first taste was compounded of Indian campfires, Pilgrim Fathers and pioneers; there were the woods and valleys of my childhood search; such boyhood dreams are very pleasant for a middle-aged man to munch on.

Such romantic sauce tended to fade as I became more familiar with this tuber-bearing perennial legume, but I still like groundnuts, preferring them to potatoes as a general thing. I like them just plain-boiled in heavily salted water and eaten with butter. They should always be eaten hot, for they become tough and tasteless when cold. Leftover boiled groundnuts will regain their flavor if they are greased and roasted a while in the oven. I have also enjoyed groundnuts in camp just washed and thinly sliced, then fried in bacon fat. Even to those who have never shared my long-drawn-out anticipation, the groundnut is one of the fine native wild foods.

Japanese Knotweed:

A COMBINATION FRUIT-VEGETABLE

(Polygonum cuspidatum)

THIS bold invader from Japan has made itself at home from New-foundland to Ontario, south to the Carolinas and Missouri. It is related to our docks and sorrels and even to domestic buckwheat, but it is very difficult for an amateur to see any resemblance.

A single clump of this propagative plant will soon spread and form a thicket, monopolizing the ground where it gets started. In early spring, it sends up numerous vigorous sprouts which superficially resemble asparagus when they first appear. These rapidly shoot up to make large hollow stems, four to eight feet high. The jointed stems have enlarged nodes, like bamboo, and each node is sheathed in a papery cufflike membrane. The leaves are somewhat ovoid, but are nearly square across the base and terminate in an abrupt point. The greenish-white flowers are borne abundantly on racemes that spring from the axils of the leaves, and in July and August the whole plant seems weighted down with the blossoms which almost cover it. I do not find these flowers particularly attractive but many consider them beautiful and it was as an ornamental that this plant was first brought to this country. When in full bloom the branches with their loads of flowers can be broken off and dried in a warm room, and the flowers can be used in dried winter arrangements in the manner of coxcomb or everlasting.

It is the young, vigorous shoot that we want for food, and these are easily located by noting the dry, hollow, last-year's stalks, which persist over winter.

This *Polygonum* so closely resembles asparagus that many are disappointed when it doesn't taste like that vegetable. Like other wild foods, Japanese knotweed has to be considered a good vegetable in its own right, and not a substitute for some familiar product.

The summits of the young shoots, a foot high or more before the leaves begin unrolling, make a pleasant vegetable, just boiled, salted and buttered, but don't taste like asparagus. They cook very quickly, in 3 to 4 minutes, and have an acid quality that survives the cooking. If you find them too tart for your taste, a little sugar can be added. These tips are also good when cooked, chilled and served as a salad with mayonnaise or French dressing.

An even better way to prepare these asparaguslike tips is to steam or boil them until soft, then put them through a food mill or colander to prepare a purée. Seasoned with butter, salt and a little sugar and served as a hot soup, this is utterly delicious. By leaving out the butter and adding a bit more sugar, this soup can be served cold as an unusual first course for a lunch or dinner on a hot spring day. This is reminiscent of the fruit soups so popular in Scandinavia.

To make a tasty Aspic Salad, add 2 tablespoons of sugar and ½ teaspoon of salt to 2 cups of purée. Soften 1 envelope of unflavored gelatin in ¼ cup of cold water, then set the cup in boiling water until the gelatin dissolves. Stir the dissolved gelatin into the purée and pour into individual molds. Unmold to serve and garnish each mound with a sprig of fresh water cress. Such an attractive and unusual salad can serve as a conversation piece to get a dinner party off on the right foot, and it tastes just as good as it looks.

Japanese knotweed, like rhubarb, can be used as fruit in making sweet sauces, jams or pies. For these purposes, select large, young stalks several feet high, with long internodes, and peel off the purple-mottled rind. Don't peel too deeply, or you will have nothing left but a large round hole, for the walls of the stems are pretty thin. The green inner walls of the young stalks should be cut into short pieces crosswise. They are very tender and have a pleasant, acid taste even when eaten raw, and can be used in this state to give an often-needed piquant touch to a green tossed salad.

To make a different kind of sweet-tart sauce, put 3 cups of peeled

JAPANESE KNOTWEED

and chopped stalks in a saucepan, add 1 cup of sugar, the juice of 1 lemon and about 1 teaspoon of finely grated lemon peel. Let stand a few minutes and the sugar will draw enough juice so no water will have to be added. Boil for only a few minutes until it is soft, and it is ready to serve, hot or cold.

To make Japanese Knotweed Jam, put 4 cups of peeled and chopped stalks in a saucepan and add the juice of 1 lemon, a little grated lemon peel and ½ cup of water. Simmer for a few minutes until the chopped knotweed is soft. Stir in 1 package of commercial pectin, let it come to a boil and stir in 4 cups of sugar. Boil hard for 1 minute, then pour into half-pint jars and seal. The first time I made this jam I didn't like its yellowish-green color, so now I stir in some green food coloring just before pouring it into the jars to give it a nice bright hue.

When I first began research on *Polygonum cuspidatum,* I experimented with many recipes, trying to make a really good pie. The less said about my earlier attempts, the better. However, I finally hit on a combination that makes a pie which everyone seems to like. In one mixing bowl, blend together 1½ cups of sugar, ¼ cup of flour and ¾ teaspoon of nutmeg. In another bowl, beat 3 eggs. Then gradually beat the flour-sugar mixture into the eggs. When this is all well blended, stir in 4 cups of peeled and chopped knotweed stalks. This completes the filling for the pie.

As in all pies, whether one fails or succeeds depends as much on the crust as on the filling. I have found that an Oil Crust is just perfect for a Japanese Knotweed Pie. To make this flaky pastry, sift together 2 cups of flour and 1 teaspoon of salt. Pour ¼ cup of cold milk and ½ cup of salad oil into a measuring cup, but do not stir. Add all at once to the flour and mix well with a fork. Divide the dough in half and form into two round balls. Dampen the table top with a sponge and smooth a 12-inch square of wax paper on the dampened area. Slightly flatten one of the balls of dough in the center of the wax paper and cover with another piece of wax paper exactly the same size as the first. Roll the dough between the pieces of wax paper until it reaches the edges and it will be just the right thickness and size. Peel off the top paper, turn the dough over, fit it into the pie pan, then carefully remove the second piece of wax paper.

Now pour in the filling, dot the top with butter and fit on a top crust, made of the other piece of dough rolled between the same two pieces of wax paper. Perforate the top crust in several places to keep it from trapping steam, and bake in a 400° oven for 50 minutes. Cool before serving.

Don't tell me that you would like to try some of these products but can't locate any Japanese knotweed. I have seldom driven on the roads or ridden the trains in any part of the area where it grows without seeing a number of clumps of this fine food plant from the window of the car or train. You only need to have access to one clump of Japanese knotweed in order to gather all that you can use.

Juneberries, Shadberries or Serviceberries

(*Amelanchier*, about 20 species)

IT SEEMS strange to me that more modern Americans don't know and use the Juneberry or, as it is known in some areas, the Shadberry. Enterprising campers, even those from the city, immediately recognize and eagerly pick blueberries, blackberries and wild strawberries, but the equally good Juneberry goes begging.

One species or another of *Amelanchier* grows from Newfoundland to British Columbia, and south to Mexico and the Gulf. All the species do not produce equally good fruit, but nearly all of them were eagerly sought by the Indians and entered many ways into their cookery. In the eastern part of our country, the Juneberry (A. *canadensis*) is the very finest of the genus. It ranges from Nova Scotia to western Ontario and south to Georgia and Missouri.

The Swamp Sugar Pear (A. *intermedia*) is another member of this family with about the same range, being a shrub six to ten feet high. It is sometimes cultivated for its excellent, sweet fruit which is somewhat pear-shaped, about a half inch long and purple with a bloom when ripe.

Another excellent species is the Northwestern Serviceberry (A. *florida*) which grows from western Ontario to British Columbia and south to Colorado and northern California. I have seen areas in the state of Washington where literally thousands of bushels of this fruit could have been collected. The recipes which we will consider were all tested with Juneberries, but they seem to work well with the other species of *Amelanchier* that I have had the opportunity to try.

The Juneberry, in adapting itself to the varied conditions throughout its wide range, has assumed a variety of forms. In eastern Pennsylvania, I have seen it growing as a good-sized tree, thirty feet high with a trunk eight inches in diameter, bearing dozens of quarts of large berries. In the high mountains of the central part of the same state, I have found it growing as a knee-high shrub, but still bearing delicious berries, identical with those of the larger plants.

JUNEBERRY, SHAD

The alternate leaves, slightly resembling those of the apple tree, are oval, rounded at the base and somewhat pointed on the other end, edged with very fine teeth. The white flowers, five-petaled, about an inch across are borne in loose bunches, appear early and sometimes almost cover the tree, making it the most conspicuous thing in the woods. This is the time to locate the trees from which you can gather the ripe fruit in late June or early July.

Most people who have made the acquaintance of the Juneberry need no instruction on how to use the fruit, but merely stand by the bush or tree and stuff themselves. The dark-red, almost purplish, berries are a fine fruit to eat out of hand, the ten soft seeds in each adding rather than detracting from their flavor. These same seeds get even softer when the berry is cooked, and contribute much to the flavor of the finished product.

They are delicious as a Stewed Fruit or Sauce, served hot or cold. Add 1 cup of sugar to 3 cups of berries and simmer for 20 minutes.

Few fruits equal the Juneberry as pie timber. To make a June-berry Pie, line a 9-inch plate with Oil Pastry and fill generously with washed Juneberries. Mix ¾ cup of sugar, ¼ cup of flour and 1 scant teaspoon of salt. Sprinkle this over the berries, dot the top with butter, arrange the top crust, perforate a pattern and bake for 45 minutes in a 400° oven.

Juneberries make wonderful Muffins, the cooked seeds imparting a rich almond flavor, but unlike blueberries, the Juneberries should be cooked before being included in the muffins. Just follow the recipe for stewed Juneberries, then drain off the sirup. In a round-bottomed mixing bowl, sift 2 cups of flour with 2 tablespoons of sugar, ½ tea-spoon of salt, 1 teaspoon of baking powder and ½ teaspoon of soda. Stir carefully from the outside of the bowl and mix the berries into the flour. Still stirring gently so as not to crush the berries, mix in 1 beaten egg, 2 tablespoons of melted butter and ¾ cup of buttermilk. Stir barely enough to dampen all the ingredients. The mixture will be thick, more like sticky dough than batter. Use a small ice-cream dipper and fill greased muffin tins half full. Bake in a 400° oven for about 18 minutes.

The Indians used to dry great quantities of Juneberries and North-western serviceberries for out-of-season use. They are easily dried on flat trays in the sun. The dried berries taste so different from the fresh fruit that they have to be considered another kind of food. They are very good used like currants in puddings and muffins, or just stewed and eaten.

The canning or freezing of Juneberries is no trouble at all. Pack the washed berries into jars, cover with a sirup made of 3 parts water to 1 part sugar, seal the jars and set in the quick-freeze section of your freezer. For canned berries, process for thirty minutes in boiling water, check the seal and store away. The frozen berries make an excellent dessert or breakfast fruit; just thaw and serve. The canned berries make pies, muffins or stewed fruit that is little if at all inferior to those from fresh berries.

I'm sure that God put Juneberries on earth for the use of man, as well as for the bears, raccoons and birds. Let's get our share.

Sweets from Trees

(The Maple Family)

> For we can make liquor to sweeten our lips
> From pumpkins and parsnips and walnut tree chips
>
> Old song quoted by Thoreau in *Walden.*

These lines seem to indicate that man once knew how to garner the vast supplies of sugar to be found in nature, but this knowledge has now largely been forgotten. It had already grown dim in Thoreau's day, for, although he considered the possibility of planting Sugar Maples to provide sirup and sugar, it apparently never occurred to him to tap the other species of maple which he mentions as growing about Walden Pond. Had he tried this, he probably would not have bothered to plant the sugar maples.

My own experiments would lead one to conclude that good sirup and sugar can be made from all the large species of maple growing in this country. This includes those which have been introduced from foreign lands, such as the Norway Maple and the Planetree Maple, as well as the indigenous species. As we shall see in succeeding chapters, sugar and sirup can also be made from the sap of some trees which are not even related to the maples.

Today, the production of maple sirup and sugar is confined to a relatively small area in northeastern United States and adjacent

117

Canada, and it never seems to occur to anyone that it might be made elsewhere. Yet in literature I find mention of maple sirup having been made as far south as Georgia and as far west as Texas. This was in early times, before other forms of sweetening became available to the settlers. Now maple sugaring seems to be a completely forgotten art in these regions. Generally, one could say that the sap sugars can be made wherever suitable trees are growing, and there are many more suitable trees than most people have suspected. This is not to say that commercial production of maple sugar would be successful in all these places, but, as a hobby and for one's own use, this interesting pursuit could be practiced over a much wider area than was formerly thought possible.

I have made sirup from the Sugar Maple (*Acer saccharum*), the Red Maple (*A. rubrum*), the Silver Maple (*A. saccharinum*), the Norway Maple (*A. platanoides*), the Planetree Maple (*A. pseudoplatanus*), and the Box Elder or Ash-Leaf Maple (*A. negundo*), boiling the sap down separately for each species. A panel of tasters was not able to detect any difference in the various products. Nor did I discover any really significant differences between the various species in amount of sap produced or its sugar content. These last two qualities vary widely from tree to tree within the same species and this makes for wide overlapping between the species. That is, a good Norway maple will be a much better sugar producer than a poor sugar maple, and this same relationship holds good for all the other varieties.

There are two other maples in this country I'd like to try as sugar producers. One of these is the Bigleaf Maple (*A. macrophyllum*) of the Pacific Northwest. I can find no record of even one experimental tap being made on this tree, and yet I'll wager that it would be a good sugar producer. The other on which I would like to experiment is the Sugar Tree (*A. floridanum*) of the Deep South. There is record that this tree was an important source of sugar until sugar cane and sorghum products became common. Today most of the people living in the areas where the sugar tree grows have long since forgotten how it acquired its name.

On reading that certain Indian tribes used the sweet sap of the Sycamore (*Platanus occidentalis*) for making sugar and sirup, I tapped a large, double-trunked sycamore that was growing on a creek bank near my home. It produced a copious flow and, with one tap in each trunk, I soon had the two gallons of sap I wanted for the experiment. But when I boiled it down I discovered that I would have done about as well had I merely dipped up two gallons of water from the nearby creek. It gave off a maple aroma as it boiled, but the entire amount produced little over a tablespoonful of very dark-colored sirup which tasted like a poor grade of blackstrap molasses. One shouldn't draw too many conclusions from this single experiment, but it does cause me to suspect that either those reported Indians are more industrious than I am, or else they had better sycamore trees than the one I used.

Sycamore   Silver

MAPLES

There has been much debate about the proper time of year to tap maple trees. I have tapped sugar, Norway, red and silver maples during a New Year's thaw, as early as January 7 in southern Pennsylvania; and there is record of the sugar harvest extending as late as May 10 in Saskatchewan from the sap of box elder. Roughly, one could say that any time is sugar time from New Year's Day until the leaves appear, if the weather is right. The maple flows best on warm sunny days following frosty nights.

The inexperienced are always amazed at the quantity of sap that will drip from one maple tree. By putting six taps in one huge maple, I once collected over ten gallons of sap from a single tree in one day. On another occasion, I collected a little over forty gallons of sap from six large Norway maples on a perfect day for sugaring. These are exceptional trees; the average good-sized maple can be expected to deliver only about a gallon of finished sirup per year.

Although collecting sap is not a tedious task, the job of boiling it down more than makes up for it. There is an old legend that long ago the Indians were able to draw thick, finished sirup directly from the trees. One of their culture heroes was afraid that being able to get food so easily would make the Indians lazy. He climbed all the maple trees and poured water down inside them to dilute the sap so his people would henceforth have to evaporate the water by boiling, thus requiring a decent amount of work to get a supply of sirup.

I think most people will agree with me that this ancient guardian of Indian character rather overdid it. It takes thirty to forty gallons of average maple sap to make one gallon of sirup and I suspect that this industrious Indian accidentally spilled his whole water supply down the sycamore.

The spigots from which the sap runs are called spiles. Manufactured ones of metal are sold in Vermont but I always make my own. This is done by cutting some large elderberry stems, sawing them in four-inch lengths and punching out the pith with a small iron rod. These are abruptly sharpened on one end so when driven in the hole they will fit the opening snugly and still not close off any of the ducts inside through which the sap flows. Near the other end a notch is cut in which to hang the pail.

With a half-inch bit pointed slightly upward, drill a three-inch deep hole on the sunny side of the tree about three feet above the ground. Gently hammer the spile snugly into place with the notch uppermost, hang on your pail and the tap is complete. That's all there is to it. Two taps can be put in most trees and more in the larger ones. I make my pails of gallon-size fruit tins with holes punched near the top on either side to fasten in a wire bail.

For reducing the sap to sirup commercial operators use large flue-type evaporators and sirup is made in a continuous process, but such equipment is beyond the reach of most amateurs. It is possible to boil down a few gallons of sap, using regular cooking pots on your gas or electric range, but if you keep close track of fuel costs you will find that such sirup comes very high. Those romantic old iron sirup kettles one sees hanging from tripods in old prints could still be used if you could locate one. Any sheet-metal worker could make you a large pan to fit your barbecue grill or outdoor fireplace. I use four 5-gallon square oil cans with the tops cut out, on an improvised fireplace made of cinder blocks. As you collect the sap you

Norway (top left)   Sugar (top right)

Box Elder (middle)

Red (bottom)

MAPLES

can gather firewood from fallen branches and dead wood. You will feel much prouder of the finished product if you forage your wood as well as the food.

There is no particular secret or recipe to making good Maple Sirup. It is simply a matter of boiling it down to a desirable consistency without scorching it. I reduce it about 20 to 1 over the outside fire, then take it to the kitchen range for the final finish. This avoids the danger of scorching there would be if the thickening sirup was allowed to boil up and stick to the sides of the can over the open fire. As it approaches the proper consistency, the sirup will boil over if not closely watched. A few drops of cream or a tiny piece of butter dropped into the pot will quiet it down.

If you have trouble deciding when the sirup has reached the best consistency, you can use a cooking thermometer. Maple Sirup, when it has exactly the right sugar content, boils at 7° hotter than the temperature of boiling water. This means that at sea level sirup will be ready to pour off when it reaches a temperature of 219°. If you live in the mountains, you can easily ascertain the correct heat for your altitude by noting the temperature of the sap when it first boils, then letting it rise 7°.

If you want to make Maple Sugar, keep cooking it a bit longer. The boiling temperature will mount more rapidly now, so watch it closely. When it reaches 234°, remove it from the fire and pour it immediately into molds. Buttered muffin tins make excellent molds for small amounts. The little sugar loaves can be removed by slightly warming the bottom of the tin.

I realize that commercial producers will laugh at my primitive methods and crude equipment, but this equipment has been assembled with no cash outlay and with it I have made many quarts of excellent sirup and many pounds of sugar. In the process I have acquired considerable knowledge and had a barrel of fun. Could anyone ask more?

I am sure I do not have to tell anyone how to make use of Maple Sugar and Sirup. However, I will give a few hints on how to combine this finest of sweets with other wild foods.

Black walnuts or hickory nuts can be combined with Maple Sirup to make Maple Nut Divinity, the most delicious confection this side of heaven. Butter a heavy saucepan and in it cook 2 cups of Maple Sirup rapidly without stirring, until it reaches 250° on your candy thermometer. Pour the hot sirup slowly over the stiffly beaten whites of 2 eggs, beating constantly at high speed with an electric mixer. Continue to beat until the mixture forms peaks and loses its bright gloss. Then quickly stir in ½ cup of chopped black walnuts or hickory nuts. Using a teaspoon, drop the candies on waxed paper, swirling each one to a fancy peak. This makes about eighteen candies and the only way they can be kept uneaten is to lock them in a burglarproof safe and forget the combination.

Since we have demonstrated that maple products are not necessarily a monopoly of the North, those who live where they can find wild pecans will be able to forage the two main ingredients for some luscious Creamy Pralines, that favorite confection of the South. If wild pecans are not available, use hickory nuts. While not so traditionally correct as pecans, the more highly flavored hickory nuts will make an even better candy.

Mix 3 cups of Maple Sirup with 1 cup of light cream and ½ teaspoon of soda. Cook it in a deep saucepan, stirring it often, until it forms a soft ball when dropped in cold water, or until it shows 234° on the candy thermometer. Remove from the heat, immediately add 1½ tablespoons of butter, then stir in 2 cups of shelled pecans or hickory nuts. Beat the mixture for 2 or 3 more minutes until it begins to thicken, then drop it by spoonfuls on waxed paper.

Or you can make a wonderful Praline Sauce. Put 2 cups of Maple Sirup, 1 cup of light cream and 1½ dozen marshmallows in a heavy saucepan. Boil over medium heat until it reaches 224°. Remove from fire and add ½ stick of butter or margarine. Cool slightly, then stir in ½ cup of chopped pecans or hickory nuts. Serve on Wild Blueberry Pudding, Persimmon Pudding or homemade ice cream. These are not low-calorie dishes, so on the evenings you serve them you had better forget about that diet and just live it up.

There are other uses for maple sap besides making sirup and sugar of it. I have often been asked if a man lost in the woods without food could live on unprocessed maple sap. *If* it were the right time of year and *if* he had or could improvise some instrument for making the taps and devise spiles and containers, the maple sap would certainly help to sustain him. However, since he would have to drink about three gallons of unreduced sap in order to get a thousand calories, I doubt that he could live long on it even if his kidneys could take the strain. If the nights were cold enough, the sugar content could be concentrated somewhat by allowing the sap to freeze, then throwing off the ice. This might lower his liquid intake within reasonable bounds.

A more practical camp use of maple sap is as a source of potable water of unquestioned purity. The sugar in solution is so dilute that only the most sensitive taste can detect its presence. Even the syca-more would furnish good water for drinking and cooking.

When maple sap has been reduced about 4 to 1 by boiling, it has about the right sweetness for making some interesting woodland teas. A cupful of chopped-up bark of the fragrant spicebush boiled for twenty minutes in 1 quart of this sweet sap will give a palatable tea that formerly had a reputation as a restorative and reliever of fatigue. Whether the tiredness of the early settlers was relieved by the sugar, warmth and rest they acquired while making and drinking this tea, or whether the spicebush actually contains some stimulant is for a more scientific researcher than I am to decide. Its pleasant flavor and invigorating effect are all the excuses I need to drink Spicebush Tea made with maple sap.

Traditionally, Sassafras Tea is the drink to be made with maple sap. Just dig a few sassafras roots and scrub them well. Some prefer to use only the bark of the roots but the entire root cut into pieces short enough to fit into the kettle works very well. Cover the roots with the partially reduced sap and boil for at least 30 minutes. This tea develops a red color as it boils and after a little experience one can tell when it has reached the required strength by the depth of the color. The sassafras gives up its flavor slowly and the same roots can be used several times.

Many people think that drinking Sassafras Tea in the spring helps the body to adjust to the changing season. Even if it could be demon-strated that it has no medicinal value whatever, I would still drink it for flavor alone. Maple sugaring in the spring just wouldn't seem right without it.

You can also make a more ardent beverage from maple sap by combining it with still another woodland product. Maple-Spruce Beer is an aromatic beverage which is highly appreciated by some.

To make this wildwood brew, take 20 gallons of maple sap and boil it until it is reduced to 4 gallons. While waiting for this to boil down, gather ½ peck of new growth from the ends of the twigs of the Black Spruce (*Picea mariana*). Wash these and put them in some kind of large container. When the sap has reached the desired volume, pour it boiling hot over the spruce twigs and let them steep until the sap has cooled to lukewarm. Strain it into a 5-gallon crock and add 1 package of activated dry yeast mixed with a little of the brew. Keep the crock covered with a cloth and in about a week, when the beer stops foaming and the cloudiness starts to clear up, bottle it and cap it tightly. In about 3 weeks it will be ready to drink.

Why don't you make some of these maple products next spring? This chapter contains all the information you need to start, and the chances are good that there are suitable trees right in your own neighborhood. There is no need to slavishly copy my poor methods. Improvise! And have fun.

May Apple, or American Mandrake

(*Podophyllum peltatum*)

> Go and catch a falling star
> Get with child a mandrake root.
>
> —from "Song" by John Donne

The original Mandrake (*Mandragora officinarum*) was easily the most famous and most revered of all the ancient medicinal herbs, and became surrounded with an unbelievable amount of superstition and folklore. It is a native of Mediterranean countries and during medieval times mandrake roots, trimmed to look like tiny human figures, were sold all over Europe, including England, where it was much used in medicine and magic—not necessarily two separate pursuits in those days.

When early settlers in America learned from the Indians that the plant we now call May Apple had a root, which, like that of the Mediterranean plant, was at once a valuable medicine and, in over-doses, a drastic poison, they transferred the name and much of the lore of the mandrake to this unrelated American plant. It was by the name of mandrake that I knew this plant as a child. When the fruit was thoroughly ripe, we ate it freely, but we regarded the rest of the plant, and especially the root, with considerable awe.

May apple roots owe their medicinal properties to their content of

MAY APPLE

podophyllin. The roots were not only used by herb doctors and in home remedies, but also became an ingredient in many patent medicines and achieved a respectable place in medicine. In *The Herbalist* * Joseph E. Meyer, the author, says of May apple:

The Indians were well acquainted with the virtues of this plant. The proper time for collecting the root is in the latter part of October or early part of November, soon after the fruit has ripened. Its active principle is podophyllin, which acts upon the liver in the same manner but far

* (Hammond, Ind.: Hammond Book Co., 1934), pp. 161-62.

superior to mercury, and with intelligent physicians it has dethroned that noxious mineral as a cholagogue.

Properties and Uses—May apple is cathartic, emetic, alternative, anthelmintic, hydrogogue and sialagogue. It is an active and certain cathartic. It can also be used as an alternative. In constipation it acts upon the bowels without disposing them to subsequent costiveness.

Dose—A teaspoonful of the root, cut fine to a pint of boiling water. Take one teaspoonful at a time as required. . . .

The *Encyclopaedia Britannica* gives this warning about podophyllin: "In toxic doses podophyllin causes intense enteritis which may end in death." It is my opinion that amateurs would do well to go slow on home dosage with this powerful drug.

Besides mandrake the May apple is also known as Raccoon Berry, Hog Apple and Wild Lemon in various parts of its range. Found from Quebec to Florida and west to Minnesota, Kansas and Texas, this is one of the most familiar of the wild flowers which beautify low, rich woods in the spring. Its horizontal roots persist in the ground year after year, and in the first warm days they send up a one- or two-leaved plant, the new leaves unfolding like tiny umbrellas. They shoot up very quickly and soon reach twelve to eighteen inches in height, growing in dense clusters that often hide the ground. If the plant has but one leaf, the stem is attached to the center. These single-leaved plants do not produce blossoms or fruit, but the yellowish-green leaves, a foot or more in diameter, with seven to nine lobes, drooping around the stem like an open umbrella, are very decorative.

The fruiting stems fork near the top and make a pair of similar but somewhat smaller leaves with the stems attached near the inner edge. The single flower, a beautiful, waxy-white blossom nearly two inches across, appears in the fork of the stem. It is seldom seen by those who only look at May apples from the windows of their speeding cars, for it tends to hide itself under the ample leaves. The flower is followed by a single fruit the size and shape of an egg, with a smooth, yellow skin when ripe, in August or early September in the latitude of Philadelphia. At this time the parent plants have mostly fallen down, and one picks up the ripe luscious fruit where it has fallen to the ground.

Most people consider the flowers ill-smelling, but I love the sweet scent of the ripe fruit with its hint of mysterious muskiness. I have often "smelled out" a patch of ripe May apples while walking through the woods in late summer.

The flavor of the ripe May apple, while agreeable to most people, is not easily described. It has been compared to the flavor of the strawberry, but I fail to see the resemblance. When I eat a thoroughly ripe May apple, I am reminded of several tropical fruits, the guava, the passion fruit and the soursop, but I can't honestly say that it tastes like any of them.

If the raw, ripe May apple doesn't appeal to your taste, don't thereby dismiss it. Remember, neither the lemon nor the cranberry is often eaten in the raw, unmixed state, but that doesn't keep them from being valuable fruits.

If you have a vegetable juicer, try extracting juice from the May apple. A jigger of this juice will give a wonderful fragrance and a new and delightful taste to a glass of lemonade. Of course, I wouldn't know about such things, but it is rumored that a mixture of half May apple juice and half Tokay wine with the addition of a little sugar makes a nectar fit for the lips of the gods.

One of the finest products of the May apple is the fragrant and beautiful greenish-amber Marmalade. You can't buy this ambrosia in a supermarket, but in early autumn, when the woods are full of ripe May apples, you can easily make your own. Take ½ gallon of ripe May apples, remove the stem ends and blossom ends, cut in quarters and put in a suitably sized kettle. Add 1 cup of water and simmer for about 15 minutes, stirring occasionally to keep any of the pulp from sticking to the bottom of the pan. When the fruit is soft enough to mash easily, put it through a colander to remove the seeds and skins. To 4 cups of this thick pulp, add 1 box of Sure-Jell and bring it to a boil. As soon as it boils, add 5 cups of sugar. While stirring constantly, let it come to a hard boil and maintain that boil for one minute. Skim off the foam and pour immediately into half-pint jars and seal. This is a unique gourmet's product that you can proudly serve to the most discriminating guest. In fragrance, flavor and appearance it is unequaled by any commercial preparation.

Surely, now that you know its virtues, you will give more attention to this beautiful wild flower when next you take a drive in the country.

The Common Milkweed

(*Asclepias syriaca*)

A GREAT many people must have heard of eating Milkweed, but very few moderns seem to have tried it, for I am more frequently questioned about the esculent properties of this plant than almost any other. Yes, the milkweed is edible, and, when gathered at any of the several edible stages and properly prepared, is really an excellent vegetable, rivaling many which we laboriously cultivate in home gardens.

The *syriaca* is the commonest and most widespread of the milkweeds. It is the one with stout stalks, large leaves, rounded umbels of sweet-scented greenish-purple, or sometimes nearly white, flowers, and a warty seed pod which splits down the side when mature, releasing the light seeds, each with its streamer of silk, which allows it to float on the wind to a new location. It is found from Nova Scotia to Saskatchewan and south to Georgia and Kansas. Its wide distribution, abundance and ease of procurement could make the milkweed an important wild vegetable if more people knew the secrets of processing its products into palatable food. The milkweed furnishes not one, but four, very good vegetables, and has a possible fifth use as food.

The young shoots, up to six inches high, make a very passable vegetable to serve like asparagus; the newly opened leaves can be served like spinach; the unopened flower buds are eaten like broccoli, the young pods can be cooked like okra. Let me warn the reader right

MILKWEED

now that, although these milkweed products are served like the domestic vegetables mentioned, they will not taste like them. All vegetables that I know have their own taste and milkweed is no exception. The taste of milkweed is different without being too strange or objectionable, and most people who try it, find it a very acceptable vegetable, but only if it has been properly cooked.

The milkweed has an extremely bitter principle that seems to permeate every part of the plant. Fortunately, this excessively bitter taste is easily removed with boiling water. All four of the milkweed vegetables are prepared by very much the same process, so we only need to describe it once for all of them. The shoots, leaves, buds or pods are put into a pot, covered with *boiling* water and placed over a high flame. When they have boiled one minute, drain and cover with fresh boiling water and return to the heat. This process is repeated at least three times, then the vegetable is boiled for about ten minutes, seasoned and served.

Those who try to cook milkweed by covering with cold water and then slowly bringing it to a boil will be disappointed in the taste, for this seems to cause the bitter principle to become fixed in the cooked product. I know that health-food enthusiasts will object to pouring off the water-soluble vitamins and minerals in these repeated water changes, but I'll bet they would never eat those vitamins and minerals anyway if they were mixed with anything as bitter as the first water from milkweeds.

The young shoots are only good in the spring, when they are eight inches high or less. Washed, bundled together with string, like asparagus, and given the hot-water treatment, they can be served plain, with salt and butter, or covered with a cream sauce and served on toast.

The young leaves can be gathered over a slightly longer season than can the shoot. Take only the tender top leaves before the plants start forming flower buds. Milkweed leaves can be mixed with other greens if they are processed with hot water first. I sometimes mix milkweed leaves, poke and wild mustard buds and put them all through the hot-water process. All three of these wild vegetables are rather strong, and profit from this taming treatment.

Most of the guests at my "wild parties" have preferred the unopened buds to any other milkweed product, and these little beaded heads do make a delicate and delicious vegetable. Gather the buds while they are still young and in tight clusters. They will appear dull and slightly woolly when uncooked, but as soon as they are covered with boiling water they become a bright green and make an attractive vegetable to look at as well as taste. After the hot-water treatment, boil the buds only a few minutes, then season with salt and butter.

My own favorite milkweed product is the young pod, but it must be gathered at just the right stage. If the pod has become tough and elastic to pressure, it is inedible. The hard, young pods should be cooked a bit longer than other milkweed products. When gathered at just the right stage and cooked properly, the developing seeds and silk inside the pod cook up into a soft and delicate mass which I find delicious. Eaten with pot roast and gravy, it is one of my favorite vegetables.

We like milkweed buds and pods so well at our house that we usually freeze a supply for out-of-season use. These are put through the usual three changes of boiling water, then quickly and thoroughly cooled in cold water, drained, packed in plastic bags or other suitable containers and placed in the quick-freeze section of the freezer. When used they are placed, still frozen, in very little boiling water and cooked for ten to fifteen minutes, seasoned and served.

There are persistent rumors that during the eighteenth century, the French in Canada made brown sugar from the copious nectar secreted by the blossoms of milkweed, but the exact process seems to have been lost. By washing the flowers in lukewarm water, then evaporating the water after the manner of maple sap, I obtained a very poor yield of thick sirup that probably contained considerable sugar, but it was bitter and unpalatable, at least to my taste. Maybe some enterprising reader will carry these experiments further.

Milkweeds are most often found along roadsides, in waste places, in fallow ground and about the edges of cultivated fields. I'm sure no farmer will object to your helping yourself to all you can use.

Mulberries: RED AND WHITE

(*Morus rubra* and *Morus alba*)

RECENTLY I was helping a couple with three small children move into a new house, and remarked that the children would no doubt enjoy the ripening mulberries on a tree in their new yard. The mother looked horrified and said, "*My* children would never eat anything like that!"

How sorry I felt for *her* children—never to know the pleasure of purpling their faces with sweet, ripe mulberries. My own childhood would have been infinitely poorer without this most familiar of all wild fruits, which persists even in and about our cities and towns. I still remember fondly some of the individual trees that enriched my boyhood, for, like all seedling fruits, the quality of the berries varies wonderfully from tree to tree.

There was one tree in which I competed for the luscious fruit with a dozen or more little Negro children, who knew a good berry when they tasted it. There was another tree on a village street where I acquired the nickname "Toes" because of my skill in climbing about the fruit-laden tree with the almost prehensile toes and feet of a barefoot boy. One of the minor tragedies of my boyhood, which seems ludicrous now, occurred when I threw a rock into the top of a mulberry, then rushed under the tree to get some of the dislodged fruit before the other children beat me to it, and was struck in the back of the head by the same stone I had thrown. Then there was a tree that bore the most delicious mulberries I have ever tasted, more than twice the size of ordinary mulberries, but they were a rusty brown color when ripe. I never allowed their unappetizing appearance to interfere with my enjoyment of them.

The native mulberry is called *Morus rubra* by the botanists and that translates as Red Mulberry, but like the blackberry it's only red when its green. When fully ripe it is dark purple. Indigenous from New England to Florida and west to beyond the Plains, it has been

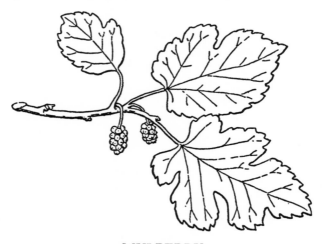

MULBERRY

introduced into most areas where it does not occur naturally, and wherever found is usually abundant. Although moderns do not appreciate this really fine fruit as much as the Indians and early settlers did, I am glad to report that not all modern children refuse to eat it. Often, I can hear the neighborhood children laughing and playing as they pick and eat the fruit from the mulberry trees that grow in my front yard, and often I, too, go out and give them some competition.

Mulberries are easily gathered in quantity if one merely spreads a plastic sheet beneath the tree and shakes the limbs. Because of the persistent stem and an axis that goes part way into the fruit, many people do not like to bring fresh mulberries to the table, but they are better food than much that comes there, despite the aforementioned handicaps. However, I still prefer to eat my fresh mulberries directly from the tree, and use the ones I gather to make some delicious pies, jellies and cooling summer drinks.

To make a mouth-watering Mulberry Pie, line a 9-inch pie plate with Oil Pastry (see page 112) and fill with 3 cups of ripe berries with the stems removed. Mix together 1 cup of sugar, ¼ cup of flour and a dash of salt, then sprinkle this mixture over the berries. Dot the top with butter, arrange the top crust and bake at 400° for about 40 minutes.

Mulberry Jelly is surprisingly good, with a delicious fruit flavor and a beautiful color. The fruit lacks pectin, so this must be added. Add ½ cup of water to 2 quarts of berries and simmer for 5 minutes. Then thoroughly crush the berries and simmer for 10 minutes more. Strain out the juice through a cheesecloth jelly bag. To 1 quart of juice, add the juice of 1 lemon and 1 package of powdered pectin. Bring just to a boil, then add 5½ cups of sugar. Bring to a boil again and boil hard for 1 minute. Skim, pour into jelly glasses and cover with paraffin, or seal into half-pint jars with sterilized lids.

A really modern food gatherer should invest in one of the new vegetable juicing machines that can extract juice from nearly anything. For a delicious summer drink this machine can extract the juice from raw, ripe mulberries. Or you can crush the ripe berries and squeeze out some juice through a double thickness of cheesecloth, but this is likely to leave your hands dyed an unfashionable shade of purple. Fill a glass ⅓ full of mulberry juice, add the juice of ½ lemon, 2 teaspoons of sugar, a couple of ice cubes and fill the glass with plain soda.

More than a hundred years ago, there was an attempt to found a domestic silk industry along our eastern seaboard, and white mulberries (*Morus alba*) were imported from Asia to feed the silkworms. Because of high labor costs, the silk venture proved unprofitable, but the white mulberry found a congenial home in our climate and rapidly established itself over much of our country. The ripe berry is white, or slightly purplish, and very sweet. The lack of acid and the excessive sweetness causes this berry to be disliked by many, but, like our native mulberries, the quality of the fruit varies from tree to tree, and I know some specimens of *Morus alba* that bear delicious berries. Small children don't object to their oversweetness, but eat them as if they were candy. One advantage they have over the native mulberry is that sometimes a tree bears berries that are almost seedless.

In parts of Afghanistan a variety of this species is, when dried, a staple food of the common people. After considerable experimentation, I have produced a palatable dried product from this species.

Gather white mulberries by shaking them down on a plastic sheet as described earlier and start the drying process as soon as possible to forestall any possible decay or spoilage. Spread the berries, one layer deep, on an old aluminum or plastic window or door screen that has been previously washed and dried. There is such an old screen in the basement, attic or storeroom of nearly any house. If you don't have one, ask your neighbor. This screen-dehydrator should be placed in the full sun and supported so air can circulate under as well as over the fruit. At night, put your plastic sheet around the screen, top and bottom, to prevent any dew condensing on the fruit. In bright, hot weather with low humidity, mulberries can be dried in this manner in two days. I found that by supporting the screen near the roof of a warm attic room I could dry the mulberries just as well in about four days. If the weather is favorable, sun drying is best, for the ultraviolet rays of the sun have a sterilizing effect which will eliminate bacteria that might cause spoilage. If you don't have an attic and the weather is not propitious, you *can* dry mulberries in your oven. Cut aluminum screening in pieces that will just fit your oven racks. Fold the edges of the screen up slightly, place them on the racks and cover with mulberries, about two layers deep. Put your oven on the lowest possible setting and prop the door partly open for better air circulation and so the moisture can escape. It will take ten to fifteen hours to dry them to the proper stage using this method, so you had better get an early start.

Using any of these methods, you can tell when the berries are sufficiently dry if one crushed between the fingers exudes no watery juice. At this stage I place the dried berries in quart fruit jars and set them in a very low oven for thirty minutes, then seal with sterilized, two-piece dome lids.

Dried mulberries can be used like dried figs or raisins in puddings, cookies or muffins. The United States Department of Agriculture analyzed a sample of dried mulberry pulp from Afghanistan and found it contained 70.01 per cent invert sugar, 1.2 per cent sucrose, 2.59 per cent protein, 1.6 per cent fat (ether extract) and no starch. I'm sure our own *Morus alba* is equally nutritious.

The Afghans have a trick of grinding the dried mulberries and mixing with ground almonds. The almonds would add protein and fat, making this a more balanced food. I tried mixing hickory nuts with my freshly dried mulberries and grinding in an ordinary, hand-powered, kitchen meat grinder and it came out a gummy, sticky mass of doughlike consistency. I formed this material into small balls and rolled them in powdered sugar to remove the stickiness and they turned out to be a delicious confection. Children love it, and I'm sure it is better for them than most kinds of candy.

Some of my Japanese friends told me of eating mulberry shoots and leaves during the war, but I wasn't anxious to try them, for during food shortages people eat many things that are not really good. Last spring, however, I pulled a tender shoot of new growth from a mulberry tree and nibbled on it. To my surprise, it tasted good, even raw. I gathered a quantity of the tender shoots of new growth together with their barely unfolding leaves and cooked them, and I have seldom eaten a better vegetable. Just boil for twenty minutes, then season with butter and salt. The firm texture and the sweet and nutty flavor make a combination that is hard to surpass. Try it sometime.

The Cult of the Mycophagists

(Edible fungi)

IN NO field will the forager find greater rewards than in the field of edible fungi, or Mushrooms. Some of the most delicious food known to man is produced by these peculiar growths. A real gourmet will know that the different species of mushroom are cooked in different ways and used for different purposes, and that all the edible species have a place in a refined cuisine, but so standardized and limited has the average taste become that we tend to judge all mushrooms by how closely the taste resembles that of the cultivated mushroom, which is only one variety of *Agaricus*. This is as ridiculous as the case of an expatriate Englishman I know who judges all vegetables by how near their taste approaches that of Brussels sprouts.

Not that I have anything against the *Agaricus*, either cultivated or wild. I take every one I can find. It is truly a delicious mushroom, but it furnishes only one of the many taste thrills which can be had from this class of plants. Let us approach each new edible fungus as a new food, and let it stand or fall on its own merits. Let's not be guilty of condemning a mushroom for its difference from the cultivated variety without judging whether that difference is good or bad.

The gathering, cooking and eating of the edible fungi is a very specialized area in the field of wild food plants, and I make no pretense of having mastered it. I regularly gather and eat more than a dozen varieties of mushrooms, but this is only a beginning, for hundreds of edible species are known to exist. The American Indians seldom ate mushrooms, perhaps because of their awareness of the danger of poisoning that exists when this class of plants is used indiscriminately. This may have been the wisest course for a people who did not have access to the complete and authoritative information that is now available on this subject, but their caution caused them to miss out on some very good eating.

Of course an uninstructed amateur who starts gathering and eating mushrooms before he can distinguish one species from another is likely to poison himself. A rash fool can find a way to kill himself anywhere, but that is no reason why sensible, prudent people shouldn't enjoy delicious and wholesome wild mushrooms. Like other wild plants, the fungi require some study before one starts using them for food. This doesn't mean that you must become an expert mycologist and know the secret name of every fungus in the field. As soon as you can certainly recognize only one edible species, you are ready to start enjoying the rewards of this interesting and fruitful hobby. Once started, I am confident that you will go on increasing your knowledge in this field.

One word of warning: don't listen when well-meaning amateurs start telling you of some short-cut test that will surely distinguish the poisonous from the edible species. All these tests are worthless and exceedingly dangerous. A silver spoon against the flesh of a mushroom tells you exactly nothing. Even the much-vaunted method of watching to see which fungi the wild mice have nibbled is completely unreliable. I have seen deadly *Amanitas* so eaten by insects as to look exactly as if they had been nibbled by mice. Besides, even if a fungus has been eaten by mice, how do you know that the mouse didn't die? There is only one reliable rule to follow when gathering wild mushrooms, and that is: *Never gather for food any fungus that has not been positively identified as an edible species.*

If you are going to study the edible fungi in books, you should make an effort to learn their Latin names, for the common names are apt to vary from area to area, and are notoriously unreliable. This is not so great a task as you might think, and is sometimes real fun. The rewards come when you discover such names as *Lactarius deliciosus,* and *Morchella esculenta.* Don't you just love to roll such succulent names over your tongue? The names are nearly as tasty as the delicious mushrooms which bear them. On the other hand, a name like *Russula emetica* is suggestive enough to make one study its bearer further before considering it as food. All this is fun, but it is not, of course, a reliable method of separating the good mushrooms from the bad. As an example, the unappetizing name, *Fistulina hepatica*, is borne by the delicious Beefsteak Mushroom.

There are so many very good manuals on the recognition of edible mushrooms that it would be presumptious for a person of my small experience to attempt writing another one. Also, space does not permit me to give the illustrations and minute descriptions that would be necessary if I intended this chapter to be used by the uninstructed to positively identify the edible fungi. Still, one couldn't present a book on wild foods that ignored these fine wild food plants. My purpose in including this section is to call the attention of the amateur to a rich source of wild food plants, and to give some instruction on the preparation of this delicious food, which can be had for the taking. For the few edible species mentioned, I have purposely kept my descriptions meager, for I do not recommend that any unaided amateur try to use this text alone to identify an unfamiliar mushroom.

For the beginner, there is a wide choice of excellent books on this subject, some of the better ones marvelously illustrated and costing a king's ransom. A simpler and cheaper, but completely reliable, guide to the wild mushrooms most commonly gathered and eaten is the Department of Agriculture Circular # 143, a little booklet by Vera K. Charles, titled, *Some Common Mushrooms and How to Know Them*, which can be obtained from the Superintendent of Documents in Washington, D.C., for thirty-five cents. I heartily recommend that every amateur who wishes to delve into this interesting subject send for this bulletin.

There are a few species of edible fungi so distinctive in form, or with such characteristic recognition features, as to be easily identified with little possibility of error. We list a few of these before going into the subject of mushroom cookery.

PUFFBALLS

The Puffballs are of two genera, the *Lycoperdons* and the *Calvatias*, each with several species. All of the puffballs *with white flesh* are good to eat and some of them are very superior. They are found throughout the temperate zone, and in some localities they become very abundant after heavy fall rains. Puffballs are good French-fried, en casserole, as fritters, or added to vegetable and meat dishes. The best way to preserve a surplus is to peel, slice and sauté them a few minutes, then pack them into jars and freeze.

MORELS, OR SPONGE MUSHROOMS

These are the *Morchellas*, of several species, including the *esculenta*, mentioned above. None of them are poisonous, but some are of better quality than others; let your taste be your guide. They are found throughout the temperate regions but are sometimes scattered and rare. Look for them in rich, open woods and other half-shade spots, and especially in burnt-over lands, where they are sometimes found in abundance. This is one of the very choicest of the edible fungi, and is best cooked stuffed and baked, or sautéed and served on toast, with a sauce made of its own rich juice. To freeze a surplus, follow the directions given for puffballs.

THE CORAL MUSHROOMS

These are the *Clavaria* of several species, all of them safe enough to eat, but some species too bitter to be palatable. They are strange-looking plants, either bushy with many simple, or forking or sometimes fused branches, closely resembling some forms of coral, or with small club-shaped bodies. There are white, yellow, brown and reddish varieties. They are found over most of the United States and Canada. The large, freely forking kinds are sometimes discovered in great abundance on leafmold or decaying wood. They are best prepared as Mushroom Soup or en casserole.

The small yellow, club-shaped, *Clavaria pulchra* (another beautiful name) is sometimes plentiful in spruce and fir woods in the northern part of our range. They have a delicate and nutty flavor when eaten raw, and should be served in Raw Mushroom Salad or in Mushroom Soup.

ELM AND OYSTER MUSHROOMS

These excellent mushrooms belong to the genus *Pleurotis* and there are three good species, all forming clumps on dead, dying or injured trees throughout the temperate regions. The *ostreatus* has white spores and the *sapidus* has pink ones, but otherwise these two species are almost indistinguishable, and both are commonly called Oyster Mushrooms. They are usually found in crowded, overlapping clumps, with large white, gray or light-brown caps, from three to nine inches across, with the short, thick stem attached to the inner margin. The Elm Mushroom, which I find more often on dying poplars than on elms, differs from the former chiefly in having long, curved stems, attached somewhat to one side of center of the many overlapping caps. I have gathered a half-bushel basket of these fine mushrooms from a single standing dead tree. Only the tender parts of the older caps should be used, though the younger ones can be used entire. These tender sections are excellent sautéed slowly in salad oil, French-fried or in Mushroom Soup. A surplus should be sautéed and frozen as with puffballs.

THE SHAGGY-MANES AND INKIES

The genus *Coprinus* furnishes three commonly eaten and very good mushrooms, the Shaggy-Mane (*C. comatus*), the Inky (*C. atramentarius*) and the Early Inky or *C. micaceus*. All of these mushrooms have black spores and, when old and inedible, the whole plant turns to a black inky mass. They are found throughout the temperate regions, the shaggy-mane and inky growing in rich, manured fields, meadows, lawns and about rubbish heaps, and the early inky springing up about the bases of old stumps and dead trees, or, occasionally, in lawns. These three little mushrooms are easily recognized and delicious to eat. The best way to serve them is sautéed in butter with a rich sauce made of the abundant and flavorful juice that cooks out of them. Don't let the black color of this juice repel you; it's one of nature's best sauces. These little mushrooms are also very good en casserole.

BEEFSTEAK MUSHROOM

This is the hearty mushroom with the unappetizing name (*Fistulina hepatica*). It forms short-stemmed, or stemless, brackets on dead stumps and logs of hardwood trees, each bracket looking like a large opened fan, or, as some seem to think, like a lobed liver, hence the specific name. Do not confuse this with the woody kinds of bracket fungi; the Beefsteak is fleshy and juicy, dark red above and yellowish or buff below. It is found throughout our range but is rare in some sections and abundant in others. The beefsteak mushroom is the nearest thing to a piece of meat that is produced by the plant world. It has an acid juice which some people find offensive, but, if it is sliced and soaked in salt water for an hour, the offensive quality disappears. The slices can then be broiled, stewed, or the best way of all, cooked in a Mushroom Shish Kabob.

THE SULPHUR MUSHROOM
(Polyporus sulphureus)

The Sulphur Mushroom is another of the bracket variety, and grows in large masses, with the brackets commonly fused at the base, on old hardwood stumps or dead trees. The overlapping brackets range in color from sulphur-yellow to orange; they are fan-shaped, and the under surface is full of minute pores. It tends to be somewhat tough, and should be thinly sliced and stewed, or sautéed in oil for a half-hour or more. The sautéed slices can either be eaten, as is, or be chopped and made into some delicious Mushroom Fritters.

THE FAIRY RING
(Marasmius oreades)

This little mushroom is found in lawns, meadows and other open, grassy places throughout the temperate regions. It gets its common name from its habit of growing in circles or rings, which sometimes contain more than a hundred individual mushrooms. These rings gradually expand in size each year and are often interrupted and sometimes entirely obscured. Look for these little dainties where the grass grows greenest. They have a white, solid stem, one to two inches high, and a cap of about the same diameter, convex or widely expanded, with a small hump in the center dull white, pink or light brown in color. They decay very slowly, becoming dry during sunny weather and freshening up again when it rains; thus they can be picked over a comparatively long period. They are slightly leathery in texture, but the flavor is hard to beat. They should be stewed or sautéed in oil. A surplus can be strung on a stout thread and dried, or sautéed and frozen.

ORANGE MILK MUSHROOM

This is the mushroom with the luscious name, *Lactarius deliciosus,* and, when thoroughly cooked, lives up to its name. Unfortunately, it is found only in the northern part of our range. Look for it under spruce and fir trees. It has a stout stem, one to two inches high, and a cap two to five inches broad, with a depression in its center. The stem is spotted yellowish-orange, and the top has orange, yellow and greenish tones, sometimes in concentric zones of color. When bruised it exudes a thick, milky, orange-colored juice with a pleasant, aromatic odor. The fact that this juice turns greenish on cooking, or even after a short exposure to air, may scare some off, but if it is baked or boiled for an hour or more, it is one of the finest of the edible fungi.

HYPOMYCES LACTIFLUORUM

This is one of the most interesting of all the edible fungi. I had long read about this curious combination of two fungi, and then one fall day, when I was walking up a trail through some dry woods in Pennsylvania, I saw several places where the leaves and needles were slightly lifted from the ground. Under one I glimpsed an orange-red color. I began lifting the raised leaves and discovered a half-dozen brilliantly colored funnel-shaped mushrooms, several of them four inches high and about the same size in diameter. They are considerably heavier for their size than most mushrooms. The botanists tell us that this is the *Lactarius piperatus* with a parasitic fungus, the *Hypomyces*, growing all over it and forming the bright red coat. All I know is that when I took my haul home, sliced it thinly crosswise and cooked it slowly in a little peanut oil and water for about an hour, it was one of the most substantial and delicious mushroom dishes I had ever eaten. This hearty dish makes an excellent substitute for meat, and, when enough is found, can be served as the main course in a wild food meal.

THE CHANTERELLES

These also are funnel- or vase-shaped mushrooms of several species. The *Cantharellus cibarius* is a dull egg-yellow color and from two to five inches in height. The gills on the outside of the often irregular or one-sided funnel are forked and connected with small veins, giving the appearance of a network. This mushroom is found in dry, coniferous forests, sometimes in great abundance. Cut in very thin slices across the gills and stew or sauté slowly in oil. These are good dried, and one can sometimes buy dried chanterelles in markets that cater to immigrants. The fresh mushroom can also be sautéed and frozen.

The *Cantharellus aurantiacus* is very like the above, except that it has a dull-orange or brownish funnel and yellow gills. It is used like the other chanterelles.

The *Cantharellus umbonatus*, which is commonly called the Grayling, is a smaller species, often little over an inch in diameter. For some reason, it only grows in carpets of haircap moss. In cool, damp woods, where this moss abounds, these little mushrooms can sometimes be gathered by the quart. They do not easily decay and can be collected until snow covers them. They are slightly tough, but, when cooked long enough, the flavor is excellent.

PASTURE OR MEADOW MUSHROOM

This is the well-known *Agaricus* with two familiar species, the *campestries* and the *arvensis*. This is *the* mushroom. Varieties of *arvensis* are the mushrooms that are cultivated and sold in the markets. The wild ones are not so white as the cultivated varieties, and are usually not so fleshy, but they are just as delicious. The general shape and recognition features of this mushroom can be learned by studying those in the markets. Remember that the *Agaricus* does not have a scaly bulb or membranelike cup at the base. It does have gills that are white in the button stage, but these quickly turn pink as they are exposed and finally turn purplish brown. The *Agaricus* can be cooked according to almost any mushroom recipe you can find. They are excellent in Raw Mushroom Salad, broiled on Mushroom Shish Kabobs, sautéed, in soup or in nearly every other way that one can eat mushrooms. Preserve a surplus by drying or by sautéing, then freezing.

MUSHROOM COOKERY

HOW TO SAUTÉ MUSHROOMS

In many recipes for the use of various edible fungi, the first step is to sauté the mushrooms. The success of the final dish is greatly dependent on this step's being done the right way. Meadow mushrooms, morels, shaggy-manes, inkies and puffballs should all be sautéed in butter, about 2 tablespoonfuls to the ½ pound of mushrooms. Use a heavy skillet over medium heat, and a broad spatula for turning them so as not to break any apart. These are all tender mushrooms and should never be overcooked. When they are brown about the edges, take them out and keep them warm until ready to use. They should never be black and rubbery.

The oyster, fairy ring, chanterelle, beefsteak, sulphur, orange milk and many other wild mushrooms are tougher than those mentioned above and need longer cooking. They should be sautéed slowly in peanut or other good cooking oil for ½ hour or more, keeping the skillet covered except when turning the mushrooms.

Seasonings should be added with a light hand, for you want the subtle flavors of the various mushrooms to dominate the finished dish. They should be lightly salted, and the addition of a little freshly ground black pepper and a pinch of ginger will improve most mushroom dishes. Monosodium glutamate, added in the latter stages of cooking, will help to bring out the flavor.

If your recipe calls for onions, sauté these first until they are clear and yellow, then remove them and keep them warm while you sauté the mushrooms in the same oil or butter. Be absolutely certain that you remove every shred of onion before adding the mushrooms, as a tiny piece of scorched onion will impart a bitter taste to the whole dish.

Most of the wild mushrooms, whether the tender or the tough varieties, will give off copious quantities of juice as they are being cooked, so the sautéing soon resembles boiling or stewing. This juice is rich in flavor and should never be thrown out. Use it in the recipe or thicken with flour and serve as a sauce.

Unless otherwise specified, most kinds of wild mushrooms can be used in the recipes below, providing they have been sautéed properly for the variety used. However, each new species will make the recipe into a new dish with a different flavor. Thus a few recipes will furnish many different and delicious dishes merely by changing the kind of mushrooms used, and you will find each seems better than the ones you tried before.

MUSHROOMS ON TOAST

Sautéed mushrooms need no further cooking to make them eminently edible. Sauté ½ pound of mushrooms according to above directions, then remove from the pan and keep them warm. To the leftover oil and juice in the pan, add 2 tablespoons of flour, ½ teaspoon of salt, a little black pepper and a tiny pinch of ginger. Stir and cook until smooth and thick, then add 4 tablespoons of cooking

sherry and ½ cup of light cream. Keep the heat low, and simmer
(do not boil) stirring constantly until it thickens. Heap the cooked
mushrooms on slices of toast and pour the thickened sauce over them,
then dust the top very lightly with paprika.

MUSHROOM FRITTERS

Sauté 1 pound of mushrooms according to directions for the variety
you have collected, drain and save the juice. Chop the mushrooms
fine. Let the juice cool, then mix it with 2 beaten eggs. Sift together
1½ cups of flour, 2 teaspoons of baking powder, 1 teaspoon of
monosodium glutamate, ½ teaspoon of salt and a little freshly ground
black pepper. Add the egg-juice mixture and the chopped mushrooms,
and mix well. Drop by spoonfuls in shallow cooking oil heated to
375°. Fry until nicely browned; this will take about 3 minutes. Drain
on paper towels and serve piping hot.

CHICKEN AND MUSHROOM SOUP

This is one of the finest soups ever made by man, and yet, when
cheap chicken parts and wild mushrooms are used, it costs next to
nothing to make. This is the way to give your family or guests a
royal treat with no strain on your pocketbook. Now that the choicer
pieces of chicken are being sold in packages at good prices, the backs,
necks and wings are going for a song. These parts actually make better
soup than do the meatier pieces.

Put 6 or 8 chicken backs in a kettle, add ½ cup of fresh celery
leaves and 1 onion cut in chunks. Boil for two hours, cooking down
until only 1 quart of broth is left. Strain, then pick the meat from
the chicken and set aside.

Next, sauté 1 pound of mushrooms, cut in small, thin slices, according to the directions given above, remove the slices from the skillet
and keep warm. To the oil and juices left in the skillet add 2 tablespoons of flour, 1 teaspoon of salt and a pinch of ginger. Stir and
blend over low heat until a smooth paste is formed, and it has lost
all raw taste. With the heat turned a bit higher, slowly add the
chicken broth, stirring until it is smooth and slightly thickened. Add
sautéed mushrooms and chicken meat to soup and simmer gently as
you stir in 4 tablespoons of sherry wine and ½ cup of light cream.
Don't let it boil after adding the cream. Stir in a teaspoon of mono-

sodium glutamate, then serve in hot bowls and dust the top lightly with freshly ground black pepper.

CLAM AND MUSHROOM SOUP

Here is another moneysaving, epicurean dish for those who live where they can dig their own clams. Add 1 pint of water to 1 quart of clams and steam until the shells have all opened. Pour the broth into a saucepan, being careful not to include any settled sand, add a few celery leaves and 1 onion cut in chunks and simmer for 5 minutes, then strain.

Sauté ½ pound of mushrooms in the manner the variety requires and add, juice and all, to the clam broth. Mince the clams finely and add them to the soup. Season with 1 cup of top milk, a generous hunk of butter, a little black pepper and a very little salt. Never boil after the ingredients are combined, but serve very hot, in scalded cups, with a small, round, buttered cracker floating on each serving.

Both the above soups are real show-off recipes that will enhance your reputation as a gastronomic artist.

MUSHROOMS EN CASSEROLE

No good cook ever has a set recipe for casserole dishes, but varies them from time to time by artistically adding a bit of this and some of that. Here is one way to prepare mushrooms for cooking in a casserole. Sauté 1 pound of shaggy-manes, inkies, corals, puffballs or pasture mushrooms in butter for only a few minutes, then cool until only slightly warm. Stir in 1 beaten egg, ½ teaspoon of salt, a little black pepper and enough crushed corn flakes to take up the juice. Turn into a casserole, dot the top with butter and bake in a 375° oven for 30 minutes. If insufficient juice cooks out of the mushrooms, add a little rich milk to the pan before mixing in the corn flakes. Sometimes I use bread crumbs instead of corn flakes and, again, I might add raw ground beef or cooked chicken to this recipe. Let your taste and your good cooking sense be your guide.

RAW MUSHROOM SALAD

Who ever heard of eating mushrooms raw? Let me assure you that the meadow mushrooms, the puffballs and the little club-shaped corals are all delicious raw when served in this salad. You will need 1 pound of mushrooms, 1 large celery heart or 2 small ones and 4 hard-cooked eggs. Don't chop any of these, but cut them into hearty, bite-size pieces. Rub a deep bowl with a cut clove of garlic and place the above ingredients in it. Add 1 finely minced sweet red pepper and 2 minced scallions, tops and all. Season to taste with salt and black pepper and toss in a dressing made of 4 parts cold-pressed olive oil to 1 part wine vinegar. Toss for several minutes, then set in the refrigerator for 1 hour or less to ripen and blend. Serve on lettuce leaves.

STUFFED MUSHROOMS

Meadow mushrooms are good stuffed, and I have even seen fairy rings with each little cap piled high with stuffing, but the best stuffing mushroom of them all is the morel. Sauté 8 or 10 large morel caps in butter until about half done, then remove and keep them warm. Next, sauté 1 finely minced onion, and the stems and rejected caps of the morels. When they look done add ¼ pound of ground beef, 1 teaspoon of salt and a dash of monosodium glutamate. Let this cook for only about a minute, then turn the heat off and add ½ cup of cooking sherry. Now stir in enough dry bread crumbs to make a fluffy mixture and carefully stuff the morel caps without breaking them apart. Set them in a casserole and bake for 30 minutes in a medium oven. Serve hot.

VEGETARIAN SHISH KABOB

Cut beefsteak mushrooms crosswise into ½-inch slices. Soak for one hour in salted water, then drain, dry and sauté in peanut oil for twenty minutes. Remove the slices, turn off the heat and add 1 pinch of basil, 1 teaspoon of dried parsley, 2 tablespoons of wine vinegar and a dash of tabasco sauce to the leftover juice and oil. Use skewers of a length that will fit into your broiler and load them, first with a piece of mushroom, then with a very small whole onion, then another piece of mushroom, then a little tomato, another piece of mushroom, then another onion and so on until the skewer is filled. Pour the juice-oil-vinegar in a shallow dish and turn the skewer in it so that the mushrooms and vegetables are all evenly coated with this sauce. Lay the skewers across a bake pan and place under the broiler, keeping them about six inches from the flame. Baste with the sauce several times while it is broiling. Serve with large chunks of warmed French bread spread with garlic butter.

LUXURY SAUCE

If you find too few mushrooms for any of the above dishes, you can still make a fancy sauce of the few you have that will perk up most any meal. Sauté 1 large finely minced onion in butter until it is yellow and clear. Remove the onion and keep warm. Add a little more butter to the skillet, thinly slice your meager supply of mushrooms and sauté to a light brown. Season to taste with salt, pepper and a dash of tabasco. Add 1 pinch of basil, 1 tablespoon of minced chives and ½ tablespoon of finely minced fresh parsley leaves. Return the onion to the skillet, then slowly stir in 1 cup of sour cream. Heat through thoroughly but do not boil. This sauce really does something for fish, fowl or meat.

I hope I have at least given you a glimpse at the possibilities of the fascinating hobby that is shared by the members of the cult of the mycophagists. If your interest has been aroused, you will have no trouble locating many fuller sources of information about the edible fungi than is contained within the covers of this book. Maybe we will meet some day out in the fields hunting wild mushrooms. Meanwhile, let me wish you good hunting and good eating. I must go now, for supper has been announced, and I know we are having Sautéed Shaggy-Manes on Toast, covered with a creamy black sauce made of their own rich juices.

Wild Mustard:

NATURE'S FINEST HEALTH FOOD

(Brassica species)

IT IS hard to write about Wild Mustard because so many different plants are called by that name. There is hardly a member of the *Cruciferae*, or Mustard Family, that is not called wild mustard in some part of its range. To this family belong some of our most valuable cultivated crops, including not only garden mustard but also turnips, cabbages, Brussels sprouts, cauliflower, radishes, broccoli and several others. We are therefore not surprised to find many of the wild relatives of these common garden vegetables are also edible.

There are about ten species of the true wild mustards, or *Brassicas*, found growing wild in this country, and all of them are perfectly safe for human food. One of the best of these, and fortunately, the most widespread and abundant of all, is the *Brassica nigra*, or Black Mustard. This excellent potherb is found everywhere in southern Canada and throughout the United States. It is often a pestiferous weed in fields of small grain, such as oats or wheat, which cannot be cultivated.

The edible leaves, or Mustard Greens, are the lower leaves which are somewhat lyre-shaped, four to six inches long, on slender stems, with large terminal lobes and several small lateral lobes along the stem, all finely toothed around the edges. The leaves that appear on the flower stalk, after it starts developing, are smaller, almost stemless and very bitter. The flower stalk quite early forms flat-topped clusters of buds, the whole cluster looking like little heads of broccoli. As the stalk shoots up, it leaves individual buds scattered thickly along its length, and these soon open to become bright yellow flowers about three-eighths of an inch across. The flower stalk may reach a height of one or two feet. As in all the Mustard Family, the flowers have four petals and six stamens, which are in two sets, four long and two short.

WILD MUSTARD

Mustard greens, to be at their best, must be gathered early, during the first warm weather of spring. If you are in doubt about the recognition of wild mustard, I'm sure any farmer will be glad to point it out to you, and he will be pleased if you gather your supply from his fields.

When picked at the right time and properly prepared, mustard greens have just the right combination of bitterness and pungency to make a tasty boiled green. You will need quite a lot, as they tend to shrink while boiling. Don't try to short-cook mustard greens as you do spinach. They should be boiled about 30 minutes, then seasoned with butter or bacon drippings and served with vinegar or pepper sauce.

A little fancier dish is made by chopping the cooked mustard greens and seasoning with crumbled crisp bacon, finely chopped onions and a topping of thin slices of hard-boiled egg. This can be served hot or cold with French dressing or plain cider vinegar.

Vinegar and chopped onion or onion juice are not only the natural seasonings for mustard dishes; they help mask some of the bitter flavor, which some relish in spring greens, but others reject.

Mustard greens are a poor dish when only half cooked, but, if you are a health-food enthusiast who deplores the loss of vitamins that inevitably occurs during cooking, then you can eat your mustard greens raw. Most tossed salads are better off for the tang and zip which can be added by including a few finely chopped, tender mustard leaves. Young mustard leaves will improve most lunch-meat sandwiches, and liverwurst and mustard greens seem to be made for one another. I am not fond of liverwurst alone, but, when some tender leaves of wild mustard are added, it becomes one of my favorite sandwich fillings.

As a health food there are few vegetables that surpass wild mustard. It is an excellent source of vitamins A, B_1, B_2 and C, as well as being loaded with many of the trace minerals necessary to good nutrition. It also furnishes healthful bulk in a pleasant, palatable form. Then, too, think of the healthful outdoor exercise you will get gathering your own wild mustard greens from the fields and roadsides.

Most country people and many of our foreign-born population eat mustard greens every spring, then forget about the plant for the rest of the year. To me, the early greens are only the start of the mustard season. As the weather warms up, the greens become bitter and inedible, but this versatile plant is a relative of cultivated broccoli, and, like that delicious vegetable, the bloom buds are good to eat. These can be gathered over quite a long season, from the time they first form until nearly all the flowers have opened. They change slightly in taste as the season advances, indeed they improve as the flowers develop. Try to gather the flower heads without including any leaves, for these upper leaves are excessively bitter.

Unlike the mustard greens, this "wild broccoli" should be short-cooked. If it is cooked too long, it becomes an unsightly, mushy mess. Boil in salted water for about 3 minutes, then drain and season with butter, finely chopped onion and a little vinegar. The taste is slightly reminiscent of cultivated broccoli but it has a pungent, mustardy flavor all its own. Healthwise, it contains even more vitamin A than the leafy greens, and, because of the developing nitrogenous pollen, it contains considerably more protein.

While the masses of bright yellow blossoms make wild mustard conspicuous, select a spot to collect a supply of mustard seed. This seed is the basis for the condiment that has come to be considered indispensable with hot dogs.

The yellow flowers are followed by little four-sided pods about a half inch long, each containing several seeds. These ripen unevenly, and as soon as they are ripe they split open and the seeds drop out. The best way I have found to collect these seeds is to gather the whole seedstalk, which has now become a pod-bearing raceme, just when the lower pods are beginning to shatter, and spread them on one of the large plastic sheets, which I have found such a handy help in foraging. After drying in the sun for a few days, they will be ready to thresh out by beating them with a flail. From one 9 by 12 sheet, piled full of ripening seedstalks, I have winnowed out ½ gallon of clean mustard seed, and that is as many as I can possibly use in a year.

The clean dry seeds can be ground in an ordinary foodchopper using a fine plate. This will give you the same kind of dry ground mustard you can see on the spice shelves at your grocer's, and it can be used in any recipe that calls for dry mustard.

To make the yellow pasty condiment that is called Prepared Mustard, put some flour in a pan and toast it in the oven, stirring occasionally until it is evenly browned. This cooking is to keep the Prepared Mustard from having a raw, starchy taste. Mix this browned flour, half and half, with ground mustard and moisten with a mixture of half vinegar and half water until it is the right consistency, and your condiment is ready to use. You can vary the amounts of mustard and flour to suit your own taste. If you like the flavor, you can also add grated horseradish, which makes it particularly good with boiled tongue or boiled beef.

As a condiment for Chinese food, I add 1 tablespoon of very pungent Prepared Mustard to ½ cup of soy sauce and mix it thoroughly. This makes a delicious sauce for vegetables which have been short-cooked in the Chinese style, but use it sparingly or it will bring tears to your eyes.

Mustard seed also has a medicinal use in mustard plasters. These can be purchased ready-made at the drugstore, and many consider them the finest remedy for a congested chest resulting from a cold.

They are also used to apply heat to sore muscles and aching backs. To make your own, mix ground mustard, half and half, with raw flour and moisten with tepid water to the consistency of paste. Spread this thinly on a piece of muslin, cover with another piece of cloth and apply to the affected part. Leave it on about 20 minutes, or until the skin reddens. The patient will usually inform you when it is time to remove it, as the sensation of heat continues to increase as long as it is left on.

A plant that can furnish us a variety of tasty and wholesome vegetables, which are potent sources of vitamins and minerals, provide a tangy condiment to increase interest and enjoyment of other foods, and also give us relief from chest congestion and aching backs, certainly should not be overlooked.

The Wild Onion Family

(*Allium* species)

A MERICA is blessed with many kinds of Wild Onions. They are one of the most abundant and widespread of all wild food plants, one or more species being found in every state from the Atlantic to the Pacific, and from Canada to Mexico. There are no poisonous species of wild onion and all may be used for food, although some kinds are much better flavored than others. Nowadays most people think of onions and garlic as seasonings or condiments, but many Indian tribes considered them hearty staples, and ate them in great quantities.

You will have no trouble recognizing wild onions. All the species grow from basal bulbs, leaves may be tubular or flat, and flowers are borne in a terminal umbel on a naked scape. The characteristic odor is unmistakable. The nose knows when it has found a member of the onion tribe.

One of the commonest and most useful members of this family is the *Allium canadense*, commonly called Meadow Garlic, Wild Garlic, or Wild Shallot. It is common from New Brunswick to Florida, and west to the Plains. Look for it in rich, low meadows. It is often abundant. Although called Wild Garlic, the bulbs do not resemble the clustered cloves of ordinary garlic but are solitary, although many are often found growing almost against one another. The leaves are tubular, or quill-shaped like the domestic scallion, or green onion, only somewhat smaller in diameter. They grow a foot high or more in good soil. In May or June the wild garlic puts up a slender seed-stalk, or scape, one to two feet high, that bears few or no flowers but rather produces at its summit a globular cluster of tiny bulblets. This spherical cluster of "top-bulbs" is about one inch in diameter and each one contains several dozen individual bulbs, each shaped like a tiny, fat clove of garlic.

The underground bulbs of this onion are sweet and palatable after being parboiled and cooked in butter, but the best way to use A. *canadense* is to gather the whole plant like scallions, before the flower scape appears. Remove the tough outer layers and use only the tender, inner parts. Boil these for ½ hour in water salted to taste. Drain and save the water. Season the boiled onions generously with butter and serve hot.

Use the drained-off water to make a delicious Cream of Onion Soup. To 1 quart of the onion water add 2 tablespoons of butter and 1 cup of rich milk. Blend 2 tablespoons of flour with a little milk until it is smooth, then add this to the soup. Cook over low heat until it just reaches a simmer, then serve hot with saltines.

The green clusters of top bulbs on A. *canadense*, when gathered before they are ripe enough to shatter, make a fine onion-flavored pickle. Leave a bit of the tough stem on each cluster to serve as a handle when they are served with hors d'oeuvres or cocktail snacks. Just pack the clusters in a pint jar, add 1 tablespoon of whole mixed pickling spices and fill the jar with 2 parts cider vinegar to 1 part water. Seal them cold, store in a dark place, and any time after a month they will be ready to use.

When gathering A. *canadense*, do not confuse it with *Allium vineale*, or, as it is commonly called, Field Garlic. The latter species is not harmful to eat, but it has a very strong and penetrating taste and odor that is not appreciated by most humans, although cows seem to like it all too well. This unwelcome immigrant from Europe infests fields and pastures in the Atlantic states. The tender young plants are greedily eaten by cows in the early spring, and they impart a garlic flavor to the milk which doesn't improve its taste at all.

Once in camp, we had no garlic, so I used some bulbs of A. *vineale* to season a pot of chili con carne. The flavor was good, but the garlicky odor and taste seemed to linger about for days. A better way to use this powerful member of the onion family is to emulate the cows and only use the young tops in early spring. A small bunch of these tender blades, chopped fine, really does something for a tossed green salad.

A member of the onion tribe which is greatly appreciated in our family is the *Allium tricoccum*, or Wild Leek. It grows in dense, rich woods, from northern New England to North Carolina, and west to Minnesota and Iowa. The bulbs are clustered, like garlic, but the cluster is not covered with a membrane, and the cloves are much larger, some being more than two inches long and as thick as your thumb. In the early spring these bulbs each send up a little cylinder of tightly rolled leaves. As these leaves start unrolling at the top, this species resembles a tiny leek and can be used in the same ways as that vegetable. They are very good, chopped fine and added to a tossed salad, or they can be boiled for 20 minutes in salted water, then seasoned with butter or served in a cream sauce. They also make an excellent leek soup, either creamed or clear.

If the plant is left undisturbed, these leaves unroll and are very unonionlike in appearance. They are flat and lancehead shaped, from one to three inches broad and from five to nine inches long. These leaves die and disappear before the naked flower scape, bearing an umbel of greenish-white flowers, makes its appearance in June or July. After the flower scape dies down, it takes a good eye to recognize the points of the bulbs sticking above the leaf mold, which is the only way to locate a cluster of wild leeks at this time.

We consider wild leek bulbs the sweetest and best of the wild onions. They have a mild onion flavor with a hint of garlic, which I find delicious. This is the ingredient par excellence for a forager's French Onion Soup. Clean the bulbs by removing the outer fibrous skin, then slice them thinly crosswise. Sauté 1 cup of these sliced leeks in 2 tablespoons of butter. Add 1 can of consommé and 1 can of water. Simmer for 20 minutes over low heat, and you'll have a good onion soup without doing any more. But if you want to make it a real occasion, add 2 tablespoons of cooking sherry to the soup and pour it into individual ramekins. Cut a round of toast for each bowl and float the toast carefully on top of the soup. Sprinkle the toast with grated Parmesan cheese and set the bowls in a hot oven for ten minutes to let the cheese melt slightly. This is the way that one who is not satisfied to be known merely as a good cook can acquire a reputation as a culinary artist.

Wild leek bulbs can improve a tossed green salad, but they are best added to the dressing. If you have a knife-type blender, pour into it ⅓ cup of cider vinegar, 1 teaspoon of salt and 2 teaspoons of sugar. Add ½ cup of chopped water cress and 2 or 3 bulbs of wild leek, cut in small pieces. Blend well, then add 1 cup of salad oil and blend until the dressing is smooth. Use this on a tossed salad of mixed greens and listen to your guests beg for your salad secret.

Wild leek bulbs also make a good White Pickled Onion with a slight garlic flavor. Just pack the peeled bulbs into a jar, cover them with 2 parts vinegar to 1 part water and seal them up. After 3 weeks they are ready to make a meal prepared from leftovers taste like a feast.

The Nodding Wild Onion (*Allium cernuum*) is another common species with a wide range. It is found from New York to South Carolina. In the northern part of its range it goes west to the Pacific Coast. In the South, I know it extends west to beyond the Plains, for I have gathered it from gravelly hills in western New Mexico.

The nodding wild onion can be recognized by its bell-shaped, rose-colored flowers, in an umbel borne on a flower scape from six to eighteen inches high, and bent back near the top, like a shepherd's crook.

The bulbs are about a half inch in diameter and more than twice that high. They are strong-flavored enough to speak with considerable authority in a soup or stew. To use the bulbs as a vegetable, parboil them in plenty of water and throw the first water away. Return the onions to the fire with very little water, some butter, salt and pepper and let them simmer for 10 minutes to absorb the seasoning. Prepared this way they are sweet and palatable.

There are many other species in this numerous family, and all of them are good for food. Try using the recipes found here with whatever wild onion grows in your locality. You might discover a prize.

The Papaw:

A TROPICAL FRUIT COME NORTH

(*Asimina triloba*)

THE Papaw looks, tastes and smells like a tropical fruit, although it grows wild as far north as Michigan. It ranges from New York to Florida, and west to Nebraska and all the way down to Texas. Local names are False Banana, Michigan Banana and Custard Apple. All its relatives are tropical fruits, for the papaw is the only member of the *Annonaceae*, or Custard Apple Family, found growing outside the tropics.

The papaw is a small, slender tree, usually eight to twelve feet tall, but occasionally reaching twenty-five or thirty feet, but even these tallest ones will have a trunk diameter of less than six inches. It has large leaves, up to a foot long by five inches wide. These leaves are shaped like lance heads with the broadest part out near the point and tapering toward the base, where they are attached to the twigs with short leafstalks. They have entire margins, are dark green above and whitish underneath.

The flowers, which appear with the leaves in late April or May, are peculiar. They have six petals in two sets, the outer three larger and flattened out, and the inner ones standing more erect and forming a cup with three points. These flowers are about an inch and a half in diameter and are at first green, but turn purple before falling off.

The mature fruit is three to five inches long and is slenderly kidney-shaped, with a smooth yellowish-green skin which turns brown a few days after the fruit is picked. Papaws have large, brown seeds which are surrounded by the sweet and highly flavored yellow pulp. In Indiana, I once heard someone ask a Hoosier lad what papaws tasted like. Since flavors are notoriously hard to describe, his answer surprised me by its preciseness. He said, "They taste like mixed bananers and pears, and feel like sweet pertaters in your mouth." I can't improve on that description.

The fruit usually falls from the tree when mature, and the best papaws are often gathered from the ground. Boys, and those first making the acquaintance of this fruit, usually prefer it dead ripe and very soft. When I was a boy I liked it this way, but after years of eating this luscious wild fruit, I have come to prefer it ripe but still somewhat firm. We used to gather papaws by the basketful and bury them among the oats in the bin to let them ripen to our taste.

Ripe papaws have a heavy sweet fragrance that seems pleasant at first, but if one is continuously subjected to this aroma for several days it becomes cloying. For this reason papaws should never be ripened in the house. The sweet odor will permeate every room. I have known people to be turned against the fruit from having to smell it too long.

Nearly all the papaws gathered in this country are eaten out of hand as fresh fruit. One can, however, cook papaws, or combine them with other materials to make some fancy and delicious desserts. The simplest way to cook papaws is to bake them in their skins. It's a method which I don't recommend too highly, but there are people who relish baked papaws. My own favorite papaw preparation is a fluffy mixture that can be used as pie filling or served in parfait glasses.

In a saucepan, mix together ½ cup of brown sugar, 1 envelope un-flavored gelatin and ½ teaspoon of salt. Stir into this ⅔ cup of milk and 3 slightly beaten egg yolks. Cook and stir the mixture until it comes to a boil. Remove from the fire and stir in 1 full cup of strained papaw pulp. Chill until it mounds slightly when spooned. This will take 20 to 30 minutes in the refrigerator. Shortly before the mixture is sufficiently set, beat the 3 egg whites until they form soft peaks, then gradually add ¼ cup of sugar, beating until stiff peaks form. Fold the partly set papaw mixture thoroughly into the egg whites. Pour into a 9-inch graham cracker crust, or into parfait glasses and chill until firm. Then lock the doors to keep the neighbors out.

The Sugar-Plum Tree:

PERSIMMON

(Diospyros virginiana)

THE Persimmon is one of the finest and most abundant tree fruits
growing wild in our country. It is found from Connecticut to the
Gulf of Mexico and west to the Great Plains, but is most plentiful
in the Middle South. The fruits vary in quality and size throughout
their range, and even from tree to tree in the same locality, but
the hardy race which is common in the mountain regions of Pennsylvania, where I gather my persimmons, seems to be fairly uniform.
These are small, as persimmons go, being an inch or less in diameter,
a dull-orange color when ripe and most of them are seedless.

It seems a shame that this excellent wild fruit is better known for
the puckery, astringent quality of the green fruit than for its rich,
luscious sweetness when fully ripe. There are few wild fruits which
offer a better prospect for a hearty meal to the hungry hiker than
a treeful of ripe persimmons in late fall or early winter. And this is
one of the most delightful things about the persimmon—it is at its
best long after all other wild fruits are gone and forgotten. Once
while hiking across crusted snow in mid-January, I came on a persimmon tree with many fruits still hanging on. With an appetite
sharpened by the long walk in the wintery air, I climbed the tree
and stuffed myself with those soft, sugary lumps of goodness. When
I could hold no more, I gave all the limbs a good shake then de-

scended and picked up from the crusted snow enough ripe persimmons to fill the plastic bag I always carry in my pocket in order
to bring home any unexpected gift which the woodland might offer.
The whole family enjoyed the persimmon pudding we had for dessert
that evening.

There is a widespread belief that persimmons are edible only after
frost, or, as some say, after a hard freeze. Believing this, some
friends of mine gathered a quantity of half-ripe persimmon and stored
them in their home freezer. When these artificially frozen persimmons were thawed, they were just as puckery and astringent as
when they were picked. It is the degree of ripeness that counts, and,

PERSIMMON

for this, frost is not necessary. It is true that this tenacious little
tropical interloper often has to hang on until long after frost in order
to achieve the requisite ripeness, but frost has nothing to do with it.
In years when winter came late, I have gathered and eaten perfectly
ripe persimmons without a trace of astringency, long before the first
frost. It is time, warmth and sunlight which bring the persimmon to
perfection and the cold which accompanies a frost only retards the
process.

I have already given a hint as to the easiest way to pick persimmons. Just shake the tree and let the ripe ones fall. There are
on the market large plastic sheets which are ideal to spread beneath
the tree to catch them on. These sheets are reasonable in cost and
take up little room, so an ardent forager will always carry a couple
of them in his car. They are the greatest shortcut ever in gathering

many kinds of wild fruit. Using this method, a half bushel of persimmons can often be gathered from a single tree in a few minutes. True, they will include some twigs and foreign matter, but even counting sorting time it is far faster than plucking them from the tree one by one.

As you sort your haul, reject all that are firm, for, to be at its best, a persimmon must be soft and gooey. This is why the American persimmon will never be a successful market fruit. One occasionally sees wild persimmons on the market but these have been picked when underripe and are usually a great disappointment to those who buy them. Those which are too firm can be placed on trays and ripened in the sun, but they will never be as good as the tree-ripened fruit.

The fact that a persimmon will cling to the tree all winter without spoiling would indicate that they are easy to preserve, and so they are. The best way is to put all the fully ripe persimmons, except the ones you want to eat fresh, through a colander to remove the occasional seeds. Pack the pulp directly into half-pint jars, seal and place in a boiling hot-water bath for thirty minutes. Check the seal, store them away and they will keep until persimmons are ripe next year.

When those you placed on the trays to ripen are somewhat dry and no longer astringent, pack them in quart jars a handful at a time, covering each layer with dry granulated sugar. Be sure the last handful is covered with sugar, then seal the jar and set it away in a dark place and they will keep the year around.

Let's hurry on to the goodies that can be concocted from persimmon pulp. I'm going to give you my recipe for Persimmon-Hickory Nut Bread, which we consider the finest way of all to use persimmons. One October day while gathering persimmons we noticed a hickory nut lying among the fruit on the plastic tarp. On looking about we saw that it had fallen from a middle-sized shellbark hickory which almost overshadowed the smaller persimmon trees. We quickly turned our attention to this and after picking up the nuts we could find on the ground, we spread our tarps beneath the tree and climbed up and shook all the branches we could reach. Over a half bushel of nuts rained down from this one tree.

On reaching home I prepared some persimmon pulp and shelled some of the sweet nuts. I then sifted 2 cups of flour and 1 teaspoon of soda together. In a separate bowl I creamed 1 cup of sugar with

1½ sticks of margarine, added 2 well-beaten eggs and dumped in the soda-flour mixture. I then put in ½ pint of persimmon pulp and ½ cup of chopped hickory-nut meats. I added no other liquid, but just stirred this mixture up into a very stiff batter. Two small oblong loaf pans were lined with waxed paper and half the batter was placed in each. It was baked 1 hour at 325° and the result was even better than anticipated. Persimmons darken as they cook, so the bread was a moist dark brown, like gingerbread, and utterly delicious. It can be eaten hot or cold, with or without a sauce, and I have yet to see the person who dislikes it.

Later, I made this bread using black walnuts instead of hickory nuts and it was equally good. Never add flavorings or spices to this bread, for persimmons and nuts are flavorful enough. Of course you could make persimmon bread with nuts you buy at the store, but for a true forager this would be somewhat like the fisherman who bought his trout at the market.

Perhaps the highest form of persimmon cookery is achieved in the Persimmon-Nut Chiffon Pie. You will need a 9-inch Graham Cracker Crust (see page 198). In a saucepan, combine ½ cup of brown sugar, 1 envelope unflavored gelatin and ½ teaspoon of salt. Slightly beat 3 egg yolks and mix with ⅔ cup of milk, then stir into the brown-sugar mixture. Cook and stir until this mixture comes to a boil, then immediately remove from the heat and stir in 1 heaping cup of strained persimmon pulp. Chill until mixture mounds slightly when spooned. This will take about 1 hour, but watch it closely toward the end. Don't let it get too stiff.

Beat the 3 egg whites until soft peaks form, then gradually add ¼ cup of granulated sugar and beat until stiff peaks form. Fold the partly stiffened persimmon mixture and ¼ cup of chopped hickory nuts thoroughly into the egg whites and turn the whole into the crust. Chill until firm and you will have a delectable dream of a pie, fluffy and light as a wisp of foam.

If, after tasting these delicious products, you don't think that persimmons are too precious to use for any other purpose, you can make a unique Christmas Pudding, using both kinds of preserved persimmons. Cream 2 cups of sugar with 1 cup of margarine. Add 2 eggs well beaten and 1 cup of sour cream, then stir in 2 cups of flour which have been sifted with 1 teaspoon of soda and 1 teaspoon of salt. Add 1 pint of persimmon pulp and mix well. Carefully fold in 2 cups of the sugar-preserved dried persimmons. Wring out a pudding cloth in boiling water, spread it in a deep dish and turn the batter into it. Tie up the cloth and suspend it over boiling water in a deep, covered vessel. Keep it steaming for 4 hours, using boiling water to replenish the supply in the bottom of the kettle as it boils away.

When you unwrap the cloth you will have a dark-brown cannon ball of luscious pudding, just bursting with nature's own sugarplums. If you want to be really festive, stick a sprig of holly in the pudding at a jaunty angle, then, just before serving, pour a jigger of brandy over the top, set it afire and carry the pudding blazing to the table. You can serve it with whipped cream or with a wine sauce if you like, but I want nothing that might mask the delicious flavor that is its very own.

To slide from the sublime to the ridiculous, you can also make Molasses, Beer and Vinegar from persimmons. These three products are mentioned together because the first part of the preparation is the same for all of them. Mix 10 pounds of wheat bran, of the kind usually fed to cattle, with 1 gallon of pulp from very ripe persimmons. Bake this mixture like pones of cornbread until it is brown and firm. Break the pones in pieces and put through a food chopper using a coarse plate. Dump the ground mixture into a 5-gallon crock and fill the crock not quite full of boiling water.

To make Molasses let this stand for twelve hours or slightly more, then drain off the liquid and boil it down to the desired consistency. It tastes somewhat like cane molasses, slightly improved by the persimmon flavor which comes through.

If it's Beer you want, as soon as the water in the crock cools until it's barely warm, stir in 1 package of dry yeast mixed with a little of the liquid, and keep the jar covered with a cloth. It will ferment furiously for a few days but keep watching it and in about a week it will start settling down. The moment it becomes still and clear, bottle and cap it tightly. Store it in a cool, dark place and in about 3 weeks it will be ready to use. 'Simmon beer has a long and venerable history and some people are extremely fond of it. I think it is a waste of good persimmons, but I have some friends who always very willingly dispose of any I make.

An interesting and mild Vinegar resembling the beer vinegars of "Olde Englande" can be made by further processing. Proceed exactly as in making beer to the point where the liquid settles and clears. Then carefully siphon it off and to the whole lot add 1 gallon of un-pasteurized cider vinegar. Keep in a warm place in gallon jugs, each plugged with a wad of cotton. The vinegar ferment will proceed rapidly and in a few weeks it will be ready to use. Don't be afraid it has spoiled if mother of vinegar develops in the jugs. When you are sure the vinegar ferment is complete, carefully decant into clean jugs and cap tightly.

A recent discovery points to a use of the persimmon which is not concerned with the fruit. It has been reported in the scientific journals that "persimmon leaves have been found to give excep-tionally high values in content of vitamin C." Persimmon Tea could help fortify your family with this protective vitamin, substituting at least in part for the expensive citrus fruits. This tea proves to have a very pleasant flavor, which is surprising in something so healthful. Tea made from the green leaves is very acceptable but that from the dried leaves is even better, having a flavor slightly reminiscent of sassafras.

Gather the leaves in summer when they are full grown and spread them on newspapers in a warm attic room until they seem thoroughly dry. Pack them in fruit jars and heat the jar in a very low oven for 30 minutes. This preheating protects them from mold and if two-piece dome lids are placed on the jars while they are still hot, cooling will cause them to vacuum seal and they will keep perfectly fresh through the year.

Finally, I must point out that the persimmon with its shiny green foliage is an exceptionally beautiful small tree and should be planted more often as an ornamental. It belongs to the Ebony Family and the dark wood can be turned on a lathe into beautiful bowls and other ornamental objects. If you are looking for food and drink, beauty, goodness and health, why don't you go 'simmon hunting?

Beating the Pigs to the Pigweeds

(*Chenopodium album*)

YEARS ago, I was very impatient with anyone using a long Latin name to designate a common, ordinary plant. I considered the use of these tongue-twisting titles to be an affectation, designed to show off the knowledge of the user. Why couldn't these high-brows use the common name, which everyone understood?

I think it was the Pigweed, more than anything else, that cured me of this attitude. Pigweeds are among the commonest of the unwanted plants in fields, gardens and barnyards in Pennsylvania. Therefore, I was not surprised to find that pigweeds were also very common in Indiana, when I traveled there. I learned that farmers in Tennessee, Texas, New Mexico, California and even Hawaii were troubled with pigweeds. Obviously these farmers should get together and learn some way of controlling this troublesome weed. The only difficulty with this procedure was that, in each of these localities, the "pigweed" was a different kind of plant. To complicate matters even more, *Chenopodium album*, the pigweed of Pennsylvania, also grew in all these other places. In some sections it was called Lamb's-quarters, in some Goosefoot and in still others it was referred to as Wild Spinach.

I began to see why the botanical classification was necessary. Many totally different plants are called pigweed in some parts of the world.

The plant I call pigweed is known by dozens of other common or folk names in different places. Therefore any attempt to use the common name in distant places would only lead to confusion. But, I can say *Chenopodium album* and a trained botanist from any part of the world would instantly know the precise plant meant. Far from confounding the confusion, these Latin names greatly simplify the task of communication in this area.

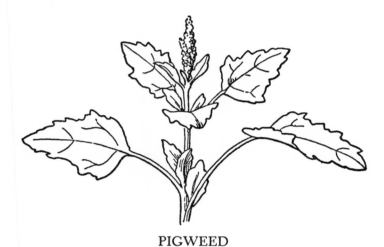

PIGWEED

More than that, the botanical name can tell me more about the plant in question than even the most descriptive common name ever could. If I had never seen this particular plant, the name *Chenopodium* should tell me that this weed is a member of the same family to which garden beets and spinach belong. If I don't have this knowledge at my fingertips, I can easily look it up in any botanical manual. About this time I'll begin to suspect that this plant might be good to eat.

This line of reasoning doesn't always work. Some very good food plants have worthless relatives. There are likely to be black sheep in any family. But in this case I was not misled; *Chenopodium album* is a valuable food plant.

Prejudice prevents many people from enjoying this excellent potherb merely because it is called pigweed. It isn't called that because it's only fit for pigs. It is just that pigs, knowing a good thing when they taste it, will eat all of this weed they can get. Pigs will also greedily eat pies, cakes, strawberry shortcake or caviar. If we refuse every kind of food that pigs love, there will be few things indeed that we are willing to eat. If we object to eating anything called pigweed, let's call this fine food plant lamb's-quarters, which at least has a more appetizing sound.

There are few better wild potherbs than this close relative of garden spinach. Only young, tender plants, less than one foot high, should be collected. Fortunately, in cultivated ground, one can find young plants, just right for eating, from midspring until frost. It requires a bit more cooking than spinach, but it doesn't need parboiling as some wild greens do. The taste of well-cooked lamb's-quarters is very similar to that of spinach.

When lamb's-quarters is young and edible, its leaves are roughly ovoid, or egg-shaped, tending to be somewhat four-sided or lozenge-shaped, with the margins roughly toothed toward the point. These leaves are a dull green with a whitish mealiness, and this white dusting is much more pronounced on the underside than on the upper surface. Before cooking, lamb's-quarters leaves are unwettable, that is, water either runs off them leaving them dry, or else it stands in drops without wetting the leaf surface. As soon as they are boiled, they lose this quality.

My sister cans lamb's-quarters for winter use, and finds her family likes it much better than spinach. The processing necessary to can greens is too long a cooking for spinach, but it leaves lamb's-quarters just about right. We prefer to blanch, package and store our off-season supply in the freezer.

In rich soil, lamb's-quarters will grow four or five feet high if not disturbed, becoming much branched. It bears a heavy crop of tiny seeds in panicles at the end of every branch. In early winter, when the panicles are dry, it is quite easy to gather these seeds in considerable quantity. Just hold a pail under the branches and strip them off. Rub the husks between the hands to separate the seed and chaff, then winnow out the trash. I have collected several quarts of seed in an hour, using this method.

The seeds are quite fine, being smaller than mustard seeds, and a dull blackish-brown color. I have heard that lamb's-quarters seed is the very finest food for caged birds. I find it pretty good food for humans, too. Finely ground in a hand gristmill, or even in a knife-type blender, and mixed half and half with wheat flour, it makes as fine a "buckwheat" pancake as you will ever taste. I have also added lamb's-quarters meal to muffins and biscuits. It makes these products very dark, but it tastes well enough.

All in all, I would say that pigweeds are too good for pigs.

Poke: WILD POTHERB PAR EXCELLENCE

POKE, the *Phytolacca americana* of the botanists, is probably the best known and most widely used wild vegetable in America. The Indian tribes eagerly sought it and early explorers were unstinting in their praise of this succulent potherb. They carried seeds when they went back home and poke soon became a popular cultivated garden vegetable in southern Europe and North Africa, a position it still maintains. In America it is still a favorite green vegetable with many country people and the tender young sprouts, gathered from wild plants, often appear in vegetable markets, especially in the South.

Poke has many local names, among them Garget, Pigeonberry and Inkberry. In the South, it is called Poke *Salad*, an infinitely better term than Poke *Weed*. A weed is a plant growing in a place where we don't want it, and I have seldom seen a poke plant I wanted removed.

This excellent wild vegetable is abundantly available over a very wide area, being found from Maine to Florida and west to the Great Plains. It is a rank-growing herb reaching a height of six to eight feet. The leaves, shaped like a lance head, five to nine inches long, are borne alternately. The greenish-white flowers found growing in long clusters opposite the leaves are not particularly attractive. The plant becomes beautiful in the fall. when the tall stems take on

POKEWEED

a lovely violet hue and are covered with long clusters of the purple-black berries which follow the flowers.

Each spring a new crop of fat young sprouts shoot up from the enormous perennial root. These can be located by looking for the old dried stalks from last year. After a little practice, dried poke stalks can be easily recognized.

Poke is best when very young, so grab the tender sprouts while they are still small. Wash and trim, leaving the unrolled clustered leaves at the top. Boil for 10 minutes in plenty of water, then throw this first water away. Return the drained sprouts to the kettle, add a very little water, some salt and quite a lot of butter, margarine or bacon drippings. Simmer slowly for half an hour so the seasoning can permeate the vegetable through and through. Served just as it comes from the kettle, or combined with cream sauce, this is a delicious vegetable. It so closely resembles asparagus that some may be fooled. I find the taste quite different, but equally good.

Poke can also be prepared as leafy greens, but, unlike spinach, it should be thoroughly cooked. Gather only the young, unfolding leaves at the top of the sprout. Some like to combine these with mustard greens, but they are very good cooked alone. Just follow the directions for cooking sprouts and you will have as tasty a dish of greens as any you ever ate.

The country people of southern Indiana eat Fried Poke. The thicker young sprouts are peeled, and this seems to obviate the necessity for parboiling. The tender, clear, inner portion is rolled in white corn meal and fried in oil or fat.

Both sprouts and greens can easily be preserved for out-of-season use. Boil for 10 minutes, drain, then package and store in the freezer. Or, after parboiling, can the greens or sprouts just as you would spinach or asparagus.

An excellent pickle can be made of the sprouts. Boil some vinegar with 1 tablespoon each of salt, sugar and mixed pickling spices added to each quart. Pour boiling water over the sprouts and let it stand 20 minutes. Drain and cover with fresh boiling water, this time letting it stand only 3 minutes. Drain quickly, pack the hot sprouts loosely into jars, cover with the boiling vinegar and seal at once. These will be ready to use in about a month.

The huge root of the poke plant has white succulent flesh that looks edible, but don't try it, for poke, besides being an excellent vegetable, is a powerful medicinal herb. The root and the old plant contain phytolaccin which is cathartic, slightly narcotic, a slow-acting emetic in large doses and, actually, poisonous. The seeds can be extremely poisonous and should not be eaten, nor should the old stems or root, which also are poisonous. When I was a child my mother used to crush 3 dozen of the berries in 1 pint of boiling water, turning it a pretty wine color. After cooling, this was strained and we were given a tablespoonful a day to "purify the blood" whenever we had boils or pimples. We also put pieces of cut-up root in the chicken's drinking water in the belief that it would protect them from disease. I don't know how efficacious either of these remedies are, but at least there seemed to be no ill effects to either children or chickens.

Because of the drug content of the mature plant, one should be chary of eating the foliage after it is fully developed, but the young leaves and sprouts are a delicious and wholesome vegetable.

Although many people do know and use poke, the supply seems unlimited. Each year thousands of tons of tender sprouts grow old and tough because no one comes to claim them. Let's resolve now to do our part to prevent this waste and at the same time enjoy some "real good eating."

Purslane: INDIA'S GIFT TO THE WORLD

(*Portulaca oleracea*)

RECENTLY a would-be humorous article was carried by one of the news services. An ignorant reporter, writing in a supercilious manner, said that he had a recipe for a "depression salad" which he would gladly give away. He had been amused to learn somewhere that it was actually possible to eat the leaves of young dandelions and peppergrass. He went on to say that if things were really hard up, one could even eat Purslane. Then he ended the article by saying, "You can have these recipes, but if you use them, don't invite me."

The attitude reflected here is, like all prejudice, based on inexcusable ignorance. It is a sad commentary on the American mind that this attitude has become the prevalent one.

I happen to know that a salad made of tender, blanched, young dandelion leaves and young peppergrass is perfectly delicious. If this ignoramus was served such a salad, without knowing its contents, as part of a fifteen-dollar dinner he would probably send his congratulations to the salad chef.

This reporter further betrayed his ignorance by the plants he selected to deride. Many acres of dandelions and peppergrass are raised on farms in New Jersey, and tons of these fine vegetables are sold each year on the New York and Philadelphia markets at premium prices.

As for purslane, this succulent plant has been eaten and appreciated in India and Persia for more than two thousand years. It is today a prized garden vegetable over much of Europe and Asia, and several different varieties have been developed. To write, as this reporter did, as if the eating of purslane was the depth of degradation is a boorish insult to the millions of people about the world to whom it is a favored food. Such thoughtless writing in our press contributes to the unpopularity of Americans in many lands.

PURSLANE

Originating in India or Persia, purslane has established itself around the world. In America it has found a congenial home, being found from the Atlantic to the Pacific, and from far up in Canada to Tierra del Fuego. Between Canada and Mexico, I doubt that there is a single township where this esculent herb could not be found.

The wild plant is a ground-hugging annual seldom reaching up two inches high, although it may be more than a foot across. It reaches its best development in rich, sandy soils and so is sometimes a bad weed in gardens and cultivated ground. Each plant has several tender stems, which radiate from the center of the plant, forking freely as they creep along the ground. The stems are about a quarter inch in diameter near their origin, and reduce in size at each forking. The tiny yellow flowers, opening only on sunny mornings, are found in the forkings of the stems.

Just seeing the specific name of this plant, *oleracea*, should indicate that here is savory food. The entire plant, stem, leaf and flower bud, is good to eat, but unless you are weeding the garden, the way to gather purslane for the table is to pinch off the leafy tips. These will quickly be replaced, and a few plants will supply a family for a season.

Purslane can be used raw, cooked, frozen or pickled. It should always be washed thoroughly, for it is apt to be gritty. The tender tips make a very pleasant salad, either alone or in combination with other salad plants. Purslane is neither pungent nor bitter; it has a mild acid taste and a fatty or mucilaginous quality which most people like, but a few find it objectionable.

It is this mucilaginous characteristic, which makes purslane a valuable addition to soups and stews, serving, like okra or the Creole "gumbo filet," to give these dishes a desirable consistency.

Purslane is probably eaten more often as a plain boiled green than in any other way. The new tips, washed and then boiled for 10 minutes and seasoned with butter and salt, make a very acceptable cooked vegetable.

An even better way to cook it is to cut several slices of bacon in small pieces and fry them in a large skillet. When the bacon is done, dump in about 1 quart of the tender tips of purslane. Stir until it is evenly coated with the bacon drippings, then cover and let it cook for 6 or 7 minutes. Season with salt and a little vinegar.

For those who object to the fattiness of purslane, a casserole dish can be made which completely masks this quality. Boil the tips 10 minutes, drain and chop fine. Stir 1 beaten egg into the purslane, then stir in as many fine bread crumbs as the mixture will dampen. Season to taste with salt and pepper, then bake in a moderate oven until the top is nicely browned.

The fat, tender stems of purslane make a splendid pickle. While searching the literature for information on this subject, I came across several old English recipes for Purslane Pickles, but they all required more work than I was willing to do. I had a very simple recipe for unfermented dill pickles, which had served me well, so I used it, substituting purslane stems for cucumbers. The pickles are crisp and tasty, and now, nine months after they were made, they are still in perfect condition.

A liquid mixture is made by stirring together 1 cup of white vinegar, 2 cups of cold water, ¼ cup of salt and ½ teaspoon of alum. This is enough to fill two pint jars. In the bottom of each jar is placed a flower of dill, a clove of garlic and a small red pepper. The jars are then packed, not too tightly, with clean purslane stems. Another flower of dill is put on top, the jars are filled with the liquid and sealed. No cooking, no processing, no fuss, no bother. Just store them in a dark place at least 1 month before using.

If you find your family likes cooked purslane, and would like to store some for winter use, freezing is the best method. Fill a large pan with washed purslane tips and cover with boiling water. Simmer for 5 minutes, then drain in a colander and run cold water over the tips until they are cool. Pack in pint jars and freeze at once.

One would think, after all the uses outlined above, that we had asked enough of one plant, but purslane has another, and this time very different, use. This world-traveling plant early invaded the sandy Southwest, where it grows luxuriously. The Indian tribes of that section learned not only to eat the fresh plant, but also that its abundantly borne seeds could be ground up and made into very good bread and gruel.

Purslane seed is produced in a peculiar manner, many seeds being packed into a little round pillbox about the size of a buckshot, which follows the flower, in the fork of the stems. When ripe, the outer half of the little box pops off, like a lid, releasing the seeds. These pods ripen unevenly, but purslane has the ability to rush the process of seed production to completion, even after the plant is pulled from the ground, using the food and water stored in the succulent stems for this purpose. Gardeners hate this propagative habit of purslane, but foragers can take advantage of it.

I wanted to try this Indian meal, and offered to pull the purslane from my brother-in-law's garden, where it was growing profusely. I spread the plants on a large plastic sheet and let them dry for 2 weeks. Then I beat them to loosen the seed, put them through a coarse sieve to remove the big trash and winnowed out the small stuff. I had left about 3 cups of tiny black seed. These were ground in a hand grist mill, mixed half and half with wheat flour and made into some dark but good "buckwheat" cakes. Eaten hot with butter and home-made maple sirup they were pronounced delicious.

The mush we made with purslane meal was not so good, but still it was worthy of the attention of a really hungry man.

Let's stop considering purslane worthless merely because it is abundant and easily procured. Not all good things are rare and costly. Maybe purslane proves there is truth in the old cliché that states that "the best things in life are free."

Raspberries and Wineberries

(*Rubus* species)

FOR those who are fortunate enough to live where they grow, the raspberries furnish some of the very finest wild fruits to be found. Because of our familiarity with the cultivated forms of some of our wild raspberries, the flavors are known and well liked.

The wild Red Raspberry (*Rubus strigosus*) is found from Newfoundland to British Columbia and south to New Mexico, but south of the Great Lakes regions it is usually found only in high mountains. I once gathered some, though only a handful, in the high Rockies of northwestern New Mexico. In the Alleghanies of central Pennsylvania, one commonly sees the canes in the forest bearing leaves but very few berries. However, where roads, trails or logging have cleared away the trees and allowed the sun to get through, they sometimes fruit abundantly. I have gathered several quarts of delicious ripe raspberries by picking along the edge of a mountain road for a mile or so.

The canes of this berry grow from two to five feet tall, the leaves are compound, with from three to five leaflets, irregularly notched around the edges, green on top and downy white beneath. The flowers are greenish-white in the spring, and the fruit is ripe in Pennsylvania in July or early August.

The flavor is almost identical with that of the cultivated red raspberry, except there is a bit more of the raspberry flavor in this slightly smaller wild fruit. If abundant where you live, the red raspberry makes some of the finest jams and jellies ever tasted. They lack pectin so this must be added, and there are good recipes for both jams and jellies of raspberries right on the packages or bottles of commercial pectin.

I like red raspberries so well as fresh fruit that I usually consume all I can find in that way. If I can find a surplus, I freeze them by putting the berries in a jar or plastic container, covering them with a sirup made of 1 part sugar to 4 parts water, and set them in the quick-freeze section of my freezer. There they keep, practically as delicious as the fresh-picked fruit until I serve them at some winter wild food party, or just take them out to give myself and my family a treat.

The Black Raspberry, or Blackcap (*Rubus occidentalis*) is much more common and of considerably wider range than the wild red raspberry. Found from Quebec to Ontario and south to Georgia and Missouri, this berry was much appreciated by the pioneers and also by the Indians who preceded them. They grow on thin, recurved canes up to six or eight feet long, that often bend back to the ground and take roots at their tips, forming a series of "croquet wickets" that make it exceedingly difficult to get through a patch of these berries. The leaves are compound with three leaflets, with double rows of teeth about their edges, green above and downy white below. There are curved prickles on the canes and leaf stems. The flowers are very similar to those of the red raspberry.

The wild black raspberry is fully as delicious as the cultivated variety, and they can often be found in great abundance along the edges of woods, about fields and along roadsides. Served with sugar and cream, there are few better dessert fruits to be found growing wild. They can be frozen by following the directions for freezing red raspberries and then you can enjoy this superb dessert any time of the year. Black Raspberry Jelly is a really fine product with a flavor that is enjoyed by nearly everyone. Add 1 cup of water to 4 quarts of crushed berries and simmer gently for 15 minutes, then squeeze out the juice through a jelly bag. This should yield slightly over 1 quart of juice. To this juice add 1 package of powdered pectin and bring it to a boil. Then add 7 cups of sugar and bring it to a boil again, boil hard for 1 minute, then pour into half-pint jars and seal.

One of my favorite wild fruits, and one that I gather many quarts of each year, is a relative of the raspberries called the Wineberry. Botanically it bears the almost unpronounceable name, *Rubus phoenicolasius,* and it is a recent immigrant from Asia, but has already become thoroughly naturalized and is becoming common over a fairly wide area. The canes grow eight to ten feet long and, like the black raspberry, they are apt to take root at the tips, thus making impenetrable briar patches. The canes are red on top and green underneath, and are covered with bristles and armed with prickles. The compound leaves have three leaflets, the outer one being much larger than the other two, and they are green and smooth on top and a downy white below. The terminal leaflet is three to four inches wide and four to five inches long. It is a rounded heart-shape and abruptly pointed. The two lateral leaflets are smaller, pointed-egg-shaped, and all the leaflets have saw-toothed edges. The leafstalk and even the midribs of the leaves have small curved prickles. The bloom is insignificant and the calyx encloses the berry, forming a husk that only opens when the fruit has reached full size. The fruit when ripe looks like a bright, shiny, light-red raspberry and has a slightly clammy or sticky feel.

I have been unable to determine the limits of the range where this berry grows in this country, but I have picked wineberries in Pennsylvania, New Jersey, Delaware, Maryland and Virginia, so it is not just a local wilding. I have not found it mentioned in other books on wild food plants I've consulted so far, probably because it is such a recent immigrant. This is one "foreigner" that is certainly welcome here, as far as I am concerned.

Where I live the wineberry is common along roadsides and about the edges of fields. It is a dependable cropper, and each year, during wineberry season, some of the neighbor's children gather the beautiful bright red fruit in berry boxes and sell them at premium prices from door to door. I have found them bearing so abundantly that I was able to pick twelve quarts in two hours from one small patch.

Wineberries have a delicious flavor and a sprightly tartness that is acceptable to almost everyone. There are few better desserts than sugared wineberries and sweet cream. I have made Wineberry Jam and Jelly by following recipes intended for the use of raspberries, but I like the fresh fruit so well that I usually freeze any surplus that I have to extend the season over which I can enjoy wineberries. Despite their suggestive name, I have never heard of anyone making wine of these berries.

The Sassafras for Food and Drink

(Sassafras albidum)

> I got so thin on sass'frus tea
> I could hide behind a straw,
> Indeed I was a different man
> When I left Arkansas.
>
> —Old Song

Few American trees are more widely known than the Sassafras. Strangely, however, very few people know the important role this tree played in the very early history of our country. Europeans first heard of sassafras through the Spaniards, and sassafras is a Spanish name. From the Spanish parts of America sassafras was traded into England where it soon acquired a great reputation as a medicinal herb and sold for a high price. In 1577, a book by a Spanish physician, one Dr. Monardus, was translated into English under the title, *The joyful newes from the West Indies,* and this volume listed the medicinal uses of sassafras, thus greatly increasing both the fame and the price of this fragrant plant product.

In 1590 there appeared the report of Thomas Hariot on Virginia, which has already been mentioned in relation to groundnuts. Hariot, in listing the valuable plants of Virginia, says:

Sassafras, called by the inhabitants Winauk, a kind of wood of most pleasant and sweete smel, and of most rare vertues in physick for the cure of many diseases.

187

In 1602, when Bartholomew Gosnold crossed the Atlantic in the good ship *Concord* and sailed down the New England coast, discovering and naming Cape Cod, Martha's Vineyard and the Elizabeth Islands, among others, there was with him one John Brereton who wrote a book called, A *briefe and true relation of the discourie of the north part of Virginia.* (Everything from Newfoundland to Spanish Florida was then called Virginia.) Brereton very modestly fails to reveal the role he played in this historic exploration, but he was probably an officer on the *Concord.*

There is no doubt, however, about Brereton's enthusiasm about sassafras. He gives a glowing description of Elizabeth Island which is now called by its old Indian name, Naushon Island, for we have broadened the name Elizabeth to include the whole group of islands between Woods Hole, Massachusetts, and Martha's Vineyard. In speaking of the riches to be found on Naushon, the largest and finest island of the group, he says, "Sassafras trees great plenty all the island over, a tree of high price and great profit."

Incidentally, Margaret Schroeder, the artist who produced the plant illustrations for this book, is now part owner of Naushon Island and makes her summer home there. Undoubtedly, many of the plants she used as models were directly descended from those that John Brereton saw and so vividly described.

In another place in the book, Brereton says of some Indians they had encountered that some of them "remained with us behinde, bearing us company every day into the woods, and help us to cut and carie our Sassafras." It seems established that sassafras was the first plant product exported from New England.

Brereton appends to his book what he calls "A briefe note of such commodities as we saw," where sassafras is mentioned several times more. Of all the commodities he lists, sassafras is the only one where a price is mentioned, and the figure is three shillings per pound. So we'll be properly impressed with this profitable price, he does a bit of arithmetic and points out that a long ton (2240 pounds) of these fragrant roots would bring the astonishing figure of 336 British pounds. In this same section he gives credit to a fellow officer for calling their attention to this source of wealth, writing, "The finder of our Sassafras in these parts was one Master Robert Meriton." We could feel very grateful to this otherwise unknown Master Meriton for discovering such an interesting and useful tree except for the fact that anyone who has ever seen the abundant sassafras growing along every fence row and roadside in "these parts" is apt to feel like the schoolboy who was unimpressed by the story of Columbus discovering America, for, as he asked, "How could he miss it?"

The commander of this expedition, Bartholomew Gosnold, was influential in securing the charters for the London and Plymouth companies in 1606, and there is no doubt that the excitement about sassafras played no small part in the formation of these companies. Gosnold himself was associated with Christofer Newport in command of the three vessels which brought the first colonists to Jamestown, Virginia, under these charters, and these first settlers expected to make easy fortunes in sassafras. Gosnold died in Jamestown Colony in 1607 of swamp fever which, ironically enough, was one of the diseases which sassafras was supposed to cure.

Sassafras grows from Maine to Florida and west to the Plains, and it is usually abundant and easily found throughout its range. Oddly, it was the great abundance of sassafras which depressed the price and prevented anyone from making great fortunes from its sale. Like most plants which have entered deeply into folklore, the sassafras has a number of folk names, being called Ague Tree, Chewing Stick, Tea Tree and Cinnamonwood in different localities. This is one case where the botanical names are as numerous as the folk names, the same species being called *Sassafras albidum, S. variifolium, S. officinale*, and even *Sassafras Sassafras*, which is getting downright silly.

This interesting plant belongs to a fascinating family, the Lauraceae, which are all aromatic plants, abounding in stimulating, volatile oils to which their qualities are due. Local kin of the sassafras are the Spicebush and the Sweet Bay, but it has more glamorous relatives in the Cinnamon of the Spice Islands and the Camphorwood Tree of China and Japan.

Both the old specific name, *officinale*, and the folk name, ague tree, point to the supposed medicinal virtues of sassafras. Once thought to cure a multitude of ills, the medicinal use of this plant has gradually declined. The essential oil, *oleum sassafras*, is still found in the pharmacopoeia, but it is in demand today mainly as a flavoring for other medicines. It is also used in soft drinks and confections.

Many country people take Sassafras Tea regularly each year as a spring tonic, believing that it thins the blood and prepares the body to better stand the coming heat of summer. I happen to like the flavor

of Sassafras Tea, so I drink it, not only in the spring, but throughout
the year. Recently, warnings have been issued that sassafras has stimulant and narcotic effects when taken in large doses, but in reasonable
amounts, such as would be taken in ordinary use, it is a wholesome
and palatable beverage.

The sassafras is easy to recognize any time of the year. It is a small
tree, often no more than a twiggy shrub, but I have seen one speci-

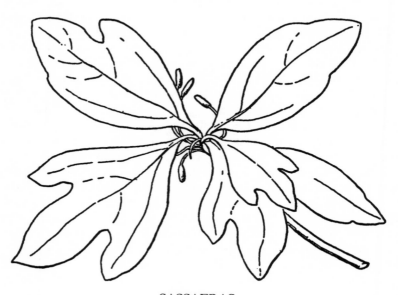

SASSAFRAS

men, in southern Pennsylvania, that was thirty feet high with a trunk
over two feet in diameter. Sassafras sends up new shoots from its
far-wandering roots, so it tends to form small thickets. The twigs have
green bark which helps us to recognize the tree in winter and early
spring. The old specific name, *variifolium*, was given to this tree because it has three kinds of leaves. Some have entire margins, some
are mitten-shaped and some have three lobes, that is, the "mitten"
has two thumbs. One often finds all three kinds of leaves growing on
one twig as shown in our illustration. The greenish-yellow flowers,
about a quarter inch across, appear with the first leaves in spring.

The fruit is a dull-blue drupe about half an inch long on red, club-shaped stems. If there is any doubt about identification, dig out a root and smell a broken end. The root-beer aroma is unmistakable. One whiff will make your mouth water and set you grubbing for more roots.

Don't be afraid that you might exterminate the plant by pulling up a few small saplings to get the roots. The sassafras is very tenacious, and has the ability to put up new plants for every one you take. A farmer who gave me permission to pull the plants which grew along his fence and were creeping out into his field said, "When you pull one, two grow back." Unless you carefully grub out every root, gathering sassafras seems to make the clump thrive.

See the section on maples to learn about making Sassafras Tea with maple sap in early spring (page 124). Other times of the year, the tea can be sweetened with ordinary sugar. The roots can be collected any time, but I find they are easier pulled from the ground while it is still soft after the spring thaws. I look for small saplings growing on banks where they can be pulled to one side, which is easier than pulling them straight up. All the roots are good, but the larger ones are harder to gather and they tend to develop a rough outside bark which must be scraped off before they are used. Scrub the roots thoroughly and cut them in pieces short enough to fit conveniently into the kettle. Use them fresh or let them dry for later use.

To make the tea, just put a handful of the roots into a kettle, add a bit more water than you want tea, and boil until it turns a nice red color. Sweeten to taste and drink hot or iced. The same roots can be used to make tea several times before the flavor is expended.

Some people object to the medicinal flavor of Sassafras Tea, but these folk have things backward. Some medicines are flavored with sassafras, but this merely means that some medicines taste of sassafras, and not that sassafras tastes of medicine.

As the old folk ballad, quoted at the beginning of this chapter indicates, drinking Sassafras Tea was once thought to make the drinker lose weight and become thin. In view of the current interest in reducing aids, those huge fortunes about which the early explorers dreamed might still be made from sassafras if it proved a real help in losing weight.

After reading *Folk Medicine* by Dr. D. C. Jarvis, my wife started serving honey and vinegar, stirred in water, with our meals. I didn't object, in fact I found the good doctor's drink quite palatable, with a sweet-sour cidery flavor. But I am an experimenter by nature, so one day I added 3 tablespoons of honey and 3 tablespoons of vinegar to 1 quart of Sassafras Tea. After setting in the refrigerator until it was ice cold, it was delicious.

There are those who claim that a better tea is made if one uses only the bark from the roots. I use the whole root when I am making tea from freshly dug roots, but I often peel some bark and dry it at room temperature for later use. An old-fashioned condiment, to be eaten with meat, is made by grating dried sassafras bark into boiling sugar and water until it is thick as paste. You really have to like sassafras to appreciate this, as it is pretty powerful.

Much more acceptable to the average palate is Sassafras Jelly. To 3 cups of very strong Sassafras Tea, add 1 3-ounce package of powdered pectin and ½ teaspoon of sour salt (citric acid). Bring this to a boil, stirring constantly, then add 4 cups of sugar. Bring to a boil again and boil for 1 minute, then pour into half-pint jars and seal. This is a spicy jelly, very good with meat, or it can be eaten with hot breads, like fruit jellies.

A different kind of Sassafras Jelly, which yields a pleasant by-product, is made with honey. If you can find a bee tree and get wild honey, so much the better. Dissolve 1 package of powdered pectin in 2 cups of strong Sassafras Tea. Bring just to a boil, then add 3 cups of strained honey and a handful of slivers of bark, peeled from sassafras roots. Bring to a boil again, and simmer for about 5 minutes. Strain out the bark, pour the jelly into jars and seal. Spread the slivers of bark on wax paper and put in some convenient place to dry thoroughly. Children, and immature adults like me, are fond of nibbling on a piece of this sweet, highly flavored bark.

Another way to make Honey-Sassafras Jelly is to add 2 tablespoons of finely grated dried root bark of sassafras to the jelly as you put in the honey. This root powder doesn't sink or rise, as so many things do when we try to add them to jelly, but remains evenly diffused through the finished product. The extra sassafras, which I recommend for the jellies where honey is used, is necessary to keep the strong flavor of the honey from masking the sassafras. When honey is used, no citric acid is necessary, as the honey furnishes the acid needed in jelly as well as the sugar.

Did you ever chew sassafras leaves or winter buds? I often do, as

I hike where this little tree grows. The young leaves have a pleasant, spicy taste and a mucilaginous quality like purslane. I often add a few tender sassafras leaves to a tossed salad, if they are available.

The dried and powdered leaves of sassafras are highly valued in Creole cookery. They are the basic ingredient of the delicious gumbo filet used in New Orleans to thicken and flavor gumbos.

To make your own filet, gather young sassafras leaves and dry them at room temperature. When thoroughly dry, crush them to powder and sift to remove the stems and veins. The mucilaginous quality of this powder will add a real smoothness to soups, stews, chowders and gravies. Use about a heaping tablespoonful to a pot of soup or stew. Put some of the powder in a salt shaker and set it on the table. Then every one can add as much as he likes to his own soup.

The fragrant wood of the sassafras, especially that of the root, repels moths, just as red cedar does. A bag of sassafras chips packed with your winter clothes will protect them from these pests. A farmer in Pennsylvania assured me that mites would never bother chickens that roosted on sassafras poles.

Now we see that sassafras is much more than an old-fashioned spring tonic. Let's stop ignoring this valuable wayside tree.

Economics of Wild Strawberries

> I wish I knew half what the flock of them know
> Of where all the berries and other things grow,
> Cranberries in bogs and raspberries on top
> Of the boulder-strewn mountain, and when they will crop.
> I met them one day and each had a flower
> Stuck in his berries as fresh as a shower;
> Some strange kind—they told me it hadn't a name.*

Prejudice prevents many people from enjoying delicious and wholesome wild food, but strangely I have never met anyone who prejudiced against the Wild Strawberry. *Fragaria* it was christened by some botanist with an appreciative nose, and there are two excellent species in the eastern part of our country, the *virginiana* and the *vesca*. Most people agree that the wild strawberry is vastly superior to the cultivated kind and is about the most delicious of all our wild fruits, the top prize for the wild food gatherer.

This is one of the widest ranging of all our wild fruits and, while it is abundant in some places, it is rare and found only locally throughout much of its range. It is more abundant in northeastern United States and eastern Canada than elsewhere, but I have picked wild

* Robert Frost, "Blueberries," *Complete Poems of Robert Frost* (New York: Holt, Rinehart and Winston, Inc., 1930, 1939). Reprinted with permission.

strawberries in a number of states, from Quebec to Texas. On the Pacific Coast I have enjoyed a closely related species, the F. *californica*, which I have picked from the mountains of California to the artillery range at Fort Lewis, near Tacoma, Washington. This species produces even smaller berries than the *virginiana*, but they are wonderfully sweet and fragrant. Once in Texas I found an open place in the center of a wild plum thicket, where a bushel of wild strawberries could have been picked from a few square rods of ground. I took my share, then informed a nearby sharecropper's family of this treasure, of which they had been entirely unaware.

Although everyone appreciates the flavor and aroma of wild strawberries, many people balk at the tedious job of picking them. The berries must be picked free of the calyx or "hull" and one must be careful to exclude leaves, sticks or trash, for the berries are small and easily crushed and picking over the day's haul would be too difficult. The care necessary to see that nothing but clean berries goes into the pail makes it fill slowly, especially since one is under constant temptation to take a toll between plant and pail.

Early last summer I drove to an abandoned orchard on a southern slope where strawberries like to grow. The season had been perfect and the berries were so thick they covered the ground, looking like a red carpet unrolled before me. I could sit down and pick a quart of berries without moving. I stayed there all day, the strawberries sufficing for my lunch. A sudden shower caught me far from the shelter of my car, so I just kept picking.

> You ought to have seen how it looked in the rain,
> The fruit mixed with water in layers of leaves,
> Like two kinds of jewels, a vision for thieves.*

The returning sun soon dried my clothes and the berries seemed brighter and fresher than before. The day was a revel in beauty, flavor and aroma, and at its close I felt that I had spent few more worth-while days in my life.

My neighbor raises strawberries in his garden. When he found how I had spent my day, he felt sorry for me. He thought it a shame that I had driven twenty miles and spent the day obtaining only twelve quarts of berries, while he had been able to gather the same quantity of cultivated berries in an hour from his own back yard.

* *Ibid.*

A friend who shared our shortcake that evening, although he appreciated the superior flavor of the wild berries, felt bad about me having spent my day at such tedious labor while he was enjoying a game of golf. He wondered aloud if it really paid to pick wild berries when one considered the labor involved, the amount of fruit obtained and the price of berries on the market.

I could have argued with these two men, but I didn't. It would have been easy to have reminded my neighbor of the many hours of spading, planting, weeding, mulching and runner-pinching he had devoted to his little strawberry patch, while I had done nothing for mine except pick them. He had put out hard cash for plants, tools, fertilizer, mulching materials and taxes on his land, while I had invested nothing but a pleasant drive in the country. To my friend, who was worried about the economics of berrypicking, I could have pointed out that my day had been far less expensive, no more strenuous and considerably more profitable than had his own day at the golf course.

I could have argued the economics of wild strawberries, but it would have been pointless. The truth is that none of us spent that day seeking economic gain. All three of us had been searching for something which is hard to put in words. In the poem at the beginning of this chapter, Robert Frost has beautifully symbolized the elusive treasure we were hunting as a strange flower without a name. Maybe my neighbor saw this flower growing in the corner of his garden, and my friend might have glimpsed its color in the rough beside the fairway. I found it mingling its fragrance with that of the wild strawberry in an abandoned orchard. I felt no need of economic profit to justify my having spent a day in its neighborhood.

> Who cares what they say? It's a nice way to live
> Just taking what Nature is willing to give
> Not forcing her hand with a harrow and plow.*

It hardly seems necessary to tell anyone how to use wild strawberries, but you do have a choice of many excellent ways in which to use this best of wild fruits. When picked far from roads and human habitation, they are safe and delicious to eat straight from the plant. Carried into the house or camp and eaten with whipped cream or even rich milk, they are superb.

* *Ibid.*

There is no need to slice wild strawberries when preparing sugared berries. Just put the washed berries in a jar or deep bowl and sprinkle on 1 cup of sugar per quart of berries. This causes the juice to flow and the berries are soon swimming in a sirup made of their own juices and sugar. Cover the jar or bowl and set in the refrigerator until used. I have kept sugared berries in the refrigerator for more than two weeks and even then it was gluttony, not spoilage, which caused them to disappear.

These sugared berries are a joy to eat with cream or milk and, as a topping for ice cream, they are a pure delight. A shortcake made with sugared wild strawberries will cause you to lose your taste for the ordinary kind.

For an easily made family-sized Strawberry Shortcake, take 2 cups of commercial biscuit mix, add 2 tablespoons of sugar and ¾ cup of light cream. Mix well, then turn the dough out on a floured surface and knead gently eight or ten times, or until smooth. Divide the dough into two equal parts and roll one half until it fits a 9-inch pie pan. Brush the top of it gently with melted butter, then roll the other half of the dough to the same size and place it on top of the first. Bake 15 to 20 minutes in a hot oven. The top layer will easily lift off. Spoon sugared wild strawberries and whipped cream between the layers and over the top. Generosity calls for at least 1 quart of berries and ½ pint of whipping cream. Cut in wedges and serve it warm, then stop envying the gods their ambrosia.

Another excellent way to use wild strawberries, either in camp or at home, is to make Wild Strawberry Roll-Ups. To 1 cup of commercial pancake mix add 1 egg, 1 cup of milk and ½ cup of rich cream. This will make about a dozen 5-inch pancakes. Heat a lightly greased griddle to 400°, or until a drop of water will dance over its surface a few seconds before evaporating. Beat the batter until smooth, then drop on the griddle, a cooking spoon full at a time. Turn them only once, when the bottom is golden brown and the top is bubbly. As soon as they are done, fill each pancake with a generous spoonful of sugared wild strawberries and roll it up. Arrange them three to a plate, sift powdered sugar lightly over them, add a dollop of whipped cream topped with a bright berry or two and serve them while still hot.

Still another delightful dessert combines wild strawberries with cream cheese in a pie which will make you the envy of all the cooks in the neighborhood. This requires a 9-inch baked and cooled pie shell. Make this with a commercial pie crust mix or make your own favorite pastry. Let an 8-ounce package of cream cheese stay in a warm place until it softens, then blend it with 2 tablespoons of lemon juice, a little grated lemon peel and ¼ cup of sugar. Spread this evenly over the bottom of the pie shell, then fill the shell to the top with well-drained sugared wild strawberries. Cover the berries with a glaze made by cooking 1 cup of the strained juice from the sugared berries with 2 teaspoons of cornstarch. Use low heat and stir constantly until it is thick and clear. Let this glaze cool to lukewarm, then pour it over the berries in the shell. Chill before serving and pass around a bowl of whipped cream for those who want it.

For some warm evening, make a Wild Strawberry Chiffon Pie, light as a summer's cloud. For a Graham Cracker Crust, crush 18 graham crackers with a rolling pin, then combine with ¼ cup of sugar, ½ cup of melted butter or margarine and ½ teaspoon unflavored gelatin. Mix well, then press evenly into a 9-inch pie plate. Bake in a moderate oven only about eight minutes, then set it aside to cool.

Soften one envelope of unflavored gelatin in a little cold water, then dissolve in ½ cup of boiling water. Let this cool slightly, then mix it with 1½ cups of crushed sugared wild strawberries. Add 1 tablespoon of lemon juice and a pinch of salt. Mix well and place in the refrigerator to chill. Whip ½ cup of heavy cream until it peaks. When the strawberry mixture has chilled till it mounds when spooned, fold in the whipped cream. Beat 2 egg whites to soft peaks. Gradually add ¼ cup of sugar, beating till stiff peaks form, then fold into the strawberry-cream mixture. Pour into the Graham Cracker Crust and chill until firm. Just before serving, cover with more whipped cream and top with whole wild strawberries.

Cooked Wild Strawberry Jam and Preserves are so superior to those made with the cultivated variety that one shouldn't mention them in the same breath, but you can do even better than that. You may have noticed that in none of the above recipes were the wild strawberries cooked. This didn't happen accidentally; I planned it that way. The fragrance of this *Fragaria* is one of its chief charms and this summery aroma is largely dissipated by cooking. It is possible to make uncooked jam and preserves which retain most of the aroma and flavor of fresh-picked fruit.

To make this superior kind of jam, you will need 2 cups of crushed wild strawberries made of fresh-picked fruit. Into a small pan measure

¾ cup of water and add ½ cup of commercial liquid pectin or 1 package of powdered pectin. Bring this liquid to a boil and boil hard for 1 minute, stirring constantly. Cool slightly, then mix with the crushed berries. Stir it well, then add 4 cups of sugar and stir briskly for 3 to 5 minutes, or until your arm gives out. Ladle into half-pint jars and store in your refrigerator if it is to be used within 3 weeks. If you want to keep it for next winter, store it in the freezer.

Uncooked preserves are really cured in the sun. Sprinkle 4 cups of sugar over 1 quart of whole wild strawberries, and let it stand overnight. Next day, drain the berries and put the juice and any unmelted sugar in a saucepan. Just bring it to a full boil, then remove it from the fire and let it cool to room temperature. Mix the sirup with the berries in a glass dish and cover with one of the commercial plastic wrapping materials you can obtain from the supermarket. Be sure the plastic is stuck tightly to the edges of the dish all around. Place the dish in the sun. Remove the plastic cover once a day and stir the preserves thoroughly but gently so as not to break the berries.

Keep it in the sun for 4 days, then ladle it into sterilized half-pint jars and seal with sterilized lids. If it has been cleanly handled, it will usually keep well just stored in a jam cupboard, but, if you want to be certain, store it in the freezer.

You can also freeze the fresh berries, if you can find the time to pick a sufficient quantity so some can be spared for this purpose. And let me say in passing that you are very unlikely afterward ever to regret the time spent in picking wild strawberries.

You can use the same kind of half-pint jars as those recommended for jams and jellies as containers for your frozen wild strawberries. Make a sirup by boiling together for a few minutes 2 parts of water by measure to 1 part of sugar. Let it cool before using it. Use only fully ripe but still firm berries, as freshly picked as possible. Wash the berries gently in cold water, pack in the jars without crushing, cover with the sugar sirup, seal tightly with two-piece dome lids and freeze as quickly as possible. Then, any time of the year, instead of just telling your friends about the superior qualities of wild strawberries, you can demonstrate them.

All these wild strawberry products are easy to make and simple in composition. But when one of these delicacies is placed before you and you see its bright color, inhale its fragrance, taste its flavor and feel its texture, you will find, if you have picked your own wild strawberries, that it is compounded of many ingredients not mentioned in the recipes. It will bring back the warm sun on your back as you bent over the plants bearing the jewel-like berries. In it you find the grateful shade of the hickory tree under which you rested, and the old pheasant hen, who, all unsuspecting, led her brood so near. There too will be the profusion of buttercups and daisies which dotted the open field. In just a small dish of frozen wild strawberries, you can recapture, in midwinter, a long and perfect day of June weather. Some of the most precious moments of my life have been spent picking wild strawberries.

The Spring Beauty or Fairy Spuds

(*Claytonia virginica*)

O
NE spring I helped an artist friend build a cabin near a trout stream in central Pennsylvania. He planned to spend much of each year in this retreat and was interested in raising and foraging as much of his food as possible, for, like all artists I know, he wasn't overloaded with money. As a place to raise vegetables, he chose a sunny little clearing near his cabin site that was literally carpeted with Spring Beauties when we first inspected it in April.

These pale-rose-colored flowers with five petals and five tiny golden stamens are familiar to nearly everyone who goes into the woods and fields seeking the first wild flowers of spring. They are borne on slender stems, seldom more than six inches high, that spring from inconspicuous plants that consist mainly of three to a dozen slender pointed leaves, four to five inches long and only about a half-inch wide. Although this is one of our best-known early wild flowers, few people seem to know that this insignificant little plant also bears an edible tuber.

I had collected a few of these Fairy Spuds before for experiments, but ordinarily I couldn't bring myself to destroy such a beautiful wild flower for the sake of the small tuber from which it grows. Now, since these flowers were to be destroyed for the sake of a kitchen garden anyway, I could dig with an easy conscience. Each evening after we had quit work on the cabin for the day, I would repair to the garden plot with a hand weeder and a pail, and in about an hour I dug all the tubers the two of us could eat. My friend would rake over the area where I had been digging and plant a few vegetable seeds. That is the only garden I ever knew to be completely spaded up with a hand weeder.

Spring beauty tubers are found two to three inches under the plant and look like little potatoes. They are from one-half to two inches in diameter, the larger ones tending to be of very irregular shape. This

SPRING BEAUTY

uneven surface usually presents a tough cleaning job, but we got around that by putting them in a covered wire basket, really an old corn popper, and setting them under a little waterfall in the trout stream. Then we could go fishing while our supper was being washed.

The simplest way to cook fairy spuds is to boil them 10 or 15 minutes, depending on size, in salted water. Drain off the water and, as soon as the tubers are cool enough to handle, just peel off the skins and pop them into your mouth. My friend described the flavor and texture as "exactly like potatoes, only much better." To me, they have the sweetness and flavor of boiled chestnuts, although they are softer and smoother in texture.

We ate them every day, sometimes twice a day, for several weeks without growing tired of them. We tried them fried, mashed, in salads and cooked with peas, like new potatoes. All these ways were completely successful, but, as regular fare, we preferred them just boiled "in the jackets." My friend grew so fond of this food that he was afraid he would experience withdrawal symptoms when the supply was exhausted.

I am glad to have had this spring beauty orgy, but I hope this account doesn't cause any of the regular displays of this herald of spring to be destroyed. The spring beauty reproduces in two ways. Besides making seed, new little tubers bud off from the older ones. In many places, where this pretty spring flower is very abundant, the careful experimenter can collect fairy spuds without harming the future floral displays if he takes only the large tubers and replants the smaller ones.

Let's not let our greediness for this food destroy or diminish this attractive plant. The tubers are good food for the body, but, after a long winter, the pale-rose flowers in early spring are food for the soul. "Man does not live by bread alone."

The Common Sunflower

(Helianthus annuus)

WILD Sunflowers growing by the roadside are a familiar sight to nearly everyone. Originally a native to the central part of our country, the hand of man has scattered the seeds until now they are becoming common everywhere. This is the parent plant of the huge Russian sunflowers which are cultivated in many parts of the world. These huge-seeded varieties have been developed by selection and cultivation and can't persist in the wild state. Where they escape from cultivation, birds and animals gobble up the huge seed of the large-seeded, single-flowered kinds and only allow the small-seeded flowers to reproduce themselves, so these escapees after a few years resemble their small-seeded ancestors.

As a food plant the sunflower is much more appreciated in eastern Europe than here. There, people eat sunflower seeds as we eat peanuts and travelers from Russia report seeing the streets littered with the shells. In America, the sunflower is largely ignored as a food plant, except by health-food enthusiasts.

The Indian tribes of the Plains made much use of the wild sunflowers which grew there in such profusion. They are reported to have first parched the seeds, then ground them to a fine meal by pounding them between two stones, which sounds as if the meal was made of the whole seed, hulls and all. This meal was used to make

SUNFLOWER

bread or to thicken soup. It is said that it was sometimes just stirred in a cup of water and drunk, and sometimes was also mixed with the marrow from the large bones of the buffalo to a doughlike consistency and eaten in that way.

Many people ask me how I find out how to prepare wild foods. I'll take you with me while I explore the sunflower and let you see my methods. I first searched the literature and came out with about the information I have already given you in this chapter. This was enough to whet my curiosity and my appetite. On a roadside near the Philadelphia Airport, I gathered an open-work onion bag full of wild sunflower heads, just before they became dry enough to begin shattering out. I hung this bag by a wire near my furnace until they were thoroughly dry. Then I threshed them out and winnowed out the trash. This left me with about four quarts of clean seed.

I didn't think I would care for a meal made of shells and all, so I set about trying to devise some method of eliminating the hulls from the finished product. By experiment I discovered that if the seeds were run through a food chopper fitted with a plate barely large enough to prevent the seed going through whole, the shells would be cracked off. I dumped the cracked mixture into a large bowl of water and stirred it gently but thoroughly, then let it stand for half an hour. The heavier kernels settled to the bottom and the hulls floated on top, where they were carefully skimmed off. Then I poured off the water and placed the coarsely ground meats in a square of muslin and squeezed out all the water I could. I placed the seed in a pan and dried them out in a slow oven, stirring occasionally to keep them from caking together. When they were thoroughly dry, I put them through a coarse sieve to separate the larger pieces of kernel from the fine stuff.

The larger bits that would not pass through the sieve were set aside to be used as nuts. They had a fine nutlike flavor and a handful of them made a delicious snack. I tried them in several cookie recipes as replacement for other kinds of nuts, and found them entirely satisfactory for this purpose. Pressed into the top of teacakes, like poppy seed, they were very good.

More than half of the original lot had passed through the sieve. This fine stuff I put through the food chopper again, using the finest plate, so that it came out almost as fine as flour. I have used this meal to replace part of the flour in recipes for cookies, pancakes, date-nut bread and muffins, and it has never failed to improve the finished product. As a thickener for soups and stews it adds nourishment and a fine flavor.

I did not care for it stirred in water as the Indians sometimes used it, but mixing it with marrowfat gave me a tasty spread. I boiled a section of beef shinbone, removed the marrow and stirred into it enough sunflower meal to make it a nice spreading consistency. With a little salt, it was delicious on rye bread or crackers.

If Americans ever learn to eat sunflower seed in quantity, they will probably use the larger seeds of the cultivated variety, but these experiments have shown that the common wild kind can be made into products that are perfectly acceptable to the civilized palate.

Wildwood Teas

I HAVE already mentioned a number of wild plants that can be used to prepare beverages to substitute for tea and coffee, such as dandelion or chicory roots, sassafras, sweet birch, spicebush and persimmon leaves. There are several dozen plants growing wild in this country that have been used as teas and all of them have their advocates. Among those that I have tried, besides those already mentioned, the following are worth a trial.

BASSWOOD
(*Tilia* species)

This fine large tree found in rich forests from New York to Florida and west to the Plains, is also called American Linden, Whitewood and Lime Tree. It has soft white wood which is the favorite material of artists for making woodcuts. The bast, or inner bark, is tough and fibrous but soft to the feel, and the Indians twisted this fiber into some strong, good-looking strings, lines and ropes. The leaves are heart-shaped, with serrate edges. The flowers, which are the parts with which we are chiefly concerned, are creamy white and hang in small cymes from stems that spring from the axils of the leaves. These flowers are very fragrant and are so filled with nectar that the basswood is a valuable source of honey. Basswood honey is light-colored, with a delicate flavor, and is one of the finest of the table honeys. When a basswood is in bloom, the number of bees attracted to the flowers sets the whole treetop into a loud hum.

To make Basswood Tea, gather the flowers on a dry day, dry them indoors at room temperature, then pack them in jars, barely warm the jars in a slow oven and seal with dome lids. Make the tea by putting 1 tablespoon of the flowers in 1 cup of boiling water, or brew it in a teapot as you would regular tea. It is sweet and fragrant with an agreeable flavor, and is supposed to aid digestion, quiet coughs, relieve hoarseness due to colds and promote perspiration to help cool fevers. Even though I know about its supposed medicinal virtues, I still drink basswood tea chiefly because I like the taste of it.

CLOVER BLOSSOM—MINT

The reddish-purple blossom heads of ordinary wild red clover (*Trifolium pratense*) which is fully described under medicinal herbs, is also used to make a tea that is relished by some, independent of any medicinal value it may have. Gather the flower heads when in full bloom and dry them indoors, then seal them in jars as directed in the section on basswood flowers. All the beverage materials used for tea should be dried out of the sun, at room temperature. They should never be dried in an oven or heated dehydrator, for the flavoring materials we want in our cups are very volatile and easily driven off by heat.

I care very little for tea made of dried clover blossoms used alone, but the addition of a small amount of dried leaves of peppermint (*Mentha piperita*) or spearmint (*M. viridis*) makes it into a very palatable and presumably healthful brew. Spearmint and peppermint were originally cultivated plants, but have escaped and are now common everywhere along streams and in wet places in all cultivated areas. They are low herbaceous perennials, and, as with all mints, they have square stems and opposite leaves. The leaves of both these species are lance-ovate with serrate margins, the peppermint leaf having somewhat deeper and coarser serrations than that of the spearmint. Both are easily identified by aroma and flavor, the peppermint being aromatic-pungent and the spearmint sweet-aromatic, but these flavors and fragrances are too familiar to need describing.

Dry the leaves as directed for other tea materials. Then mix 4 parts of crushed dried clover blossoms with 1 part of dried crushed peppermint or spearmint leaves and use in about the same amounts as you use oriental tea.

BLACKBERRY, RASPBERRY AND STRAWBERRY LEAVES

The leaves of these three familiar fruits have long been dried and used for tea and in home remedies. Gather the leaves while the plant is in flower and dry them as directed with other tea materials. One word of warning: be sure these leaves are thoroughly dry before you use them as tea, for, as the leaves wilt, they develop a poison which is driven off or altered in composition as the leaves get thoroughly dry. There have been cases of livestock being poisoned by wilted berry leaves, but when these leaves are contained in fully dry, cured hay they cause no ill effects.

Berry-leaf Tea is probably the most effective home remedy for diarrhea but, aside from its medicinal uses, it is also a pleasant beverage and wholesome in reasonable quantities. It contains tannin (as does Oriental tea) and has a pleasant aroma; the flavor differs slightly according to which species is used but all of them make an acceptable substitute for tea.

CATNIP TEA

Catnip, or catmint (*Nepeta cataria*) is another member of the mint family that originally came from Europe but has run wild over here and is very common around dwellings, old farmsteads and abandoned gardens. Like all mints it has square stems and opposite leaves, but this one is a bit more robust than the other mints that have been described, growing one to two feet tall. The leaves are a little larger than peppermint leaves, oblong-heart-shaped, downy green above and downy white underneath, with an aromatic, minty smell when crushed.

Gather the leaves any time during the summer and dry indoors with no artificial heat, then store in tight jars. This is the plant that cats love. They will roll in a bed of catnip and seem to go slightly wild over the dried leaves, rolling over in them and acting very happy and excited. They will even eat a leaf or two. With human beings, catnip is supposed to act as a mild sedative. It doesn't taste at all bad, and a teaspoon of the dried leaves to a cup of boiling water, sweetened with a little honey, makes a pleasant nightcap and you may find it an aid in getting a restful night's sleep.

NEW JERSEY TEA
(*Ceanothus americanus*)

This is probably the best-known substitute for tea among our native plants. It is a low shrub that dies back to the woody base each winter, and puts up new stems each spring. The root is red. The leaves are alternate, oval-pointed, about three inches long and half that wide, finely serrate about the edges and with somewhat blunt teeth. These leaves have three strong ribs, the center one running to the point and the two side ones curving around and almost reaching the apex. The white flowers are borne in a cluster at the ends of the leafy stems, are quite attractive, and appear in June or July. It is found in sandy or gravelly soils from Maine to Florida and west to the Plains.

The leaves of New Jersey tea should be gathered while the plant is in bloom, and dried and stored as directed with other tea plants. New Jersey tea more closely approaches the taste of Oriental tea than does any plant we have considered. It contains no caffeine nor theine and therefore is not a stimulant, but it is a nice-tasting beverage which can be used over a long period of time without one's growing tired of it.

SWEET GOLDENROD
(*Solidago odora*)

Among the many species of goldenrod that lend charm to the autumn scene, there is one, the Sweet Goldenrod, that makes a good tea. It can be distinguished from other species by the one-sided panicles of flowers that otherwise look like other goldenrod blooms; and by its slender pointed leaves, three to four inches long and usually under an inch wide with entire margins. The leaves, when held to the light, are seen to be covered with tiny translucent spots, which, when crushed, smell faintly of anise. This goldenrod grows two to three feet high but when in flower it often reclines on the ground. Gather the leaves when the plant is in bloom, dry and store as directed for other tea materials and use like Oriental tea. It has a sweet-aromatic flavor and aroma which is pleasing to some people. The sweet goldenrod is found from Massachusetts to Florida and west to Texas.

WINTERGREEN, TEABERRY, CHECKERBERRY OR GROUND HOLLY
(*Gaultheria procumbens*)

This interesting little plant is found in acid soil, usually in the shade of evergreens, from Maine to Georgia and west to Minnesota. The little plants we see, standing only three to five inches high, with glossy green oval leaves and bright red berries that hang on all winter, are really only the leafy fruiting branches of the slender stem which creep extensively on or just under the surface of the ground. When the ground is free of snow in the winter, I often gather a handful of these dry berries to nibble on for their sweet, wintergreen flavor. The freshly picked foliage of this plant can be used any time of the year to make a pleasant, wintergreen-flavored tea. Children especially seem to enjoy this beverage with sugar and cream. Unlike the other tea materials we have considered in this section, wintergreen loses much of its flavor on drying and should always be used soon after gathering. However, as noted in the section on sweet birch, the bark of that tree has a flavor that is identical with wintergreen and by careful drying much of that flavor can be preserved. Commercial wintergreen flavoring is usually synthesized today, but formerly it was made by distilling the bark and twigs of the sweet birch.

Once I was taking a young lady student from Sweden for a walk through some woods in central Pennsylvania. I picked some wintergreen berries for her to taste, and later I peeled off a sliver of bark from a sweet birch and asked her to taste that. She did, then exclaimed, "There's that American taste again! It is in the chewing gum, candy and toothpaste, and now I find it is in the plants and trees that grow over here."

Walnuts and
Hickory Nuts
(*Juglans* and *Carya* species)

I HAVE already mentioned Black Walnuts and Hickory Nuts in so many recipes in this book that it hardly seems necessary to write a separate section on these fine nuts which the alert forager can usually have for the gathering. However, I am just back from an afternoon's nutting which netted a friend and me a bushel of black walnuts and half a bushel of Shellbark Hickory nuts. We could easily have gathered more black walnuts but decided a bushel was as much as we would use. I have already collected persimmons this fall, so tonight we had Persimmon-Hickory-Nut Bread (see recipe pages 166-67). I am writing these lines after dinner, so you might say I am full of my subject.

There are two excellent wild walnuts growing in the United States, the Black Walnut (*Juglans nigra*) and the Butternut (*J. cinerea*). There are at least three other species of black walnut growing farther west, and all are appreciated where they grow. The black walnut is a large wide-spreading tree with dark-brown, roughly furrowed bark; the leaves are compound, with from fifteen to twenty-one leaflets, all except the terminal one in pairs. These leaflets are from four to six inches long, lancehead-shaped, with a long tapering point and serrate edges. The nut is enclosed in a husk while on the tree, and the whole fruit is spherical and from two to three inches in diameter.

213

Today we saw many trees with comparatively small nuts but passed them by. We finally located two trees with very large nuts. One of these was growing right beside a dirt road in the country and the road was littered with the fallen nuts, many of them already husked by being run over by the tires of passing automobiles. We cracked a few and saw that this would be a fairly easy nut to shell (for a black walnut), so we started loading our baskets. I have heard of many ways to remove the hull from a black walnut, but the easiest method I have found is to wear a heavy pair of shoes while gathering nuts, and to grind each nut under your heel right where it lies under the tree. This will break off the husk and one can toss the hard-shelled nut into a basket. Always wear a pair of rubber or plastic gloves, for, if the freshly hulled nut is handled with bare hands, it will leave a brown stain that is almost impossible to remove.

Black walnuts *are* hard to shell, there's no denying it, but the meat is oily and highly flavored, and this flavor comes through in baked products beautifully, so I believe the black walnuts are well worth the trouble. I know no short-cut method of shelling them; one just takes a heavy hammer and a nutpick and the rest of it is just work.

The flavor of black walnut combines so well with chocolate that this is the nut to use in Fudge. Here is the recipe that we like best. Butter the sides of a large saucepan and in it put 4 cups of sugar, 1 tall can of evaporated milk and ½ pound of butter or margarine. Mix this together and cook until a drop of it will form a soft ball when dropped in cold water, or until it reaches 236° on your candy thermometer. Remove from heat and add 2 cups of semisweet chocolate bits, 1 pint jar of marshmallow topping and 1 cup of black walnut meats. Beat until chocolate bits are melted and blended then pour into a bake pan to cool. Score in squares while still warm.

For those who dislike chocolate, here is a Brown Sugar Fudge that I have found to be very good. In a buttered, 2-quart saucepan place 1½ cups of granulated sugar, 1 cup of brown sugar, ⅓ cup of light cream, ⅓ cup of milk and 2 tablespoons of butter. Heat and stir until mixture comes to a boil, then cook until it reaches 238° (soft-ball stage) stirring only when necessary. When the thermometer shows that it has reached the proper heat, remove from fire and cool until it is barely lukewarm without stirring again. Then beat until the candy thickens and loses its gloss. Quickly stir in ½ cup of black walnut meats and spread the candy on a platter to cool. Score while warm and cut after it cools.

Black walnuts can also be included with profit in many kinds of cake, cookie, nut-bread or muffin recipes, for no other nut contributes so much flavor to baked goods as does this native wilding.

The Butternut, called the White Walnut in some sections, is borne on a tree that greatly resembles the black walnut except that it is not so large and the bark is of a slightly lighter shade. The nuts are borne on clusters at the ends of branches and they are elliptical rather than spherical in shape. The oily, rich-tasting kernel of the butternut is even harder to extract than the meats of black walnuts. They are used in the same way as black walnuts, and I know some cooks who actually prefer them to the black walnut for baking.

They have another rather unusual use, which is the making of Pickled Walnuts. For this purpose the young nuts are gathered when they have reached nearly maximum size but before the shell has started to harden. If you can push a nutpick or an ice pick straight through the walnut, husk and all, they are still young and tender enough to pickle. Pour boiling water over the nuts, then rub off the fuzz on the outside of the husk. Place the nuts in a large kettle and cover with water and boil until the water discolors badly. Pour off this water and add fresh boiling water and continue cooking. Keep boiling and changing water until the water remains clear. Then pack the nuts in quart jars, including 1 flower of dill, 3 walnut leaves, as much mixed pickling spices as you can get on a teaspoon, 1 teaspoon of salt and ¼ teaspoon of alum in each jar. Fill the jar with boiling cider vinegar and seal. In a month or more you will have a pickle that some people consider the finest product of the walnut tree.

Not all species of hickory bear edible nuts, but the fine, sweet kinds grow from New England to Nebraska and south to Florida and Texas. All hickory nuts are edible if they taste good. The Pecan is, of course, a hickory, but we will not consider wild pecans here. Any forager worth his salt can be trusted to make full use of any wild pecans he can find. Besides pecans there are several species of hickory that produce excellent nuts, but in my opinion the Shellbark (*Carya ovata*) is king of them all. Today we found five large shellbarks growing in the center of a pasture, just dropping a bumper crop of nuts. These trees were from seventy to ninety feet high and wide-spreading. The leaves, mostly gone now, are compound, usually with five leaflets, the two inner ones much smaller than the outer three. The bark on these old giants has split into long strips and the strips have broken away from the trees on both bottom and top, giving the tree trunk a shaggy, unkempt appearance that somehow does not detract from its dignity. The nuts differ from walnuts in that the husk is four-valved and splits off, allowing the nut to fall free. The nuts are light tan in color, about an inch long and an inch wide, slightly flattened and about three-fourths inch thick. The shell is thin and well filled with one of my favorite nut meats. Two of us managed to pick up a full half bushel of clean nuts under these five trees in little over an hour.

The most obvious way to use hickory nuts is merely to crack them with a hammer, shell them and eat them raw, and few nuts are better for this purpose, but the hickory nut has a place in cooking too, especially in cookie recipes, where the hickory nut has no peer.

Hickory-Nut Date Cookies are made by sifting together 1¾ cups of flour, ½ teaspoon of baking powder, ½ teaspoon of soda, ¼ teaspoon of salt, 1 teaspoon of cinnamon and ½ teaspoon of nutmeg. In a separate mixing bowl cream together 1 stick of margarine and 1 cup of brown sugar, then add 1 egg and beat well. Add this mixture, plus ¼ cup of buttermilk, to the dry ingredients. If you don't have buttermilk, add 1 teaspoon of vinegar to ¼ cup of milk and use that. Now, add 1 cup of hickory-nut meats and 1 cup of chopped dates. Stir only until all ingredients are dampened and evenly diffused, then drop on cookie sheets by heaping teaspoonfuls and bake in a 375° oven 10 to 12 minutes.

As a child, my favorite cookie was the Oatmeal-Hickory-Nut. Sift together 1¾ cups of flour, 2 teaspoons of baking powder, ½ teaspoon of soda, 1 teaspoon of salt, 1 teaspoon of cinnamon and 1 teaspoon of nutmeg. In another mixing bowl cream together 1 cup of shortening, 1½ cups of brown sugar and 2 eggs. Mix and beat until soft and fluffy, then beat in a ½ cup of milk. Combine liquid and dry ingredients, then stir in 3 cups of quick-cooking rolled oats and 1 cup of broken hickory-nut meats. Drop from tablespoon two inches apart on a cookie sheet, and if hickory nuts are plentiful, top each cookie with halves or large pieces of the nuts. Bake in a hot oven (400°) 8 to 10 minutes. Allow to cool slightly before trying to remove them from the pan.

The Hickory-Nut Brownie is a delectable cross between a cookie and a confection. Melt ½ cup of shortening and 2 ounces of unsweetened chocolate in the top of a double boiler, then allow it to cool. Sift together ¾ cups of flour, ½ teaspoon of baking powder and ½ teaspoon of salt. Beat 2 eggs until light and fluffy, stir in 1 cup of sugar, then blend in the chocolate-shortening mixture. Stir in the flour mixture and 1 cup of hickory nuts. Bake in a greased 8- by 8-inch baking pan for about 30 minutes in a 350° oven.

Hickory-Nut Pie is closely akin to Pecan Pie but I consider the distinctive hickory-nut flavor a decided improvement. Make an Oil Pastry (see page 90) and fit it into a 9-inch pie plate. Beat 3 eggs slightly, then add ¾ cup of sugar, ½ teaspoon of salt, 1 cup of dark corn sirup and ⅓ cup of melted butter or margarine, then beat thoroughly. Stir in 1½ cups of hickory nuts and pour into the unbaked pastry shell. Bake in a 350° oven for 50 minutes. Cool before serving.

The Indians had methods of using hickory nuts that are seldom practiced today. There are many early accounts of the southern tribes pounding hickory nuts, shell and all, and boiling them in water to make a kind of nut milk or oily liquid. This milky liquor was called, in one Indian language, *powcohicora*, and it is from the latter part of that name that our term, hickory, comes.

Recently I experimented with these pounded, unshelled nuts with at least partial success. I first cracked the nuts to make sure I didn't get a rotten or wormy one in, then pounded them up until the meats seemed pretty well loosened from the shells. I put 1 quart of these pounded nuts in a kettle and poured boiling water until it stood an inch above the nuts. Right here I made my first discovery. The nut meats are lighter than the shells and float above them, so all but the finest bits and parts still stuck to the shells could have been skimmed off. I left them in for the time being and boiled the mixture for 15 minutes. By this time the liquid was thick as bean soup and a light-brown color.

At this point, I carefully dipped out some of the liquid with the floating nut meats, added a little salt and a dash of pepper and ate it as soup, with a salted cracker. While it wasn't the best soup I ever ate, it was pretty good, and it must be very nourishing.

I then skimmed off a little of the oily top part of the liquid, strained it into a bowl to remove the nut meats and set the bowl in the refrigerator until it cooled. The thick, oily part rose to the top leaving clear liquid at the bottom. This oily, nut-meal mush, spread on a cracker, made a very tasty substitute for butter.

As I was experimenting with this *powcohicora,* I was reminded of the times in Hawaii, when I had poured boiling water over the grated meat of ripe coconuts and squeezed out an oily milk or cream. The Hawaiians use this milky liquid to make a pudding called *haupia,* which is always one of the dishes served at a *luau* or Hawaiian feast. I still remember how *haupia* is made, so I decided to combine the goodies of two primitive cultures and try my hand at making *powcohicora-haupia.* Using a large cooking spoon I carefully skimmed off liquid with its floating nut meats, so as not to include any shell, then strained the rest of the liquid from the shells through a double thickness of cheesecloth. As I poured this liquid nut-meat mixture back in a kettle, I noticed that the powdered shell which had passed through the cheesecloth had settled to the bottom and it was easy to drain the liquid off it without including any of this shell material. I had 3 cups of this liquid-nut mixture left. I mixed 6 tablespoons of cornstarch and ½ cup of sugar with just enough of the liquid to make a thin paste. Then I brought the liquid in the kettle just to a boil, then stirred in the sugar-starch mixture and kept stirring until the pudding became quite thick. Next I stirred in a little vanilla extract, and poured it into a fancy mold. When it had cooled and set, I turned it out on a cake plate and served it for dessert, and all six people, who were there for dinner that evening, pronounced it delicious.

I'm sure that walnuts and hickory nuts have still other possibilities that are waiting to be explored. They are fun to gather, good to eat and wonderful in cooking. Let's go nutting.

The Nose Twister:
KING OF WILD SALAD PLANTS

Water Cress (*Nasturtium officinale*)

WATER CRESS, exactly like that offered in small bunches at exorbitant prices on the salad shelves at your supermarket, can be found growing wild in every state of the Union, and all the way across the southern half of Canada. I say *every* state, for I have eaten wild water cress from several streams in Hawaii, and a friend whom I trust has assured me that he has gathered wild water cress from a stream near Ketchikan, Alaska.

Not only does this welcome Old World immigrant have a wide range; it also has the longest season of any salad plant I know. Although it is more plentiful in the warm months, I have gathered enough water cress for a salad in every month of the year except January. This was in Pennsylvania. Farther south, it can be gathered throughout the year.

Being originally a cultivated plant that ultimately began growing wild, water cress is seldom found far from the haunts of men. If there is none growing in the stream handiest to you, this situation is easily corrected. A handful of stems pulled from any bed of water cress and tossed into the stream at a favorable spot will rapidly take root and spread. If you don't know where you can get water cress to transplant, several of the seed houses handle water cress seed. These should be soaked overnight, so they will sink, then scattered thinly in a running stream where the water is from one to six inches deep, but not where the water is running too swiftly. Using either method in a suitable stream will soon give you all the "wild" water cress you can use.

The botanical name of this plant (*Nasturtium*) can be roughly translated as "nose twister," a reference to its pungency. The specific term, *officinale*, means that it was once included in the official list of medicinal herbs, a place it well deserved, for there are few plants richer in vitamins and minerals needed by the human body.

In late years the name, *Nasturtium*, has been stolen by the very different *Tropaeoleum*, the well-known garden flower that is commonly called Nasturtium. Taste some leaves or petals from this plant, and you will see why popular usage has transferred this descriptive title. A good argument could be made that the garden flower is equally entitled to the name, as it does fully as good a job at nose twisting. Incidentally, the garden flower is perfectly wholesome to eat. Its leaves will give a pleasant zip to a salad, and the flower petals make a very decorative and tasty garnish. But this is supposed to be a book about *wild* foods.

In gathering wild water cress, do not pull up the whole plant. Twist, pinch or snip it off at the surface of the water. The below-water parts of the stem bear white roots at the nodes, which are tough and unpalatable. One word of caution: if water cress is growing in polluted water, it may carry disease germs. If you are in doubt about the water in which it is growing, soak the water cress in water in which has been dissolved a water-purifying tablet, such as can be purchased from handlers of camping supplies. If water cress is thoroughly cooked, this precaution is unnecessary.

The use of water cress as a salad, garnish and filling for bridge-party sandwiches is familiar to nearly everyone. We need other recipes to enable us to include this healthful food in our diets more often. Wild water cress, wherever found, is usually abundant, so the sharp-eyed forager never lacks a supply.

Water cress cooked alone is better "boiling greens" than many for which we pay good money. Cook, season and serve it exactly as you would spinach. A handful of water cress added to mixed boiling greens never fails to improve the flavor.

Of course, long cooking destroys many of the vitamins we should have. I asked a friend from Hawaii, who is of Chinese ancestry, for suggestions on cooking water cress and he said, "Don't really cook it; just Chinese it." Anyone who has ever eaten the crisp, short-cooked vegetables served with a good Chinese meal will know what he meant. He gave me the following recipe, which we find the very best way to eat water cress in quantity.

Heat 2 tablespoons of cooking oil in a large skillet. Sprinkle 1 tablespoon of grated fresh ginger root in the hot oil. Let this cook about 2 minutes, then add 1 pound of well-washed water cress all at once. Cook and stir for 4 minutes, to wilt the water cress and coat it with oil. Remove from the heat, toss with 2 tablespoons of soy sauce and serve immediately.

WATER CRESS

Water Cress Soup is a tangy appetizer which will be appreciated at the beginning of any lunch or dinner. Make a smooth paste of 2 tablespoons of flour and 2 tablespoons of milk in a medium-sized saucepan. Slowly stir in 3 cups of milk, 1 teaspoon of salt and 1 tablespoon of minced onion. Cook, stirring constantly until mixture thickens and just barely comes to a boil. Remove from heat, stir in 2 cups of finely chopped water cress and serve immediately. If you prefer a puréed soup, liquefy the water cress in a blender before adding it to the soup. Serve this soup in heated earthenware bowls, each garnished with a fresh sprig of water cress.

You don't need recipes in order to use lots of water cress in salads. Almost any salad—tossed, jellied, arranged, or even potato—will be improved with the addition of water cress. A very simple salad that we like is made from 1 cup of cabbage, 1 cup of water cress and 1 small onion, all finely chopped. Just before serving, this is dressed with 2 parts sour cream to 1 part lemon juice and a little salt.

A hearty Sandwich Filling can be made by mixing 1 chopped hard-boiled egg with ¼ cup of chopped water cress and 1 tablespoon of chopped chives. Moisten with mayonnaise and season with salt and pepper.

To make some snooty little sandwiches for an afternoon tea, butter some thin slices from a small round loaf of rye bread. Make the filling from 1 cup of chopped water cress; ¼ cup of chopped hickory nuts, pecans, or walnuts; some mayonnaise and a little salt. If these sandwiches are to be served at a card party, cut the slices of bread into hearts, diamonds, spades and clubs with cookie cutters.

Finally, there is good Herb Butter, for which you will find a thousand uses. Cream ¼ pound of butter at room temperature until it works easily. Then gradually blend into it 1 tablespoon each of finely chopped water cress, parsley and chives. Work in ¼ teaspoon of salt at the same time. When well mixed, place in the refrigerator to harden. This butter can be used to spread small slices of rye bread or little round crackers, for canapés or cocktail snacks. A melting lump of it on steaks or chops is delicious, and does not mask the flavor of the meat. A floating lump of herb butter on top of flat-tasting broth or soup will turn it into something you will be proud to serve.

Let's stop letting the abundance of wild water cress in this country go to waste. I think it is a poor reflection on Americans that it is mainly our foreign-born population which uses and appreciates the wealth of wild water cress in this land, and that it is largely ignored by the native born.

Wild Rice: EPICUREAN DELIGHT

(*Zizania aquatica*)

WILD RICE is easily the best cereal grain found growing wild in North America. Once a stable of many Indian tribes, it is now harvested by the descendants of these same Indians and sold to white gourmets at fantastic prices. The grain in the little quarter-pound boxes for which you pay more than a dollar in the supermarket, was probably gathered by Indians in the Great Lakes region. There, several states and provinces protect the Indian's right to this wild crop by forbidding the white man to harvest wild rice for sale.

Few people seem to know that this same valuable plant grows over a large part of the United States, and could be collected for home use in hundreds of areas where it is presently ignored. Indigenous from New Brunswick to Manitoba and southward to the Gulf, it has been planted by sportsmen in many areas, where it does not occur naturally, to attract waterfowl. The area where this valuable grain could be gathered by alert foragers is constantly extending. You will not be robbing the wild fowl when you take some of the rice for yourself, for wild rice grows better and extends itself faster when it is harvested, thus making more for both birds and men.

Wild rice is a very large, reedlike grass, found in shallow lakes, sloughs and ponds. It will grow well in three or four feet of water and is often eight or ten feet tall, with a long broomlike flower cluster on top. The grain looks somewhat like oats and, like that grain, has a husk which must be removed before it is eaten.

The grain must be watched closely in late summer, so it can be garnered at just the right time. If it is too green it will not thresh out, but, if left a few days too long, most of it will shatter out and be lost. You are not likely to improve on the Indian method of harvesting wild rice. Take a clean canoe or flat-bottomed boat out among the rice plants, pull the heads over the boat and strike them sharply with a stick to dislodge the grain. I have gathered many pounds this way in such far-separated places as New Jersey, Illinois

WILD RICE

and Arkansas, and, had I figured the rice at prevailing prices, I would have been making excellent wages at this task.

When you get the rice home, spread it in a warm, protected place until it is thoroughly dry. Then put it in shallow pans in a hot oven for 1 hour or more, stirring occasionally so it will parch evenly. After parching, the husk can be loosened by pounding or rubbing through the hands, and the trash winnowed out. Store in tight jars until used.

When used, wild rice should first be thoroughly washed or it will have a disagreeable, smoky taste. It can then be boiled and used in the same ways as domestic rice, being considered especially good with wild game. A quail, duck or pheasant stuffed with cooked and seasoned wild rice is an epicurean dream.

While you have wild rice on hand, be extravagant at least once and cook it as a breakfast cereal. Served with light cream and maple sugar it is pure bliss.

You can also grind wild rice and use the flour to make some superior muffins and pancakes. As little as 25 per cent wild rice flour added to your pancake mix will make the cakes extraordinarily delicious. Serve them with homemade maple sirup if possible.

If you will keep your foraging eye peeled, the chances are good that you find a spot where you can gather your own supply of this luxury food right in your own area.

Winter Cress:
THE FIRST WITH THE MOST

(*Barbarea vulgaris* and *Barbarea verna*)

WHERE I live in suburban Philadelphia, the first sign of spring is not the returning wild geese winging high, nor the robins on the lawn. These harbingers are always preceded by the Italians, swarming out from town to gather Winter Cress from fields and ditches.

You would think that the suburbanites would catch on to the fact that they are missing out on a good thing and learn something from this annual event. But they never do. They pay exorbitant prices for tasteless greenhouse produce and week-old vegetables from Florida or California, and never realize that they have driven their station wagons past tons of much better vegetables on the way to the super-market. They feel smugly superior to the rummaging people they passed along the way.

Why? There's nothing smart about eating poor food and getting gypped in the bargain, when nature is offering much better fare for the taking. If I followed one of those buxom Italian women home, I'll bet I would get a much better dinner than I would if I had to eat the force-grown, sprayed, processed, refrigerated, devitalized prod-ucts for which the suburban housewife thought it smart to pay good money.

The suburban dweller seldom bothers to identify the plant which

WINTER CRESS

the immigrants are so eagerly collecting. Such knowledge is strictly for squares. He is satisfied to refer to it merely as "some weed the Italians eat." We have come to a poor pass when we think that allowing ourselves to be bilked because of our own ignorance contributes to our status. And still we think we have a mission to teach the rest of the world "the American way." Heaven forbid this kind of thinking. We do have some things to teach, but we also have many things to learn from other cultures. Unless we realize that cultural exchange is a two-way street, we shall fail, and much of the ancient and precious wisdom now residing in the simple peoples of the world will be lost.

Wow! Who would have thought that such a sermon could be dug out of an insignificant plant of the Mustard Family?

Barbarea was so named because it was formerly the only green plant that could be gathered and eaten on Saint Barbara's Day, which falls on the fourth day of December. The specific term *vulgaris* merely means the plant is common. *Barbarea verna* sounds like a contradiction of terms, for the *Barbarea* refers to early winter and the *verna* refers to spring, but this term very nicely indicates the season over which the plant is good for food.

Barbarea has many common names, being known as Winter Cress, Spring Cress, Upland Cress and Yellow Rocket. Many country people refer to it merely as Mustard Greens, and it is a member of the *Cruciferae*, or Mustard Family, but I dislike this term, because it tends to confuse this plant with the *Brassicas*.

Barbarea verna is often cultivated from New York southward, appearing on the market as Scurvy Grass or Belle Isle Cress. The canny truck farmer sows the seed in the fall and reaps a crop when his land would be useless for any other purpose.

B. vulgaris is found in low rich ground, often near streams and ditches, while *B. verna* finds its favorite home in fallow fields and cultivated lands. In rich garden soil, I have found the two species growing together. They look much alike, have the same season, and both species are equally good for food, so they can be gathered indiscriminately.

These perennial members of the Mustard Family form thick clumps of smooth green leaves, growing six to eight inches long and springing directly from the crown of the perennial root. They have an extraordinary ability to grow vigorously during any warm spell in winter and from them the forager can often gather fresh salad material or boiling greens in midwinter if the ground is free of snow. However, it is in late February and early March that winter cress becomes best and most abundant. It forms dense, bright green clusters before any other green thing shows.

These leaves have from two to eight pairs of small lateral lobes along the stem and a much larger terminal lobe. The lobes have entire margins and smooth, shiny surfaces without the hairiness of the mustards. In April, the plant puts up a seed stalk which eventually reaches from one to two feet high and bears many bright yellow flowers, about a quarter inch across and evenly spaced along the stem. These flowers, like all members of the Mustard Family, have four petals and six stamens.

To be edible, the leaves of winter cress must be gathered early, while the weather is still cold. Those who complain of the bitterness of this plant are usually those who gathered it too late in the season. When gathered early enough, winter cress is no more bitter than the best leaf lettuce, and far less so than endive or escarole. As soon as the frosty nights are past, this plant becomes too bitter to eat. Fortunately, by this time, one can select from a number of other wild salads and potherbs.

I have made an excellent wild salad in early March by combining equal parts of the blanched center leaves of winter cress, new tips of water cress and the crisp, underground shoots of day lily, with a very few wild garlic tops. These were all chopped fine and served with a bleu cheese dressing.

If you have plenty of winter cress growing near your home, as I have, you can give nature a hand to produce some real luxury-type salad material. Tie each large cluster into a tight bundle right where it's growing, then invert a flowerpot over each bunch. Stop the hole in the bottom with a bit of sod to exclude all light, and in ten days or two weeks the cress will be beautifully blanched. Excluding the light keeps the bitter principle from developing, lightens the color, gives it a crisp texture and a delicious flavor. This blanched winter cress can be mixed with other salad materials or eaten alone.

There is no need to blanch the leaves if they are to be used as boiling greens. In winter or very early spring, these leaves can be cooked and seasoned just as you would prepare spinach. A little later, when the bitter principle starts to develop, winter cress will still make good greens if it is boiled in two waters, throwing the first water away. When the bloom stalk appears, the leaves become too bitter to eat, but winter cress compensates by immediately producing edible heads of bloom buds. This is another of the wild broccolis and one of the best.

The buds first appear in a compact cluster, then the bloom stalk pushes upward, still bearing a cluster of buds at the top, and leaving opened blossoms along the growing stem. The bud clusters can be gathered for food from the time they first appear until the last buds open, so the season extends over several weeks.

This wild broccoli is neither tedious to pick nor difficult to prepare. Just pull the whole bud clusters and never mind if you get a few opened blossoms; they're good too. Place the dry clusters in a kettle and pour boiling water over them. Let stand about ½ minute, then drain. Cover the buds with fresh boiling water, place on heat and boil for about 3 minutes. Drain again, season with salt and butter, then serve. The whole cooking operation takes only about 5 minutes.

Next spring, let's join that cavalcade of Italians when they head for the country and enjoy some delicious and healthful food plucked at no cost from the fields and roadsides. There is plenty of winter cress for us all.

A Wild Winter Garden in Your Cellar

A FTER the first frost but before the ground freezes, is one of the most fruitful seasons for the forager. This is the time when he will gather in a supply of walnuts, butternuts, pecans, hickory nuts and hazelnuts. Persimmons, papaws, cranberries and wild apples are now at their best. Crab apples are begging to be made into spiced fruit and sweet butters. Now is the time to delve for Jerusalem artichokes, and shallow streams and ponds can be made to pay a tribute of arrowhead tubers and cattail roots. This is the season of the wild grape with its promise of jelly, conserve, delicious juice and sparkling, heady wine.

Even when the snow covers the countryside and the ponds and streams are all frozen, there is no need for the neoprimitive food gatherer to lay his hobby on the shelf. If he has been industrious and thrifty, there will be no vacant shelf on which to lay it. The shelves, cupboards, freezer and cellar will all be loaded with canned, dried, frozen, preserved and pickled products of field and forest. This is the time to enjoy the fruits of your foraging labor. Experiment with new menus, combinations and recipes, using your hoard of wild food products. Develop your culinary skill, for the larger part of successful foraging is in the tasteful and appealing preparation of the food you gather. Treat the family to a wild food dinner, and give the regular cook a rest, if that happens to be someone besides you. Combat the winter's chills with hot herb beverages and mulled elderberry wine. Bring up a bottle of golden dandelion wine and enjoy a taste of summer. Eat, drink and be merry.

But if you still long for spring and your hands itch to gather some new plant, try forcing wild plants right in your own cellar. Then you can continue to pick delicate, delicious "wild" salads and vegetables straight on through the winter. There are several wild plants which are easily adapted to cellar forcing, and the leaves and sprouts produced this way are real luxury items.

Our old friend the poke (*Phytolacca americana*) is one of the best plants for this kind of culture. Beneath the rank, purple stalks in late autumn, you will find the huge perennial root, large as your leg. Plant a dozen or more of these in a box of dirt. If any of the roots are too long, make them fit the box by lopping off the lower end. You can't hurt a poke root. On the crown of each root, you will see a circle of dozens of incipient buds. Each of these buds is capable of producing a sprout which will be the equal of the best, blanched asparagus.

It is best to leave the boxes outside until after a hard freeze before bringing them into a warm basement. This is to fool the plants into believing that winter has passed, and that it is time to start growing again. It is a scurvy trick, but it works.

After freezing weather sets in, place the box, with the root crowns barely covered, in a warm, dark part of your cellar and keep it well watered. In a few weeks the box will literally be covered with fat blanched poke sprouts. Cut them for use when they are six to eight inches high, and another crop will immediately spring up. You can get one cutting per week for three months. Cook and serve these sprouts just as you would asparagus. They make a welcome addition to the midwinter menu.

Do you want to try some of the finest salad greens ever produced? Then try forcing some dandelions in your basement. Just dig up the roots and set them in boxes as directed for poke. To make the work pay on both ends, you can dig the dandelions from your lawn, but don't use the roots from ground where chemical weed killers have been used.

When you bring them in, place the box in a warm, dry place and keep it well watered. In a few weeks they will produce an abundant crop of crisp, pale yellow leaves which make the best salad I know. The French have followed this practice for generations, and I suspect this is one reason why France is noted for its good food.

With little attention except cutting and watering, the roots will produce several crops of leaves. If you want to have these luxury greens all winter prepare several boxes of roots and leave them outside. Then when production starts tapering off in one box, you can bring in another.

I know you will consider these forced dandelions precious salad material, but be sure to try them as cooked greens at least once. They are so tender they need only a few minutes cooking. I have known people who thought they didn't like cooked greens to go wild over winter-forced dandelions.

The deep, yellow roots of dock (*Rumex*, about fifteen species) can be treated the same way. I don't care for a salad of dock greens alone, but I like them as a decoration on top of other salad materials. These roots are difficult to dig, and for best results they should not be shortened. Take the front out of the box you are using, and lay the roots in tiers with the crowns facing the open side, sprinkling soil between the layers of roots. This will form a stack with a backwards sloping top and a rounded face which will bear the colorful leaves. Cover the roots well with soil, and leave outside until after a hard freeze. A few weeks after being brought into the warmth, these roots will begin to produce pale, translucent, curled leaves of all colors. Snip and wash these vegetable rainbows carefully to prevent bruising. Tastefully arranged on top of a salad they make a dish that looks almost too pretty to eat.

Again, it is to the French that we owe our knowledge of *Barbe de Capucin* and Witloof, two other salad dainties that can be grown in the cellar. Both of these fancy foods are products of the chicory root.

For *Barbe de Capucin*, handle chicory roots exactly as described for dock. Don't set them too near the furnace; a temperature of about 55° is ideal. Keep them watered and in 3 weeks you will have a crop of loose blanched leaves that can only be compared to forced dandelions.

For witloof, you will need a deep box. Trim the bottoms of chicory roots to a uniform length and set them in soil in the bottom of the box, with the crowns just showing. Cover with at least eighteen inches of sawdust. After being kept warm and watered for about 5 weeks, the witloof, looking like small, close heads of romaine lettuce, will be formed. Slice one of these into a tossed salad and you'll see why Americans go to France.

When you remove the sawdust and cut the witloof, don't throw the chicory roots away. Water them and you will be able to cut a crop or two of *Barbe de Capucin* from the same roots.

One more cellar trick, and this time one that gives an abundant yield with little work. When a late-winter warm spell thaws the ground, go to some fallow field and pull a dozen or so of the largest clusters of winter cress you can find. Pack these with their adhering soil tightly against one another in a box, and place in a totally dark place. In two weeks you will have a large quantity of nicely blanched greens which can be used raw or cooked. Either way, they're mighty good eating.

Wild Honey

ALL my life I have been fascinated by wild bees, and charmed with their honey. That unaided nature, utilizing a strange and complicated, symbiotic relationship between insects and flowers could create such a perfect sweet, still seems to me very wonderful indeed. Each time I cut a dripping square of wild honeycomb and eat it, wax and all, I marvel at its perfection, which no processing could possibly improve.

My grandfather always kept a few hives of bees, and was known through the country as an expert bee man. Any neighbor who happened to locate a bee tree would usually report it to Grandpa rather than risk getting stung by attempting to rob it himself. Grandpa, and any of my maternal uncles who happened to be home, were always eager to tackle a new bee tree and bring in the stores of wild honey, and even sometimes enhive the bees and add them to the apiary, a delicate and difficult procedure. Whenever I was visiting there, I always went along on the expeditions, though at that age I usually watched the operation from a safe distance.

Grandpa was one of those rare men who have a way with bees. Instead of wearing heavy clothes, a veil and lineman's gloves, he always rolled up his sleeves and opened his collar when working with bees, wild or tame. I remember watching him and one of my uncles looking over a bee tree and estimating how low the hollow section would extend. Grandpa bored into the tree with a brace and bit, and on the first try his bit came out covered with honey. He tried again a bit lower and this time struck only solid wood. At this point they cut through the tree with a crosscut saw and felled it. This excited the bees, so the two men came away for a quarter of an hour to let them settle down. Then they went back and sawed the tree through just above the hollow.

Now even my uncle retired to a safe distance, and Grandpa worked the bees alone. He drilled another hole into the hollow, put some burning cotton rags into a bellows bee smoker and poured smoke into the hive. Then he tapped some iron wedges into one end of the section of log that housed the bees and started splitting it by hitting the wedges, one after another, with a sledge. When the log cracked open, my grandfather poured more smoke into the crack, then walked away to let the bees settle again. Finally the section of log lay in two pieces, with the honeycomb torn and exposed. The confused bees buzzed about, gorging themselves with their own honey.

As Grandpa wanted to capture this colony of bees as well as to take their store of surplus honey, he next set up a hive on the sawed-off stump. Then with his smoker and honey knife he tackled the opened halves of the bee tree. What a memorable sight he made, the old man, his hands smeared with honey, cutting through the comb with slow deliberate movements. Each section was held up to the sun to detect any pollen or brood cells and all objectionable parts were trimmed away. The good honey was dropped into a wash boiler and all brood comb was deposited in the new hive.

My grandfather cut a leafy twig to brush the bees from the comb and began closely examining the interior of the tree. My uncle said he was looking for the queen bee. Then Grandpa signaled that he had found her, and transferred the piece of comb on which she had been located to the new hive.

All this time the bees swarmed around and over the old man, crawling about on his hands and face. Once he came out of the fog of smoke and bees in his slow deliberate way and brought me a piece of light-colored, crystallized honeycomb, which he said the bees had made from cotton blossoms. It tasted better than any candy I had ever eaten. He then obtained a match from my uncle so he could fire up his pipe before returning to the tree. It seemed that the bees had been crawling so thickly over his glasses that he was having difficulty seeing, and he knew the tobacco smoke would keep them off.

Finally the tree was cleaned out, and Grandpa was satisfied that the bees would settle down in the new hive he had provided. We left the hive sitting on the stump and proudly carried home our wash boiler full of wild honey. Most of it my grandfather cut in chunks and packed into wide-mouthed jars. The people in that part of the country prefer their honey brought to the table in the comb. All odd bits, mashed section and crystallized honey, were placed in a pail and set in boiling water for about an hour. This melted the wax, which congealed on top of the honey when it cooled. When the wax was removed the honey was strained and sealed in jars. A week later Grandpa went back to the bee tree at night and stopped the entrance to the hive, in which the bees were now perfectly at home, and brought it back to his apiary.

Since that time I have robbed many a colony of wild bees, but I have never become as adept at the game as my grandfather was. I always wear heavy clothes, gloves and veil, and I feel certain that I would be stung to death without them. Whenever I open a tree and the bees start beating viciously against my veil, I am very glad for its protection. Even with all my armor I usually manage to get stung at least once for each colony I rob.

Although it was only a few years ago that I learned a technique of locating bee trees, it is amazing how many colonies of wild bees I robbed over the years that were just accidentally discovered. Two of the best hauls of wild honey I ever took were not from bee trees but from old buildings. Once some friends of mine bought a lakeside cottage that had been unoccupied for several years, and discovered that the walls were full of bees. They appealed to me for help, so I assembled my gear and went after them. The house was of double-wall, board-and-batten construction, and the bees had found a home between the studs inside a wall. I drilled several holes into the hollow space and pumped smoke in until the house looked as if it was on fire. Then I extracted the nails from the boards with a nail puller and simply opened up the section where the bees were. This huge colony had been there for several years and the hollow walls had given them unlimited room for expansion, so an unbelievable amount of honey was stored there, some of it a year or more old and completely crystallized. I obtained more than a hundred pounds of this finest of sweets from this one venture.

Another time, a contractor of my acquaintance had agreed to dismantle an old building, then found that bees in the wall chased his workmen away. This house had horizontal siding so I drilled holes between the studs near the top of the wall and sawed out the siding, carrying the honey-filled sections down the ladder and ignoring the angry bees which were beating against my veil. I made it possible for the contractor to finish his job, for which I was paid a day's wages, and for which I also obtained as much honey as my family could use in several months.

Not all my bee-hunting adventures have been so successful. Once a companion and I spent two days cutting down and splitting open a huge eucalyptus tree in Hawaii, and actually obtained less than one pound of honey for our efforts.

After many years of such haphazard honey-hunting, I read a fascinating magazine article about bee-hunting.* I immediately saw that the technique for locating bee trees described by the author could vastly expand this hobby which heretofore had depended on chance. There were directions for making a rather complicated bee box with sliding panels, partitions and windows with darkening shutters. I planned to make such a box but kept putting it off. However, when I went camping the next summer, I did take along my bee equipment, some old honeycomb, a little bottle of anise oil and some blue carpenter's chalk.

While fishing in a pond near my camp, I noticed that a nearby patch of blooming milkweed was swarming with honeybees, so I set out to improvise some tracking device. In camp, I found a square of masonite that had been painted bright red and an aluminum cake cover that fitted well over my large square of old black honeycomb. I made a sirup by putting 1 cup of sugar in a bottle with 2 cups of water and shaking it until it dissolved. Returning to the milkweed patch, I rubbed the top of the honeycomb with a corner of the cork from the anise bottle, filled the empty comb with sirup and placed it on the square of masonite, which I rested on a stone. Then I returned to my fishing.

* G. H. Edgell, "Bee Hunter," *Atlantic Monthly*, CLXXXIV (July, 1949), 47-51.

A half-hour later I checked my bee bait and, sure enough, the bees had deserted the flowers and were swarming over the sugar-filled comb. I stood and watched them come and go for many minutes, until I was satisfied that they were all leaving in the same direction. I kept them in sight as long as my eyes could pick up the flash of sun on their wings, and, by sighting over my honeycomb in the direction they were going, I picked out some landmarks to establish my beeline.

Now I knew in which direction the parent colony lay, but I also wanted to know how far away it was. Taking a pinch of powdered carpenter's chalk, I mixed it with a drop of water with the tip of a camel's-hair brush. Then, when a bee had his head buried in a honey cell, I dabbed his rear end with the blue chalk. He didn't like it much, but, after doing an angry dance across the honeycomb, he took on a load of sirup and flew away. I noted the exact time that he left and anxiously awaited his return. In just over six minutes, there was my blue-bottomed bee, upending himself on the honeycomb and drinking up more sirup. According to my mentor, this meant that the tree was less than a mile distant, and the trail led first across an open field.

Now it was time to make the first crucial move in the actual tracking process. Waiting until a dozen or more bees were on the honeycomb at the same time, I suddenly clapped on the aluminum cake cover, picked up the board with my trapped bees and carried it across the field to a fence post which I had picked out as being directly on the beeline. Balancing the red masonite on the top of the post, I waited a few minutes for the bees to settle down, then lifted the cover. They flew out, circling and figure-eighting in all directions, so I really couldn't see in which direction they flew when they finally left.

A long ten minutes went by. I refilled the honeycomb, renewed the anise with a light touch and waited while the anxious interval passed. Then a bee darted down and buzzed suspiciously around the bait. Another one joined him. Then temptation overcame one and he dropped down on the comb. In twenty minutes the bees were coming and going regularly. I even saw my blue-spotted bee come in for a load, which satisfied me that I was still running the same beeline.

I made three more moves along the line. On the last move, the bees almost deserted me. When they finally settled down to carrying away sirup, they moved off in the opposite direction toward which they had formerly been going. This was it! Now I knew that the tree was between this spot and my former setup. Sighting back along the line I spotted a likely looking beech tree. Walking to it, I circled it again and again, looking first high, then low, without seeing a thing. Finally, when I was about ready to give up, I caught the flash of the setting sun on wings as a bee came in for a landing on the side of a large limb. I had found my bee tree.

Next day, I returned and removed two water pails of honey from the tree without incident, except that I received my usual one sting in a part of my anatomy over which my trousers were tightly stretched as I was bending over cutting out the comb.

I wish I could report that my jury-rigged bee-tracking equipment had been uniformly successful ever since, but I'm afraid I must confess that I had a bit of beginner's luck that first time I used it. Sometimes the bees fail to return after one of my moves, and I have to return to the starting place and begin again. A few times I have lost the trail altogether. The quality most valuable to the bee hunter is infinite patience. However, my improvised bee-tracking gear has worked well enough so that I have never bothered to construct a regular bee box. I have a theory that the bright red color of the masonite base, which I have continued to use, helps the bees to relocate the bait after a move, although my uneven successes and failures prove nothing of the sort.

I hope that I have said enough to indicate to the enthusiastic forager the possibility of gathering his own honey from the wild, as well as some fruits, meats and vegetables. If you secure more honey than you can consume on griddle cakes and hot biscuits, there are dozens of recipes in every cookbook calling for honey. Learn the secrets of successfully using honey in cooking. It is not merely a substitute for white sugar, but brings its own distinctive flavor, aroma and other qualities to the finished product. Because honey attracts moisture, baked goods sweetened with it will stay fresh far longer than when sugar is used; indeed, some honey-sweetened baked goods are actually improved by a day or so of aging. Use honey with discretion in jams, jellies and preserves, for there is danger that the subtle flavors of the fruit may be overpowered by the stronger honey flavor. For medicinal uses of honey, I refer the reader to the excellent book,

Folk Medicine, by Dr. D. C. Jarvis,* who has made a lifetime study of the uses of honey and vinegar among the country folk of Vermont.

Speaking of vinegar, an excellent vinegar can be made of honey, right in your own kitchen. To make a sample-sized batch of honey vinegar, stir 1 pound of wild honey into 3 quarts of water and boil for 10 minutes. Allow to cool until it is barely lukewarm, then stir in 1 teaspoon of activated dry yeast, dissolved in a little of the liquid. Use a glass jar or small crock in which to ferment it, as metal is very dangerous in this process. Cover the jar with a cloth and keep it in a cool place for about 3 weeks. Then add 1 pint of unpasteurized cider vinegar and keep the jar in a warm place for 10 days. This should complete the vinegar ferment, and the finished vinegar can then be carefully decanted into bottles, tightly capped and stored in a dark cupboard.

Wine or Mead can also be made of honey, and it's much better flavored than most home brews. Is there anything that has not been used as the base of an alcoholic drink? My recipe for Mead can be used to make a gallon or a barrel of this potent brew. To each gallon of water, add 4 pounds of honey, 6 cloves, 2 sticks of cinnamon, and the juice and peel of 1 lemon, sliced thinly. Boil all together for 30 minutes, then strain into a crock that will hold it with a little room to spare. When cooled, add 1 teaspoon of activated dry yeast for each gallon, dissolved in some of the liquid. Allow to ferment in a cool place—55° is ideal—until it ceases bubbling and the liquor clears, then bottle, cap tightly and store in a cool, dark cellar. It should not be used for at least a month, and longer is better. Mead, unlike many other drinks, does not improve with really long aging, so it should be consumed within a year of the time it was made.

Surely the sophisticated neoprimitive will add bee-hunting to his foraging repertoire. Few endeavors offer greater rewards in fun, food and drink. Here is a great addition to the hobby of a wild food gatherer who is not terrified at the thought of an occasional bee sting.

* D. C. Jarvis, M.D., *Folk Medicine* (Greenwich, Conn.: Fawcett Publications, Inc., 1961).

How about the Meat Course?

MOST people will at least try a new kind of vegetable food if it is appetizingly prepared and included in a dish that looks somewhat familiar. Prejudice against vegetable foods exists, but it is comparatively weak, and disappears altogether when one encounters such commonly accepted wild fruits as blackberries, wild raspberries and wild strawberries. Prejudice reappears and is apt to be quite strong against some of the seldom-eaten wild fruits, such as prickly pear, May apple, and papaw; but even these, when presented in familiar disguises, such as pies, jams or marmalades, become perfectly acceptable. With few exceptions, people will at least tentatively try a new food of vegetable origin. It is when we try to introduce an unfamiliar kind of meat that we sometimes encounter a wall of prejudice.

Prejudice is by definition unreasonable and illogical. A reasoned dislike or a logical objection is not a prejudice, although false reasoning and pseudo logic are often found in the service of prejudice. Prejudice is invariably a symptom of a character defect, but tragically it is one that is shared in some degree by us all. Race, national and cultural prejudice is being recognized by thinking men as the great evil which has brought us to the brink of destruction. Prejudice which finds its focus in the accents, manners and styles of others is passed off as comparatively innocuous, but even this brand of prejudice does more to divide men than does any real differences in ideals and aspirations.

Have you ever thought how closely food prejudices are related to the other kinds? Long ago, during the controversy about the United States' joining the League of Nations, I saw a jingoistic orator whip up a frenzy of hatred and disgust against the French because they ate frog's legs and snails. During the late war, when a patriotic speaker wanted to emphasize how alien the Japanese were to our way of life, he would always mention the fact that they ate octopus and raw fish. Only yesterday I saw a newspaper article in which the reporter seemed to think that he had found the final argument against communism because he had discovered that some of the peoples in Asiatic Russia were eating horse meat. The fact that the horse had been the chief meat animal of these people for a thousand years before communism was ever heard of, was, if it was even known to him, irrelevant. An American governor of the Philippines once told one of the non-Christian tribes there that the American people could not like them as long as they persisted in eating the flesh of dogs. It is a sad commentary on the American mind that what he said was perfectly true.

I was fortunate in being brought up in a family that ate a broad spectrum of meats. Opossum, raccoon, squirrel, frog's legs, turtle, crayfish and even armadillo sausage were not only eaten in our family but were considered great delicacies. Even meat to which I was unaccustomed never seemed to repel me as it did some people. Once, in a wild section of New Mexico, when we had been without meat for some time, my buddy and I shot a fat young burro from a herd of feral animals, wild as any deer, that roamed the dry hills. I thought burro meat delicious at the time, and ate it cooked in several ways with great relish. At another time, on a hunt, finding game scarce, I killed and dressed a porcupine. The meat, cut from the bones and soaked overnight in salt, vinegar and water, then parboiled for 10 minutes and dredged in flour and sautéed, was very good. I cannot claim, however, that I am entirely free of this kind of prejudice. Once a companion and I shot a large bobcat. We had no fresh meat in camp, so we carefully dressed the big feline and fried some of the loin chops for supper. Surprisingly, the meat was clear and white, tender and delicate, as the breast of a quail. The taste was mild and good. As we were eating our unusual fare, my companion remarked,

"The *bob* part of this meat sure is good, but I'm having trouble swallowing the *cat.*" Frankly, I was having the same difficulty.

I'll wager that the mere reading about these strange meats has caused a queasy feeling in the stomachs of some of my readers. This points up one of the illogical facts about food prejudice. Had I described a thick sirloin beefsteak, turning to a rich brown as it broiled over hickory charcoal, I would have excited your salivary glands and aroused your appetite, yet such a mental picture would be utterly disgusting to a Hindu. Ham, sizzling in a frying pan with some new-laid eggs, is a tempting sight to most Westerners, but it would be nauseating to an orthodox Moslem. And yet we are not really different. An Indian or Arab baby, brought up in an American home, would feel just as we do, and any of us, had we been raised in their culture, would share their prejudices.

I am not trying to maintain that all food likes and dislikes are based on prejudice. For instance, I care very little for veal, yet I have eaten veal all my life and still eat it when I can get nothing else, so my dislike is not based on prejudice. It simply doesn't titillate my taste buds as pleasantly as does beef, pork or lamb.

Wild game in America is easily divided into two kinds. One kind, which includes deer, rabbit, upland game birds, duck and goose, is universally hunted and the meat is acceptable to nearly everyone. The other kind, which includes opossum, raccoon, muskrat, woodchuck, bullfrog and turtle, is eaten in only certain areas and refused elsewhere.

If the forager could enlarge his meat horizons to include those animals which are considered delicacies in only some part of our country, then he would vastly increase his chances of finding edible game to go with his wild plant food. I would expect the neoprimitive food gatherer, unless he happened to be a vegetarian, to take all of the conventional wild game he could get, or that the laws of his state allow. I would also expect him to treat this meat as game, not as butcher's meat. In no other culinary art is the skill of the chef so important as in the cooking of wild game. Unfortunately, lack of space prevents my making more than a cursory mention of the subject. A book of this size could be written on game cookery alone; in fact, several very good ones have been written. A very reasonably priced one that I can recommend is a little paper-bound volume simply called *Wild Game Cook Book* by Martin Rywell, which can be purchased for one dollar from Pioneer Press in Harriman, Tennessee.

Beyond the conventional game and fowl usually brought in by the hunter, I would expect the clever forager to enjoy, and offer to his guests, such transcendental gastronomic creations as Roast 'Possum with Maple-Nut Stuffing, Raccoon Pie, Maryland Potted Marsh Rabbit and Woodchuck in Sour Cream. Besides the recognized game and food fishes, he should be aware of such mouth-watering morsels as Crayfish Tails Tempura, Carp Chunks, Bluegill Fillets, Chicken-fried Frog's Legs, and Snapper Soup.

We laugh at the old English recipes that begin, "First you catch the hare—" but that is exactly where a wild game recipe should begin. The success or failure of a wild game dish depends largely on how the meat is handled from the time it is killed until it is cooked. I have developed a procedure that seems to work well with opossum, raccoon, muskrat, woodchuck and porcupine. As soon as the animal is killed, the jugular vein should be cut so it can be completely emptied of blood. Then, as soon as possible, it should be skinned and eviscerated. Save the liver of the opossum, for it makes a tasty addition to the stuffing. When the carcass is cleaned, carefully remove four waxy-looking little pear-shaped glands that are found, two in the small of the back and one under each foreleg on the opossum, raccoon, woodchuck and porcupine, and one under each fore- and hindleg on the muskrat. Put the cleaned animal into a deep bowl or jar, and cover with cold water to which ¼ cup of salt and ½ cup of vinegar has been added. The meat should soak in this solution for 24 hours and twice that time will not hurt, if the water is kept very cold. If you want to keep the meat for a special occasion, remove from the soaking solution after 48 hours, wipe dry, put the carcass in a plastic bag and put it in your home freezer. Freezing after soaking actually improves the flavor of the meat. It is only when the animal has been properly bled and cleaned, the glands carefully removed and all the gamey flavor soaked out and a good flavor soaked in, that you are ready to proceed on any of the following recipes with any assurance of success.

OPOSSUM AND RACCOON

I mention these two together because they have largely the same range and are taken by the same methods; often you will capture one when you are hunting the other. Even the recipes for cooking them are interchangeable, although there is a pronounced difference in the flavor of the two meats. Originally southern animals, they have thrived in the neighborhood of man, and have extended their range until now they can be found from southern Canada to Florida and west to the Plains. They are nocturnal animals and are usually hunted at night with one or more hounds, but a good, cold-nosed 'coon hound can often point out a tree in which a 'possum or 'coon is hiding during the day. They are easily taken in steel traps, or, much more humanely, in box traps or live traps, baited with bread, fried bacon, or just the camp garbage.

The esculent properties of these two excellent meat animals are highly appreciated in some sections of the South, but they are seldom eaten elsewhere. For meat purposes, they should be hunted in the autumn, between the first frost and the winter freeze-up.

One October I captured a fat young opossum, and, wanting to make him the *pièce de résistance* of a wild food dinner, I decided to concoct a stuffing of wild plants, as nearly as possible. I cooked and mashed 2 cups of wild Jerusalem artichokes, added 1 cup of diced wild apples, ¼ cup of homemade maple sirup, ¼ cup of chopped hickory nuts, a few celery leaves, the 'possum liver chopped fine, ½ stick of margarine melted and a little salt. It seemed a bit soupy, so I added crushed corn flakes, about a cupful, until it was the right consistency. I used this to stuff the ready-cleaned and soaked opossum, fastened him with skewers, dusted him on the outside with paprika and salt, then put him in the roaster. Around the meat I placed some peeled raw artichokes, and poured in a cup of water and a tablespoon of Worcestershire sauce. I kept the oven heat high until the 'possum was browned on the outside, then I lowered the heat and cooked him slowly for 2 hours more. This was one experiment that came out exactly right the first time I tried it. I have never eaten better 'possum, nor have I ever eaten better Jerusalem artichokes. If you can't get the artichokes, use sweet potatoes, and if you can't get the hickory nuts, use pecans. This same recipe will work beautifully with 'coon and with woodchuck. Each dish will taste differently but all will be excellent.

To make a Raccoon Pie, disjoint a young 'coon and soak the pieces in a salt-vinegar solution as outlined above. Next day, put the meat and the soaking solution in a kettle and boil for 30 minutes, then drain. Put the meat back in the kettle with fresh water and simmer until the meat is fairly tender, then add 2 onions, 4 potatoes and 3 carrots, all diced. When the meat and vegetables are perfectly tender, take them from the broth. Remove all bones and sinews from the meat and dice it. Brown 2 tablespoons of flour in 2 tablespoons of butter and use that to thicken the broth. Season to taste with black pepper and salt. Place the meat and vegetables in a baking dish and pour the thickened broth over them. Make a soft dough from commercial biscuit mix, roll it ¼ inch thick and spread it over the top of the pie, perforating a steam escape with a fork. Bake in a hot oven until the biscuit dough is nicely browned. This recipe also works well with meat from any of the other animals mentioned in this section.

MUSKRAT

The muskrat is an excellent meat animal with an unfortunate name. I have seen muskrats for sale in fancy butcher shops under the euphemism of marsh rabbit. They are almost strictly nocturnal animals but are easily caught in steel traps or in box traps baited with a carrot and set on a small raft or piece of timber and anchored just offshore in a pond, lake or quiet stream. After dressing and soaking the meat as outlined in the general directions above, it can be cooked in any way you would prepare rabbit, and you will find it good. To make Maryland Potted Marsh Rabbit, remove the muskrat from the soaking solution, cut into pieces, pour boiling water over the meat, stir thoroughly, then drain. Put the meat in a thick iron skillet, iron pot or Dutch oven, add ½ cup of water, ½ teaspoon of chili powder, 1 level teaspoon of salt, 1 pinch of sage and ¼ cup of bacon drippings. Place enough small, peeled potatoes for the meal around the meat. Sprinkle a little flour over all and bake in a moderate oven until very tender, basting the meat with the pan juice several times while cooking.

WOODCHUCK

The Woodchuck, or Ground Hog, is usually considered a pest, eating the farmers' crops and digging holes in which livestock are apt to break their legs. Shooting ground hogs with high-powered rifles, fitted with telescopic sights, is in the way of becoming a popular sport. They can also be caught by setting steel traps in the mouths of their dens and in box traps baited with green beans. A young ground hog killed in September or October, when he is well fattened for his winter's hibernation, is good eating, the meat being beautifully marbled with fat. After proper dressing and soaking, a wood-chuck can be prepared any way that you would cook 'possum, 'coon or rabbit.

To make Woodchuck in Sour Cream, remove the animal from the soaking solution, cut him in pieces, cover with fresh water to which 1 diced onion, 1 bay leaf, 1 tablespoon of vinegar and 1 teaspoon of salt has been added, then boil for about 3 hours until the meat slips easily from the bones. Remove the meat and throw the boiling water away; the ingredients in it were merely to flavor the meat, not to eat. Remove all bones and sinews from the flesh and dice it fairly fine. Now mash the yolks of 2 hard-boiled eggs, add 1 teaspoon of prepared mustard, 1 cup of sour cream, the coarsely diced whites of the 2 hard-boiled eggs, 1 teaspoon of flour, 1 dash of nutmeg and a little salt. Heat all this together until it boils, stirring constantly, then add the chopped woodchuck meat and let it all simmer for about 20 minutes, then serve.

These are only a few of the animals and the barest sample of meat dishes that can be enjoyed if you put prejudice aside. An ingenious forager, who is also a clever cook, need never go without some kind of tasty wild meat. There is always good hunting and good eating for the true neoprimitive who has a strong stomach and weak prejudices. Surely a people who eat chocolate-covered ants and fried maguey worms for cocktail snacks can learn to eat the delicious wild game dishes described above.

Spinning for Bluegills

ASK any sport-fisherman the name of the first fish he ever caught and, if he can remember so far back, he will tell you it was a Bluegill, nine times out of ten. He may call it a Sunny, Sunfish, Sun Perch, Gilly or Pumpkin Seed, but these are only a few of the local names for the same little fish, the *Eupomotis* of several species. This little denizen of quiet streams and ponds more often falls prey to the juvenile fisherman than all other breeds of fish in America put together.

Most adult fishermen consider the bluegill a "confounded little bait-stealing nuisance" when they don't call him something completely unprintable. I feel the same way about the undersized sunny that steals my bait when I am angling for bigger game, but we're really maligning a great little fish. Not only does he serve to introduce youngsters to the greatest sport in the world, but, with the right tackle, he can still give seasoned fishermen plenty of fun.

A quarter-pound bluegill will give you as much fight per ounce as any game fish in America. He is beautifully colored with extremely intricate markings. His flesh, what there is of it, is as sweet and delicious as any fish that ever came to the table. In fact, the bluegill has everything but size.

This fish has been known to reach a length of twelve inches and weigh more than a pound, but don't expect to catch one as big as that every time you go fishing. A pond full of six-inch bluegills can provide a lot of fun, and some good eating.

The obvious solution to this size problem is to scale down your tackle to fit the fish. I have landed bluegills on every kind of rig from sewing thread on a willow wand, with a bent pin for a hook up to the finest fly-fishing equipment, but I never knew how much fun this little fish could furnish until I started spinning for them.

Ordinary, general-purpose spinning gear is far too heavy to permit the bluegill to demonstrate his ferocity. You need the lightest and smoothest-working tackle you can buy; a light, limber rod and the lightest spinning reel made, wound with one-pound test, monofilament line is about right. A pear-shaped casting bobber with a ring at each end, called a "fly-caster," will give you just the right amount of weight for long easy casts. Now take a three- to five-foot piece of the same line, the length depending on the depth of water in which you expect to fish, and tie a No. 10 hook on one end and a light snap-swivel on the other. Don't use a swivel on the hook end of the line, for you want to avoid even this tiny weight near the hook. You can fasten the bobber to your line with a swivel if you wish, or just tie it on. Snap the swivel of your leader line into the lower end of the casting bobber. Bait the hook with a small worm or a dough ball and you're ready to fish.

It is the terminal end of this tackle, the unweighted hook, that is the big secret. When bluegills are really biting, anybody can catch them on anything, but to be sure of catching enough for supper, any afternoon after work, from early spring until late fall, needs some skill and the right outfit.

One hot summer afternoon several of us were fishing my favorite bluegill pond, but nothing was even nibbling. I lay down on a swimming pier and peered down through a crack. In the clear, shaded water below me, I could see a hundred or more bluegills, lazily swimming around. I was using a snelled hook fastened to the line with a light snap-swivel, and had a split-shot sinker on the leader. I baited with a fresh worm and dropped it among the ones I could see. They shied away from this rapidly sinking rig, and, when I let it hang right among them, several dozen bluegills formed a circle around the bait, all looking at it hungrily, but none coming forward to try it.

I then took another worm from my bait can and dropped it through the crack. It started sinking slowly, but before it was a foot down, a bluegill had it and was shaking it like a terrier with a rat. Taking the hint, I removed the weighted outfit and tied a hook with no sinker directly on the end of the line. I baited up and dropped it among the fish I was observing, and, sure enough, they fairly raced one another to take it. I started catching bluegills as fast as I could remove them and get my hook back in water. When I passed the word around, all the others began catching fish too.

The spinning outfit described above has never let me down. The plastic bobber furnishes ample weight for long casts with this smooth-

BLUE GILL

working rig, and I can lay it anywhere I like in the two-acre pond that is my favorite fishing hole. The unweighted hook will settle slowly and naturally, and in any decent fishing hole a bluegill will have it before the line straightens out. If he doesn't grab it within fifteen seconds, quickly reel in a few feet of line and let it settle again. I know a half-dozen ponds where I can practically guarantee to get a bluegill on every cast, when weighted baits are being completely ignored.

On this ultra-light outfit, a seven-inch bluegill, hooked a hundred feet away, will make you think you have a ten-pound bass on the line. Of course, bystanders may laugh when they see you land such a tiny fish after such a terrible battle, but what's wrong with giving someone a good laugh now and then?

If you are strictly a meat-fisherman, or if you resist investing in so much expensive equipment, I'll let you in on a secret. You can catch bluegills just as fast and efficiently on a rig that can be assembled for less than a dollar as on the fancy gear described above, though you might not find it as much fun. Get a light, slender bamboo pole, twelve to sixteen feet long. Such poles can be purchased in some fishing supply houses, but I cut my own from a clump of hardy bamboo that grows in a friend's garden. Tie a piece of line on it the same length as the pole, fasten a No. 10 snelled hook on the other end of the line and snap a light, plastic bobber on the line, three or four feet above the hook, varying this distance according to the depth of water in which you are fishing. Bait the hook with worms or dough balls, toss it out as far as it will go and start pulling in the fish. The reason for the long pole is to get the hook far enough away from you so the fish will not be afraid to approach it. A bluegill can see a man on the bank; this fact is very easily verified by walking along the shore of a clear pond and watching the bluegills run away into deeper water as you approach. If you sit perfectly still for a while, they will again come near you, but the least movement on your part will send them darting away. But with the long pole described here you can get the hook far enough away from you so they will not hesitate to bite, and this rig is a very efficient meat-getter.

The best thing about the bluegill is his availability. I'll bet there is a perfectly wonderful spot to spin for these gamey little fighters not too many minutes' drive from where you are right now. There are thousands of ponds and quiet streams everywhere, which provide excellent bluegill fishing, and there are more all the time. Most farm ponds are now being stocked with bluegill and bass, as the terminal end of a food-life chain. Everybody likes to catch the bass, but in every such pond I know the bluegills tend to become overcrowded. If you promise not to poach the bass, most pond owners will gladly give you permission to fish for the bluegills. Bass will seldom take the tiny bait on the outfit I have described, though they often strike at the bobber. Once, a huge bass swallowed the bluegill I was reeling in and then snapped my line. Better take along some extra hooks and swivels.

To help reduce the bluegill population in these ponds we must carry our catch away, and here's the rub. Everyone agrees that the bluegill is delicious, but very few think it is worth the effort required to clean, cook and pick the meat from among the bones. I don't agree. To me, cleaning, cooking and eating bluegills is an essential part of the pleasure I derive from this colorful little fish. Properly cleaning a bluegill is an art well worth learning. I not only clean and skin them, I fillet them. Yes, I really do, and I'm not a surgeon either. My whole family considers these little half-ounce fillets the finest fish I ever bring home.

If the head of a bluegill is removed by cutting just back of the gills, the paired pectoral and ventral fins come off with it. Just cut through the backbone, then tear the head off the rest of the way, and you won't have the messy contents of the entrails to contend with. A short slit down the belly to the vent, allows you to pull out all the offal with the head. Now, slice off the dorsal and anal fins. The skin then comes off easily, in two pieces. To get boneless fillets, make an incision around the rib case, then slice the meat from the bones, beginning at the forward end and working toward the tail.

This may sound difficult and complicated, but it is really easier done than explained. After years of practice, I find that I can finish ten fish in fifteen minutes, producing twenty tiny fillets of the finest fish that ever sizzled in a frying pan.

To pan-fry bluegill fillets, first shake them in a paper bag with white corn meal and a little salt and pepper until they are evenly coated, then fry in very hot fat for only a minute or two, until they are lightly browned.

We can borrow a trick from the Japanese and make these tasty little fillets go farther by making Bluegills Tempura. Make a batter of 2 beaten eggs, ¼ cup of water, 1 cup of flour and 1 teaspoon of salt. Dip the fillets, one by one, in the batter, then quickly drop them in very hot fat. They will puff up hugely and cook to a golden brown in about 2 minutes, and you'll find that everyone likes them.

Another good fish stretcher that everyone likes is Fish Fritters. Dice about 20 fillets, add 1 beaten egg, 1 tablespoon of water, 1 diced onion and 1 teaspoon of salt. Stir in commercial biscuit mix until the mixture is thick enough to form into patties. Fry these a bit more slowly, until both sides are evenly browned. Serve piping hot and cock your ear for compliments.

A very few bluegill fillets can give a meal a festive air when served as a cocktail. This is very easily prepared. Just drop a few fresh fillets into boiling water, let them cook for only 2 minutes, then remove and chill. Toss the chilled fish in a commercial, seafood cocktail sauce, or make your own sauce by following the directions given in the section on crayfish. Spoon the sauce-covered pieces of fish into cocktail glasses lined with the tiny heart leaves of lettuce and serve.

If you are as ardent a bluegill fisherman as I am, you are likely to accumulate a surplus of these tasty little fish. They can be kept indefinitely if the fillets are packed in small plastic freezer bags and quick-frozen. Or you can do as I do and make some fine Pickled Bluegill Fillets that rival the best Bismarck herring. I experimented a long time with various mixtures of spices and condiments trying to get the right formula for flavoring pickled bluegills; then one day when I was in a supermarket I noticed a mixture of spices that were sold in permeable bags like teabags, called a crab-boil mixture, intended to spice fresh crabs and shrimps. On reading the list of ingredients I felt sure here was a mixture of spices that would be good in pickled fish, and so it turned out to be. These spices have another advantage in that, being in bags, they can flavor the pickle without little flecks of spices clinging all over the fish.

To make this epicurean pickle, first soak the fillets in a brine made of 1 quart of water to ½ cup of salt, for 2 days. Then wash the fillets in fresh water to remove as much salt as possible. Put a crab-boil spice bag in the bottom of a quart jar and cover it with onions sliced very thinly. Then put in about a dozen fillets, then another layer of onions and so on until the jar is loosely filled. Fill the jar with wine vinegar diluted half and half with water. Keep in the refrigerator, and they will be ready to eat any time after 3 weeks.

The bluegill will never furnish the big thrills of fishing, but for solid, continuous fun and some delicious eating the bluegill can't be beat. I like to catch big fish as well as the next man, but going after them usually involves a long trip, expensive lodging and equipment and considerable time. I have neither the time nor the money to make such expeditions often, but I can go out and catch a mess of bluegills any afternoon after work. I entirely agree with the lazy farmer who defended his neglect of his crops by saying, "When God made this earth, He covered it with three times as much water as land. Therefore it is obviously His will that I should spend three days fishing for every one day I spend plowing."

This must be why God populated our waters so densely with blue-gills. I am grateful to this bantam-weight fighter for the hours of pleasure he has furnished me, for the many tasty ways in which he has appeared on our table, and for enabling me to make a nearer approach to doing the Lord's will as revealed by that inspired farmer-prophet.

How to Cook a Carp

(*Cyprinus carpio*)

WHEN I was a lad of about eighteen, my brother and I were working on a cattle ranch in New Mexico that bordered on the Rio Grande. Most Americans think of the Rio Grande as a warm southern stream, but it rises among the high mountains of Colorado, and in the spring it is fed by melting snows. At this time of the year, the water that rushed by the ranch was turbulent, icy-cold and so silt-laden as to be semisolid. "A little too thick to drink, and a little too thin to plow" was a common description of the waters of the Rio Grande.

A few species of fish inhabited this muddy water. Unfortunately, the most common was great eight- to ten-pound carp, a fish that is considered very poor eating in this country, although the Germans and Asiatics have domesticated this fish, and have developed some varieties that are highly esteemed for the table.

On the ranch where we worked, there was a drainage ditch that ran through the lower pasture and emptied its clear waters into the muddy Rio Grande. The carp swimming up the river would strike this clear warmer water and decide they preferred it to the cold mud they had been inhabiting. One spring day, a cowhand who had been riding that way reported that Clear Ditch was becoming crowded with huge carp.

On Sunday we decided to go fishing. Four of us armed ourselves with pitchforks, saddled our horses and set out. Near the mouth of the ditch, the water was running about two feet deep and twelve to sixteen feet wide. There is a saying in that part of the country that you can't get a cowboy to do anything unless it can be done from the back of a horse, so we forced our mounts into the ditch and started wading them upstream, four abreast, herding the carp before us.

By the time we had ridden a mile upstream, the water was less than a foot deep and so crystal clear that we could see our herd of several hundred carp still fleeing from the splashing, wading horses. As the water continued to shallow, our fish began to get panicky. A few of the boldest ones attempted to dart back past us and were impaled on pitchforks. We could see that the whole herd was getting restless and was about to stampede back downstream, so we piled off our horses into the shallow water to meet the charge. The water boiled about us as the huge fish swirled past us and we speared madly in every direction with our pitchforks, throwing each fish we managed to hit over the ditch bank. This was real fishing—cowhand style. The last of the fish herd was by us in a few minutes and it was all over, but we had caught a tremendous quantity of fish.

Back at the ranch house, after we had displayed our trophies, we began wondering what we were going to do with so many fish. This started a series of typical cowboy tall tales on "how to cook a carp." The best of these yarns was told by a grizzled old *vaquero*, who claimed he had made his great discovery when he ran out of food while camping on a tributary of the Rio Grande. He said that he had found the finest way to cook a carp was to plaster the whole fish with a thick coating of fresh cow manure and bury it in the hot ashes of a campfire. In an hour or two, he said, the casing of cow manure had become black and very hard. He then related how he had removed the fish from the fire, broken the hard shell with the butt of his Winchester and peeled it off. He said that as the manure came off the scales and skin adhered to it, leaving the baked fish, white and clean. He then ended by saying, "Of course, the carp still wasn't fit to eat, but manure in which it was cooked tasted pretty good."

There were also some serious suggestions and experiments. The chief objection to the carp is that its flesh is full of many forked bones. One man said that he had enjoyed carp sliced very thin and fried so crisp that one could eat it, bones and all. He demonstrated, and you really could eat it without the bones bothering you, but it was still far from being an epicurean dish. One cowboy described the flavor as "a perfect blend of Rio Grande mud and rancid hog lard."

Another man said that he had eaten carp that had been cooked in a pressure cooker until the bones softened and became indistinguishable from the flesh. A pressure cooker is almost a necessity at that altitude, so we had one at the ranch house. We tried this method, and the result was barely edible. It tasted like the poorest possible grade of canned salmon flavored with a bit of mud. It was, however, highly appreciated by the dogs and cats on the ranch, and solved the problem of what to do with the bulk of the fish we had caught.

It was my brother who finally devised a method of cooking carp that not only made it fit for human consumption, but actually delicious. First, instead of merely scaling the fish, he skinned them. Then, taking a large pinch, where the meat was thickest, he worked his fingers and thumb into the flesh until he struck the median bones, then he worked his thumb and fingers together and tore off a handful of meat. Using this tearing method, he could get two or three good-sized chunks of flesh from each side of the fish. He then heated a pot of bland vegetable shortening, rubbed the pieces of fish with salt and dropped them into the hot fat. He used no flour, meal, crumbs or seasoning other than salt. They cooked to a golden brown in a few minutes, and everyone pronounced them "mighty fine eating." The muddy flavor seemed to have been eliminated by removing the skin and the large bones. The forked bones were still there, but they had not been multiplied by cutting across them, and one only had to remove several bones still intact with the fork from each piece of fish.

For the remainder of that spring, every few days one or another of the cowboys would take a pitchfork and ride over to Clear Ditch and spear a mess of carp. On these evenings, my brother replaced the regular *cocinero* and we enjoyed some delicious fried carp.

The flavor of carp varies with the water from which it is caught. Many years after the above incidents I attended a fish fry at my brother's house. The main course was all of his own catching, and consisted of bass, catfish and carp, all from Elephant Butte Lake farther down the Rio Grande. All the fish were prepared exactly alike, except that the carp was pulled apart as described above, while the bass and catfish, being all twelve inches or less in length, were merely cleaned and fried whole. None of his guests knew one fish from another, yet all of them preferred the carp to the other kinds. These experiences have convinced me that the carp is really a fine food fish when properly prepared.

Carp can, of course, be caught in many ways besides spearing them with pitchforks from the back of a horse. In my adopted home state, Pennsylvania, they are classed as "trash fish" and one is allowed to take them almost any way. They will sometimes bite on worms, but they are vegetarians by preference and are more easily taken on dough balls. Some states allow the use of gill nets, and other states, because they would like to reduce the population of this unpopular fish, will issue special permits for the use of nets to catch carp.

A good forager will take advantage of the lax regulations on carp fishing while they last. When all fishermen realize that the carp is really a good food fish when prepared in the right way, maybe this outsized denizen of our rivers and lakes will no longer be considered a pest and will take his rightful place among our valued food and game fishes.

The Crayfish: A REAL LUXURY FOOD

(*Cambarus* and *Astacus* species of the order Decapoda)

THERE are dozens of species of these little fresh-water relatives of the lobster which are found in streams, lakes and ponds, from the Great Lakes to the Gulf of Mexico and from the Atlantic to the Pacific. They are called Crayfish, Crawfish, Crawdads, Fresh-Water Crabs and Fresh-Water Lobsters in various sections of the country. If I listed all the names they are called by fishermen whose bait they steal, this book would be banned by the censors. Some species in the South destroy crops, and these also are called some unprintable names.

Despite these long-suffering farmers and fishermen, I have a warm spot in my heart for this little crustacean because of the way he enriched my boyhood. The first edible creature I ever pulled from the water was a crawdad. From as early as I can remember, I was an ardent crawfisherman. My equipment consisted of a long stick, a piece of grocery twine with a small square of bacon rind tied on for bait, and an old nut or washer tied in the string for a sinker. I fished in roadside ditches, small streams or little ponds. When the bacon rind was rested on the bottom, a crawdad would come along and seize it with his pincers. Then I very gently lifted him ashore. I still don't know whether it was stubborn greediness or merely slow reflexes which prevented him turning loose of the bait before I had him safely landed. I do know that before I was seven years old, I had captured literally thousands of crawdads by this simple method.

At this time I knew only two ways of preparing crawdads to eat. The simplest way was to simply drop them into boiling salted water and watch them turn from a gray-green to a bright red. Then we just shelled out the meat and ate it. Like a shrimp or lobster, the only really worth-while piece of meat is in the tail. The claws also contain edible meat, but, unless they are extra large, it is barely worth the work of getting it.

The other way in which we prepared crawfish was to roll the shelled-out tails in corn meal and fry them. The latter was my favorite way of eating crayfish, and at that age I thought no food in the world quite equaled fried crawdad tails.

When I was about eight years old, we visited my grandparents who lived several hundred miles away. There they had another species of crayfish, much larger than the little green ones I had been catching. These did not live in streams or ponds, but in burrows dug down to water level below the low-lying fields. The mud they removed in digging was deposited about the mouth of the burrow, building a sort of clay "chimney" which often stood a foot high or more. These were vegetarian crawfish and very destructive of crops.

My grandfather was an astute observer of the habits of wild creatures, and he taught me a way of catching crawdads that made my former method seem very tame and inefficient. His "bottom field" was covered with crawdad chimneys, and on a warm, rainy night, when the corn was only a few inches high, we donned slickers and rubber boots and went down to the field carrying lanterns and two 5-gallon covered pails. The rays of our lanterns caught the tiny, reddish eyes of the crawdads and showed us where they were attacking the young corn. They didn't try to run away, but threw up their fierce-looking pincers and offered battle. Grandpa showed me how to grasp them by the back, behind the pincers and drop them into the pails. There was just enough danger of getting nipped by those sharp claws to add zest to the game and make it seem fair to the crawfish. In an hour we had filled both pails with crawling, fighting crawdads.

After the small species I had been catching, these fierce creatures looked huge, although they were really only about six inches long. They were red in color, looking as if they had already been boiled, but they acted very much alive and positively belligerent. We spent most of next morning cleaning the tails, and at the midday dinner that was the custom at my grandparents' house we had a huge meat platter piled high with crawdad tails. I had never seen that many cooked crawdads at one time before. To a boy who had always thought of these dainty morsels as mere luxurious tidbits, this was a thrilling sight.

I wish I could give you a sure-fire method of taking crayfish, but all my foolproof techniques only make a fool of me when I try to demonstrate them in a new area. The Lake Crayfish of coastal Washington were easily taken on ring nets. These were ordinary wire barrel hoops with half-inch fish net laced inside them, and a bridle and lifting string of mason's line. I found the closing box, the double ring, the deep net and other innovations extolled by ingenious amateurs were unnecessary. My little flat nets would consistently take more crayfish than their cumbersome inventions. I have caught five hundred crayfish in an afternoon from a lake that lies wholly within the city limits of Seattle.

In Hawaii, I tried the ring nets in the irrigation reservoirs which were teeming with crayfish, with no success whatever. Later, when the reservoirs were drawn down, I found the crayfish walking around on land in the mud and wet leaves at the edge of the ponds. At these times, one only had to pick them up and drop them into a deep pail.

In Indiana, along the Brandywine, I first reverted to the bacon-rind method of my childhood, then I found that they could be caught by dozens in little traps with funnel entrances which were easy to enter and hard to leave. I made these traps myself of galvanized hardware cloth, and baited them with little fish I caught along the stream. The traps looked something like little lobster pots or old-fashioned rattraps. By leaving them in deep holes along the stream overnight, I found that I could depend on having up to a dozen crayfish in each trap the next morning.

In northern Indiana, and in three different streams in Pennsylvania, I have caught large numbers of crayfish by just wading in the stream and grabbing them with my hands. If you are afraid of the nips they sometimes give with their claws, you can protect yourself by wearing an old pair of heavy leather gloves.

However you catch them, there is a definite technique to cleaning them efficiently. Cover them with boiling water and let it stand about 3 minutes, then drain and cool quickly with cold water. This scalding loosens the shell and kills them quickly. This is really the most humane way to kill crawfish, as they die very quickly; whereas, if one dismembers them, the individual parts will move about for some time. Remove the tail from the carapace by wiggling it gently from side to side. If this is done just right, the meat that is inside the body will come out with the tail. The body can then be discarded, and the tail cracked with the fingers and the meat removed in one piece. Hold the meat, with the dorsal side toward you, and apply pressure along the sides with both thumbs until it splits open and exposes the mid gut or "vein." Remove this, wash the meat under running water, and it is ready to cook.

The cleaned tails can be rolled in crumbs, corn meal or any of the commercial chicken-fry mixes, and fried. However, since crawfish tails are usually in short supply, we can take a hint from the thrifty Japanese and fry them in tempura batter. This makes a wonderful dish and enables one to feed a number of people with a few crayfish. Beat 2 eggs slightly, add ¼ cup of water, then stir in 1 cup of biscuit mix, ½ teaspoon of salt, ½ teaspoon of monosodium glutamate and a little black pepper. Dip the cleaned crawdad tails in this batter, one at a time, and drop them into smoking hot fat and fry to a nice golden brown. Drain on paper towels and serve hot. They puff up wonderfully in cooking, making a little go a long way.

Crayfish, when boiled before shelling, will make the finest of salads and cocktails. For these purposes, drop the live crayfish into boiling salted water; boil for 10 minutes, then cool and clean as described above.

To make a Crayfish Cocktail, line cocktail glasses with crisp lettuce and fill with chilled crayfish tails, sliced crosswise into 3 or 4 pieces per tail. Since I usually find water cress when I go crayfishing, I use it to make this nippy Cocktail Sauce. Into your blender put 1 cup of tomato catsup, the juice of 1 lemon, 1 teaspoon of Worcestershire sauce, 1 teaspoon of salt, a discreet dash of tabasco and 1 cup of chopped fresh water cress. Blend until smooth, then chill. Use about 1 tablespoon of this sauce on each crayfish cocktail.

I seldom use set recipes for salads, but move through their manufacture by instinct and taste, using materials I have on hand. One of these almost unconsciously prepared salads, which we liked was made with 1 cup of sliced crawdad tails, ½ cup of chopped ripe olives, ⅔ cup of diced celery, 1 cup of chopped water cress and about ¼ cup of mayonnaise plus some salt, pepper and a little monosodium glutamate. All this was stirred together, then generous spoonfuls were served on romaine lettuce leaves.

Whether fried or made into cocktails or salads, I still think the crayfish has the finest and most delicate meat of any of the crustaceans, far surpassing lobster, crab or shrimp.

On Eating Frog's Legs

FROG'S LEGS, with a flavor and texture more delicate and delicious than any fried chicken, are one of the finest meats known to man. They are highly appreciated in many countries, and in many sections of our own country. They can be purchased in the markets and finer restaurants of all our larger cities, and always command a good price. Happily this luxury item is also the wild meat that is more often readily available to the camper and forager than almost any other.

How often have I heard vacationers complaining because bullfrogs made such a din about their camp site that they could hardly sleep? Make the bullfrog the object of your hunt, consider him the chief reason for camping there, and his deep-throated "jug-o-rum" will become sweet music that will fairly lull you to sleep as you dream of tomorrow's frog hunts.

Frogs can be hunted with a spear, bow and arrow, sling shot, air rifle or a .22 rifle. They are most easily taken at night with the aid of a light, if your state allows that kind of hunting. Unfortunately mine doesn't. Only a few days ago, I saw a boy about twelve years old on a bicycle, with a homemade bow and a quiver of arrows over his shoulder and at least a dozen frogs tied to his handlebars. I once knew another boy who made all his spending money during the summer by hunting bullfrogs with an ordinary rubber-band slingshot and selling the dressed legs to fancy restaurants. These are boys who know their way around. I feel that they are much better occupied in this pursuit than they would be out "playing war" with their home-made weapons.

Once I stopped my car by a roadside stream, and in ten minutes speared eight large frogs. A good way is to get right into the stream, wearing old clothes or fishing waders, and walk up the middle of it, spearing or shooting frogs on either bank.

A head for a frog spear can be bought at most any sporting goods store. It is a small three- or five-tined fork looking something like the trident carried by Poseidon. Many frog-hunters will disagree with me but I think the best handle for a frog spear is made of a good stout piece of bamboo ten to twelve feet long. Such a rig looks as if it were all handle and no spear, but I have walked along narrow streams spearing frogs on the opposite bank with such a long-handled spear very successfully.

The Leopard Frog (*Rana sphenocephala*) and the Green Frog (*R. clamitans*) are both edible, but they are usually too small to amount to much. It is the giant bullfrog (*R. catesbeiana*) which is sometimes eight inches from nose to vent, that is the real meat animal. The skin slips easily off frogs, so they are handily cleaned and prepared for the pan. I have been asked why one eats only the hind legs and not the whole frog? Such a question would never be asked by a person who has ever dressed a frog. The hind legs are prac-tically the whole animal. There isn't enough meat on any other part to bother about.

Strangely, I only know one way to cook frog's legs, and that is to fry them like drumsticks of chicken. I suspect that the first person ever to try frog's legs cooked them this way, and since that time, everyone has found them so perfectly delicious that no one has been tempted to experiment with other ways of cooking them. You can vary the coating, using bread crumbs, commercial chicken-fry mixes or just plain flour seasoned with salt and pepper. In camp I have cooked them with no coating at all and still found them very good. If a coating is used, dip the frog's leg in the coating, then in a beaten egg and back into the coating again, then pop it into a hot skillet with ¼ inch of cooking oil on the bottom. Just fry until they are nicely browned, then serve.

The next time you are camping and bullfrogs are keeping you awake, don't fret or become angry. Just lie there and plan a menu for next day's dinner that includes plenty of brown, crispy frog's legs. You'll be surprised how much difference it will make in that sound.

Turtles and Terrapins

SNAPPER Soup and Terrapin Stew are usually found only on the menus of the finest and most expensive restaurants, and they are traditionally thought of as food for the most discriminating of gourmets. And yet the raw materials for these delicacies are meats often available to the camper, fisherman and alert forager. Snapping Turtles of several species are found throughout the eastern half of our country and everywhere in the Missouri-Mississippi drainage. One species or another of edible Terrapin is found over the same range. Where I live the Snapper and Red-leg Terrapin are common, and in other areas the Painted Terrapin, Diamond-Back Terrapin, soft-shelled Turtle and several other species will furnish material for the finest of soups and stews.

Both snappers and terrapins are sometimes caught on hooks while one is fishing with angleworms, but this is usually not a dependable way of securing a supply of these creatures. They are found in slow streams, ponds and marshes, and the snapper, especially, is considered a great pest in farm ponds, as they feed on young fish, ducklings and goslings. Nearly any pond owner will gladly give you permission to catch them.

In summer, they are easiest taken by "jug fishing." Fasten a good stout hook to a length of wire leader and fasten the other end of the wire to a good-sized chunk of light wood. Make up a number of these, then some evening about dark bait the hooks with small pieces of raw meat and launch them from the windward side of your snapper hole. Some people leave the hooks out overnight and remove the catch the next morning, but I find it eerie fun to tend snapper hooks from a boat by flashlight. Painting the float in bright colors helps to locate it when a turtle pulls one off into the weeds. This method is called "jug fishing" because glass jugs were once used as floats, but it is now illegal in some states to use a shatterable material.

As cold weather comes on, turtles retreat into the cozy mud around the borders of ponds. In early winter, before the freezeup, these hibernating turtles can often be located and captured by probing in the mud with a light iron bar. One soon learns the difference in the feel of a dormant turtle and a rock or some other object, and, after a few trys, a mistake of this nature is seldom made. When you strike a turtle, leave the bar against him and dig down beside it until you can lift out the turtle. The snapper will not move when the water is 40° or colder and can be picked up with no danger of getting a nip from his beak. Using this method I have enjoyed fresh Snapper Soup at Thanksgiving.

Sometimes terrapins are caught by one or the other of the above methods, but I get most of my terrapins by just wading in a stream and picking up the ones I see. I know a dozen streams where one would not be likely to wade a mile without having the opportunity to catch at least a half-dozen terrapins. Unlike snappers, these are not dangerous to pick up, as they tend to retreat into their shells rather than offer battle.

Snapper Soup is steeped in tradition, and every expert chef has his own idea about how it should be made. My own method has been worked out over the years and has cost many turtles their lives. I grasp the live snapper by the tail and hold him over a chopping block. He very conveniently sticks out his neck and I chop his head off with a hatchet, then hang him up by the tail to allow him to bleed thoroughly. When the body stops moving I give the snapper a real bath with Castile soap and a stiff brush. After rinsing the soap off completely under running water, I lay him on his back and cut out the bottom shell. Then I slit the skin back to the tail. I remove sandbags, stomach, intestines, heart and lungs and keep any eggs and the liver. The gall bladder must be carefully removed from the latter. It is a small green bag on the left of the side of the liver.

The turtle is rinsed off again, inside and out. Then he is placed on his back in a kettle and the eggs, liver and lower shell put inside the shell. Cover with 6 cups of water for an average-size snapper, and season with 1 bay leaf, ¼ teaspoon of dried thyme, 2 cloves, a pinch of allspice, the juice and peel of ½ lemon, ½ teaspoon of salt, a little black pepper and just a smidgin of cayenne. Boil until the meat will slip from the bones, then remove the turtle and let it cool until you can handle it. Remove all bones, claws, shell and black skin, chop the turtle meat with the eggs and liver and return to the broth.

In a skillet sauté 2 onions and 2 cloves of garlic in 2 tablespoons of oil until they are just yellow, not brown, then stir in 1 tablespoon of flour. Cook until the flour is slightly browned, then add 1½ cups of tomato juice or strained canned tomatoes. Cook for 10 minutes, stirring constantly, then add to the turtle mixture. Bring the soup to a boil and serve, stirring 1 tablespoon of sherry into each bowl and garnishing the top of each serving with a thin slice of lemon and several thin slices of hard-boiled egg. With this soup serve a tray of saltines, each cracker covered with a very thin slice of red currant jelly.

Terrapins average a bit smaller than snappers, so you will need more of them. Two 6- or 7-inchers will make an excellent Terrapin Stew for four people. Scrub the terrapins with Castile soap and a stiff brush, rinse thoroughly and drop into boiling water alive. Boil for 10 minutes, then put in cold water and scrub all dark skin from the legs and head with a stiff brush. Put the whole terrapins back in a kettle and just cover with salted water. Add 1 bay leaf, 1 chopped onion, 1 sprig of parsley, 1 handful of celery leaves, 1 diced carrot and 2 cloves of garlic. Boil 1 hour, then remove the terrapins and allow them to cool enough to handle. Pull out the claws, turn the terrapins on their backs and remove lower shells. Strain inside juice into a container and save. Discard the heads, tails, entrails, lights, sandbags, heart and all inside white muscles. Save any eggs and the liver but carefully cut away and discard the gall bladder. Remove all bones and shell, chop the meat, liver and eggs, and mix them with the inside juices.

Press the yolks of 5 hard-cooked eggs through a ricer and work them into a paste with 2 tablespoons of butter. Now combine the terrapin meat and juices with 1 cup of the stock in which it was cooked and simmer for 5 minutes. Stir in the yolk-butter mixture and stir and simmer for 5 minutes more. Add 1 cup of scalded cream and ½ cup of sherry, salt to taste and dust discreetly with cayenne. Serve hot, but do not boil after adding the cream.

It's time we stopped considering turtles and terrapins as mere luxuries for wealthy gourmets. The vacationing forager can often procure these creatures with either no equipment or some very easily assembled gear. Snapper Soup and Terrapin Stew are very hearty and satisfying foods, as well as being rare taste treats. Let's start getting our share.

Herbal Medicine from Wild Plants

SAGE WINE

Take four handfuls of red sage, beat it in a stone mortar like green sauce, put it into a quart of red wine and let it stand three or four days close stopped, shaking it twice or thrice, then let it stand and settle, and the next day in the morning take of the sage wine three spoonfuls, and of running water one spoonful, fasting after it one hour or better; use this from Michaelmas to the end of March;—it will cure any aches or humors of the joints, dry rheums, keep off all diseases to the fourth degree; it helps the dead palsy and convulsions in the sinews, sharpens the memory, and from the beginning it will keep the body mild, strengthening nature, till the fullness of your days be finished;—nothing will be changed in your strength except the change of the hair; it will keep your teeth sound that were not corrupted before; it will keep you from the gout, the dropsy or any swelling of the joints or body... and on and on and on.

from
THE FRUGAL HOUSEWIFE
OR
Complete Woman Cook
wherein
the Art of dressing all Sorts of VIANDS, with
Cleanliness, Decency and Elegance is explained
by
Susannah Carter
of
Clerkenwell, London
1796
272

The above recipe is typical of those found in old books on herb medicines and home remedies. No, not quite typical, for most of them would claim that their pet remedy would also stop falling hair and prevent its turning gray. Marvelous curative and preventive powers were ascribed to the simplest home remedies. These virtues were always stated positively and emphatically, as though there were no doubts or exceptions. One suspects that this was done to increase the patient's faith in the medicine, and one also suspects that this faith played no small part in the cures effected by these simple remedies.

If you would like to try this ancient miracle drug, you might be interested to know that the "red sage," which is the chief ingredient, is only a variety of the common Garden Sage (*Salvia officinalis*) which has escaped from cultivation and abundantly naturalized itself in many places in the United States. I can see a patch of this wild sage from my study window as I write. The Latin name of this plant shows how highly it was regarded in former times as a medicinal herb. *Salvia* is derived from the Latin verb, "to save"—an allusion to its reputed healing properties, and *officinalis* means it was on the list of official medicinal herbs. Today we consider this magical plant of the ancients no more than a pleasant cooking herb to flavor meat and fowl. Dried and ground, it is a common item on the spice shelf of your grocer.

The science of healing herbs has a venerable history. All primitive peoples seem to have specific remedies for all their ills compounded of wild plants growing about them, and we may surmise that our own ancestors, all the way back to the cave-dwelling days, also had their simples and compounds. The early Greeks compiled lists of curative herbs and wrote books on herbal medicine before the time of Christ.

The preservation of some of these books is a romance in itself. Shortly after the time of Alexander the Great, Greek schools were founded in Syria. From these centers, Greek knowledge, including the teachings on medicinal herbs, was handed on into Persia and Arabia. Copies of Arabic translations of these Greek works traveled with the Moslems as they made their great conquests hundreds of years later. By way of North Africa and Spain, these Greek works found their way back into Europe, where science had fallen far behind during the Dark Ages. During the Renaissance these Arabic books were translated into Latin, and some of them were even re-translated into Greek, and in these forms they found their way into Western Europe. Some of these ancient, hand-copied manuscripts are to be found in the libraries of the monasteries of Mount Athos, where the monks still use them in preparing their home remedies, even to this day.

We must not despise these ancient tomes just because in them the science of herbal medicine seems badly entangled with superstition, witchcraft and magic; this was the condition of all sciences at the time they were written. We sometimes forget that astronomy sprang from the fortune-telling astrologers of early times and that chemistry originated among ancient alchemists trying to transmute base metals into gold. Not one, but two great modern sciences, botany and medicine, had their beginnings among the humble herb gatherers of long ago.

When these ancient Greek texts had completed their circuitous route and returned to Europe, they helped to revive interest in herbal medicine, and a number of new "herbals" were written. The invention of printing, in the fifteenth century, spread copies of these books over the land and stimulated much new research in this field. However, the science was still burdened with many erroneous theories and superstitions that slowed its advance for generations.

One of the most widespread, and, from our point of view, quaintest of these erroneous beliefs has come to be known as the "doctrine of signatures." According to this discipline, any medicinal herb would bear on itself a visible sign to indicate its use. Heart-shaped leaves or flowers indicated that the plant would cure heart diseases; kidney-shaped seeds must be the signature of a plant to cure kidney ailments, and so on through the list of organs. The walnut furnishes a perfect example of this kind of signature. Both in shape and construction it resembles a miniature human head. The kernel resembles the human brain and was given for mental illness, the shell resembles the skull and was thought to cure skull injuries and deformities, while the husk was used for any scalp ailment from dandruff to graying hair. Strangely enough, walnut hulls will correct gray hair, working in much the same manner as the widely used modern "cures" for this condition. Walnut hulls contain a strong brown dye of great fastness, and, if a poultice of damp walnut hulls are left on the hair overnight, there will not be a single gray hair left.

When the herb doctors could see no resemblance between a plant and a body organ, they looked for other signs. A plant might re-semble the disease it was supposed to cure; thus a yellow plant was used for jaundice, a bloated one for dropsy and one with a rough, scaly bark for dermatitis. Again, a plant might resemble the cure, and then one would use a limber plant for stiffness of the joints, one with a bright red flower for paleness or anemia and a strong robust one for weakness. Still another kind of signature pointed to the cause of the trouble, that is, a plant which resembled a serpent was used for snake-bite and one shaped like a scorpion was used for scorpion sting.

When the doctrine of signatures was combined with astrology, the confusion was compounded. Astrological botany was another of the ancient beliefs that slowed the advance of medicine. By a com-plicated and almost incomprehensible system, each plant was assigned to a certain star, luminary, planet or sign of the zodiac. By an equally confusing system, each organ and part of the body was also assigned to a heavenly body. By an ingenious method of combining these two "facts," the herb doctor was reputed to be able to figure out which herb would cure each disease.

Let us not be too hard on these ancient practitioners of the heal-ing arts. If we still had only their knowledge and beliefs about the origin and nature of the cosmos, I doubt that we would do much better. Everyone without exception at that time accepted the belief that all species of plants were created simultaneously on the third day of time, and that these plants were expressly made for the use of man, for had not the Creator said, "Behold, I have given you every plant yielding seed which is upon the face of the earth." The ancients reasoned that a benevolent Maker, when creating herbs for the use of man, would surely include some sign to indicate their utility. When viewed in their light, this seems a very reasonable assump-tion. The only real difficulty with these theories was that they simply didn't work.

While these pseudoscientific theories were at the height of their influence, America was first being explored and trade with the Far East was being reopened, bringing Europe in contact with the herbal medicines of other cultures. Many of the new medicines that began pouring into Europe were widely acclaimed and eagerly purchased at outrageous prices. Especially was the American Indian thought to be wise in herbal lore. We may think it strange that a civilized people in a conservative age would so unhesitatingly accept the medical science of savages, but it wasn't as silly as it sounds at this distance. European medicine, because of reasons outlined above, was in a very bad way, and it was probably true that these Amerindian medicines were actually better than anything that was being compounded by European practitioners.

Of course, Indian medicine wasn't entirely free from superstition and magic, but, compared to European medicine of that day, it looks almost like a pure empirical science. The Indian medicine man, when seeking a certain kind of herb, would not take the first specimen he found, but would bury a little tobacco at the base of the plant, sit and meditate for a while, then go on in perfect confidence that he would soon find an ample supply of the plant he was seeking. This sounds like a very dignified procedure, compared to the superstitions and pseudo science that surrounded herb gathering in Europe at that time.

The exaggerated respect accorded Indian medicine died very slowly. The early settlers in this country wheedled, tricked and traded the Indians out of their herbal secrets, and every household made its own medicines. Many of these remedies, compounded by pioneer housewives with loving care, to administer to their own family's ills, probably had real merit. It was not these home remedies, nor was it the advancement of science, that finally brought Indian medicine into disrepute.

It was the actions of certain unscrupulous charlatans, out to make a fast buck, that almost gave Indian medicine a death blow. These quacks, observing how people respected Indian medicine, began touring the country in medicine shows, selling Chief Rain-in-the-Pants Kidney Cure, or Squaw Spit-in-the-Brew's Magic Elixir. The only connection these worthless and sometimes harmful drugs had to real Indian medicine was in the names dreamed up by the peddlers for their products.

Inevitably, there was a reaction. Laws were passed and regulations enforced which drove these free-lance operators from the field and their products from the market. Eliminating quacks with fake cures was a good thing, but, in an overreaction to them, doctors tended to label all herbal and folk medicine as superstition and quackery. The profession, in effect, closed the medical canon to any further contributions from this source for several decades. During this time, any researcher who dared to investigate the claims of a folk cure was risking the ridicule of his colleagues. There is no doubt that this thoroughly unscientific attitude of the scientists held up the advance of medicine for many years.

Then came the discovery of penicillin, with its plain demonstration that the folk remedy of applying bread mold to wounds to prevent infection was not a silly superstition, but actually in advance of scientific medicine. The quick unfolding of the whole science of antibiotics followed.

It was directly from the folk medicine of India that modern medicine learned to use reserpine, extracted from the Rauwolfia plant. This was the first of the modern tranquilizing drugs and its use has led to the discovery of a whole series of drugs that are widely used, and often misused, today.

One could recount the story of cortisone and its debt to African herbal lore, or of curare, the contribution of South American Indian tribes, which is presently helping to relieve and restore the victims of paralysis, but the above examples are enough to show that the canon of scientific medicine is again open to contributions from herbal and folk medicine.

There are even signs that sections of the general public are swinging too far in the other direction. Books on folk medicine, home remedies and herbal lore are enjoying unprecedented sales. The "natural" remedies as opposed to the "chemical" (that naughty word!) drugs are being extolled. The modern herb doctor seems to be on the verge of another heyday.

I sometimes hear people who should know better saying that we would be healthier if we depended solely on herbal remedies and refused to take the synthetic drugs purveyed by modern scientific medicine. Nonsense! A large part of modern medicine *is* herbal medicine. Browse through a pharmacopoeia and see how many of the medicines prescribed by doctors and sold by druggists are prepared from plants. Quinine for malaria, ephedrine for asthma, cascara for constipation, digitalis for heart conditions, atropine for eye examinations and a great host of other valuable medicines in constant use came directly from folk herbal medicines, and are still prepared from wild plants or those recently brought under cultivation. Many more of the preparations now synthesized in chemical plants were originally discovered as herbal products.

If accepting herbal medicine means rejecting the discoveries of modern medicine, then, "No, thank you." For one thing, modern medicine already has most of the efficacious herbal remedies safely in its own kit and is rapidly acquiring more.

I consider the attempt to divide medicine into natural and chemical cures a very confusing and artificial separation. The drugs that are produced "naturally" by wild plants are just as "chemical" as anything that ever came out of a laboratory. A plant is a veritable chemical factory, synthesizing wonderfully complex and sometimes useful molecules from simple raw materials. Man, by observing nature, has sometimes succeeded in synthesizing these same molecules. If the processor sometimes leaves behind harmful residues of his refining agents, or refines away some of the beneficial agents in the plant, these are imperfections in the science which we must work to correct. Meanwhile, let's not throw out the baby with the bath by demanding that the chemist cease tampering with drugs altogether.

On the other hand, the doctor who sneers at all herbal remedies without testing them is merely displaying his ignorance. True, most of these home remedies haven't been subjected to scientific tests to determine their value, but there is often a great deal of empirical, clinical evidence that they do have some worth. Let the doctor remember the vast contributions this kind of medicine has already made to his science, and that the lists are not closed. There is every reason to believe that the science of securing pharmaceuticals from wild plants is still in its infancy. Botanists have named and described more than a quarter of a million wild plants throughout the world. Only a tiny fraction of these have ever been investigated to determine what contributions they could make to the welfare of the human race. When we consider the amount of medical history that has been made by the few wild plants that have been thoroughly explored, we surmise that untold medical wealth awaits the researcher out among the herbs.

Most of us, however, are not research scientists or doctors. We only want to know if there are wild herbs which we can take for our ills right now. My answer to this is an emphatic yes. I take wild herbs almost every day of the year, and I believe my health is greatly benefited thereby. I usually don't think of these herbs as medicine, but rather as food. Unlike medicine, the preparation of food is still largely in the hands of laymen, with only occasional advice from the doctor, dietician and nutritional expert. I daresay the food we eat has far more to do with our health than does the medicine we take.

This whole book could have been written as a treatise on herbal medicine, for nearly all of the plants which appear in these pages have been included in one or another of the many lists of medicinal herbs. But since we tend to associate medicine with sickness and food with health, I would rather emphasize the food value of wild plants than their curative properties.

It is in the field of nutrition that the wild herbs show greatest promise. While it is true that comparatively few of the wild food plants have been tested for nutritional properties, the results from those tests seem to indicate that there are real treasures of vitamins and minerals among the wildings. This is not surprising, for we should expect that plants growing under natural conditions, neither forced nor sprayed, eaten fresh from the fields with a minimum of processing, would be rich in nutriments. It is the vitamin and mineral content of wild herbs that give them their greatest curative powers, and these are better taken as food than as medicine. This does not deny that there are times when the body needs certain drugs to restore it to normal activity, but even these can often be taken in the same way. When I eat a large helping of greens to relieve constipation, drink a glass of blackberry juice to correct diarrhea or the water from boiled asparagus as a diuretic, it is their drug content I seek, as well as the fortifying vitamins and minerals they contain. I would much rather ingest these drugs in wholesome and palatable food and drink than take a pill.

I also prepare and take a few herbal medicines for minor ills and pains. I don't feel this practice in any way replaces the services of my doctor. He doesn't want me running to him with every twinge of discomfort, even if I could afford it. Home remedies for minor ills still have their place, and it is here that a knowledge of wild medicinal herbs will prove valuable.

The high cost of drugs and medical care might tempt some to use more wild herbal medicines that would be wise. Don't be fooled into believing that all herbal medicines are mild and gentle in their action. Nature provides a fairly complete drugstore for the thoroughly initiated, but some of her remedies are as powerful and drastic as anything on the druggist's shelves. Those who would practice the art of herbal healing on themselves or on their families are warned to proceed with extreme caution.

Besides the notes on the medicinal values of the plants that appear in the food section of this book, I am offering a very brief list of medicinal herbs with recipes for their use. These are in no way intended to replace needed medical care. Since this book is intended primarily to introduce the reader to the wild *foods* provided by nature, the medical section must be kept short. Perhaps these few simple recipes will give you a glimpse of the possibilities in herbal medicine and arouse your interest in the useful plants that are growing all around us.

COUGH SYRUP

An effective cough remedy is made from 1 cup of the blossoms of red clover (*Trifolium pratense*), 1 cup of finely cut sprigs of new growth of white pine (*Pinus strobus*), 1 cup of finely chopped fresh leaves of mullein (*Verbascum thapsus*) and ½ cup of finely chopped inner bark from any of the wild cherries. Place all four ingredients together in a saucepan and cover with 1 quart of water. Simmer gently for 20 minutes, then strain out the herbs and add 1 pint of honey to the juice. Bring this juice to a second boil, then pour into sterilized bottles and cap tightly. Take 1 teaspoonful at a time whenever needed for cough.

The recognition features of the wild cherries will be found in the food section. Use a carpenter's scraper or a knife blade held perpendicular to the surface to remove the outer bark. When a section of the live, inner bark is exposed, shave off as much as you need. The bark from a medium-sized limb is better than that from an old trunk or a small twig.

Mullein (*Verbascum thapsus*) is a common roadside plant producing, early in the season, large rosettes of heavy, silvery leaves that feel like velvet. Later it produces a large flower stalk that may reach four or five feet in height, bearing its yellow flowers in a long, dense, cylindrical spike. It is also known as Velvet Dock, Aaron's Rod, Adam's Flannel, Blanket Leaf, Candle Plant, Feltwort, Flannelleaf and Wild Tobacco.

White pine is probably the tallest of our eastern conifers, sometimes reaching 160 feet in height. It can be distinguished from similar evergreens by having soft, long needles, growing five in a cluster, and by the slender, cylindrical pine cones, four to eight inches long which you will find under the tree.

Red clover is the commonest of clovers, growing everywhere in fields, meadows and vacant lots. It can be recognized by its egg-shaped purplish-red head of bloom.

All the ingredients of this cough sirup can be collected in June or July; this time has nothing to do with astrology, but is rather the time when the plants are all in the right stage of growth.

AN EVEN SIMPLER COUGH MEDICINE

Common Horehound (*Marrubium vulgare*) is a member of the mint family that has escaped from cultivation and established itself in many parts of the country. It is a low herb, growing in dense clusters, with whitish wooly leaves having wrinkled surfaces and rounded teeth about the edges. As in all mints, it has opposite leaves and a square stem. The bitter-aromatic flavor and the cough-drop odor are unmistakable.

To make your own cough drops, simmer 1 cup of the leaves in 1 pint of water for 10 minutes. Strain out the leaves and add 2 cups of sugar to the juice. Boil until it will spin a thread when dropped from a spoon, or until it will form a hard ball when dropped into a glass of cold water. Pour onto a buttered cookie sheet and cut into cough-drop sizes before it hardens.

I know a man who keeps a hive of bees in the middle of a patch of wild horehound. When the horehound starts blooming, he removes all accumulated honey from the supers where bees store surplus honey; then, when the plants have finished blooming, he takes out the honey that has been made from the horehound blossoms. The taste and smell of horehound is quite noticeable in this honey. When any of his family has a cough, he gives them a tablespoon of this natural cough sirip at bedtime. He claims this not only prevents coughing during the night, but also acts as a harmless and effective sedative that enables the sufferer to sleep easily through the night. Sounds reasonable and sounds good, I wonder why more people don't try it.

WILD GINGER: MEDICINE, CANDY AND SPICE

In northeastern United States and adjacent Canada the Wild Ginger is a common wild flower that grows freely in rich woods in early spring. It is a beautiful little plant with two large heart-shaped leaves rising from the base, deep green above and light below, soft, woolly and handsomely veined. Between these two leaves is the small, dull red flower on a short stem that barely raises it from the ground. The long horizontal root is almost on the surface, which makes it easy to collect. This little flower is not related to the plant which produces the ginger of commerce, but the root has a similar taste and odor. The early settlers used to dry the root and grate it, as a substitute for the commercial product. This can still be done, if you would like to forage your spices.

WILD GINGER

Medicinally this herb is used for flatulency. Scrub the roots thoroughly and cut in short pieces crosswise. Keep barely covered with water and simmer until tender; this will take at least an hour. For each cup of ginger root add 1 cup of sugar. Boil another 30 minutes, then drain. Both the leftover sirup and the candied root are effective medicines. Bottle the sirup and cap tightly. Let the candied root dry for a day or two, then roll in granulated sugar and store in tight jars. This makes a delicious, pungent nibble, much like the candied ginger of commerce.

When you are serving fresh fruit, beans or other foods which tend to form gas, nibble a few pieces of candied wild ginger at the end of the meal and the trouble will be eliminated. Or you can stir 1 tablespoon of the sirup in a glass of water and drink that and it will be just as effective.

POISON IVY
(Rhus toxicodendron)

This most common of American poisonous plants grows sometimes as a vine and sometimes as a shrub. In some sections the leaflets assume a softer, oaklike appearance and the plant is known as Poison Oak, though this is only a variant of the same species as our familiar nemesis. Poisin Ivy would actually be a beautiful plant if we could only look at it with an unprejudiced eye. It is easily recognized by having three beautiful, glossy, dark green leaflets on a single stem. These same leaves color up with many shades of red as autumn approaches.

A bad case of ivy poisoning is not to be taken lightly. I have known of several cases that had to be treated in a hospital. Poison ivy does not affect everyone equally. Some people are only affected at the spots where they contacted the plant, while others need only touch it, or even walk by it, to break out all over their bodies. A few seem to be completely immune to ivy poisoning, but this natural immunity is not to be trusted, for it may expire at any moment.

Prophylactic measures and cures for ivy poisoning are legion. There is probably no other disorder, except the common cold, on which you can get so much free advice. Most commonly people are warned to stay completely out of the woods where poison ivy grows, but this I refuse to do. I long ago lost a bay horse, a hound and a turtle dove out there, and must be about the business of seeking them. To me, a life without going into the woods would be a very poor life indeed.

Fortunately, I was never so badly affected by poison ivy as some, although I used to get touches of it several times each summer. When I knew I had touched it, I could usually prevent an outbreak by washing the exposed part in gasoline or even with hot water and soap. Then I discovered Jewelweed.

Jewelweed *(Impatiens biflora)* is an interesting plant of very tender and succulent growth standing three to four feet high and often growing in extensive patches in damp woods. Orange-colored juice will exude from a broken stem. It has unwettable leaves, that is, rain will stand in drops or run off the leaves but they will never get well all over, as with most plants. Jewelweed is also known as Touch-Me-Not or Snapweed. These common names refer to the unusual seed pods which are shaped like a slipper and which, when they are ripe, burst at the slightest touch with an audible snap, curling back and throwing the seeds for some distance.

Jewelweed grows in the same kind of habitat as poison ivy, and the two plants are often found growing close together. This is either a fortunate coincidence or a handy arrangement by Providence, for many outdoor people believe that if they have accidentally touched poison ivy, they only need to rub the exposed spot thoroughly with a handful of juicy jewelweed and poisoning will not develop. This seems to work well with many people. Perhaps it is due to the mechanical washing away of the poison with the copious juice, or there may be an actual antidote for poison ivy in this interesting plant.

When I was in the Pacific Northwest I heard stories of how the lumberjacks acquired immunity to ivy poisoning by eating young poison ivy leaves in the spring. That is the land of Paul Bunyan, and many of the stories of the loggers are best taken with a very large grain of salt. However, I found this rumor very persistent and widespread. I found a report that the eastern Indians had followed the same practice. When I came East, I kept hearing of this method of immunization, and finally I met a man who practiced it.

This man not only ate poison ivy himself, but he gave it to his wife and five children each spring. None of them appeared to have suffered any ill effect and all of them claimed to be untroubled by poison ivy, although a great deal of this dread vine grew near their house and they were exposed almost daily. He told me his dosage, and, since I am a rash experimenter, I tried it. It seems one must start on this course when the first tiny leaflets appear in the spring. Three of these first, tiny, newly opened leaflets are simply pulled off, chewed and swallowed. The next day one takes three more and continues this daily dose for three weeks. Of course, the leaves are growing all this time, so the dosage is actually increasing. By the third week, according to this discipline, one should be able to eat three full-sized leaflets without suffering any harm.

Does it work? Well, it seems to work perfectly on me, so far. I have religiously followed this rite for the last two years, and I haven't once been bothered by ivy poisoning. I have become almost contemptuous of the plant, pulling it from flower beds and off shade trees with my bare hands, with no more precaution than merely washing my hands afterward. However, the effects of poison ivy vary so from person to person that I don't feel this remedy can safely be recommended for general use until further experiments are made.

There are extracts of poison ivy on the market, both in liquid and pill form, with instructions on how to take them. A complete immunization course is rather expensive, but it may be that by following the method I have outlined here, real, rugged foragers can gather their own, and take it in the more unprocessed form.

Another interesting rumor, which I have heard but haven't had the opportunity to verify, is that goats love poison ivy and, if one regularly drinks the milk from a goat that is feeding on poison ivy, one will acquire immunity to the plant. To the highly susceptible this should prove a less risky way than merely eating the leaves, as I do.

SOME DISTILLED MEDICINES

Very often in books on herbal medicines such directions are given as "Reduce to one-fifth by distillation," or "Take one ounce of a distillation of . . . Such directions are all very well for a chemist with a well-equipped laboratory or a hillbilly moonshiner, but most of us don't have a still in our kitchens or even in our cellars.

There is a way, however, to distill small quantities of herbs using only common kitchen equipment. You will require a fairly deep kettle of stainless steel, or one of the flameproof crockeries, with a domed lid. Under no circumstances use iron, aluminum or especially galvanized ware, or you may distill a poisonous product.

Study the diagram on page 286 to see how a still works. The domed lid is inverted over the pot containing the heated herbs and filled with cold water, which is kept cold by constantly dipping out the water as it becomes warm and replacing it with cold. Many of the volatile substances which we are seeking to extract from the herbs vaporize at a lower temperature than water. As these vapors come in contact with the cold lid they condense, run to the center of the dome and drip into the bowl below. The cool drops falling into the distillate keep it cool enough to prevent its revaporization. You can check the bowl occasionally by slightly lifting the lid. The bowl will fill faster than you expect. Here are some of the medicines best prepared as a distillate.

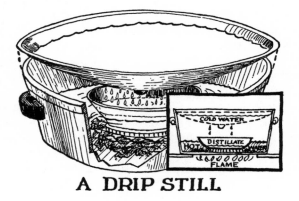

A DRIP STILL

WITCH HAZEL
(*Hamamelis virginica*)

This common American shrub is found growing in rich woods from Maine to Florida and west to the Plains. This is a tall shrub, sometimes reaching ten to twelve feet in height, with oval, wavy-toothed leaves having straight veins. These leaves are somewhat downy when they are young. This plant reverses the usual order of things by blooming in the fall. The flowers are a dull yellow, slightly resembling those of forsythia. Gather the leaves after they are full grown and spread them in a warm place to dry.

Put 4 cups of the dried, crushed leaves and ½ gallon of water into your kettle still and distill off 2 cups of liquid. Don't try to get more, or you will be getting mainly distilled water with very little medicinal value.

To the 2 cups of distillate, add ½ cup of rubbing alcohol. Use as a rub-down for aching backs and sore muscles.

CHICORY FLOWERS
(*Chichorium Intybus*)

This is the same plant so highly praised as a source of spring greens in the food section. The medicinal part comes from the pretty blue flowers, sometimes called Ragged Sailors. Put 1 quart measure of the fresh flowers and 1 quart of water in your kettle still and condense 1 cup of liquid. To this cup of chicory distillation, add ½ teaspoon of boric acid and bottle it tightly. For sore and inflamed eyes, lie down and place pads of absorbent cotton squeezed in this solution over the eyes for half an hour.

DISTILLED TEAS

Another use of the kettle still described above is in making certain wildwood teas. The flavoring and medicinal substances in plants, such as spicebush, wintergreen, sweet birch, spearmint, peppermint, sweet goldenrod and a number of others, are so volatile that they largely escape into the air when tea is made by merely infusing them in boiling water. When using your homemade still for this purpose, the brick and bowl are removed and the distillation is allowed to drip back into the infusion which is kept at a temperature just below the boiling point.

Some of these teas have real medicinal value, but, since they are mainly esteemed as flavorful, fragrant and bracing beverages, I will not implant a prejudice against them by labeling them as medicines. You will find directions for making these agreeable brews under the various plant names.

STRONGER "TEA"

An unscrupulous person *could* also use the kettle still to make small quantities of brandy by distilling one or another of the wild fruit wines described in these pages, but don't tell anyone I told you. In fact, this device first came to my attention when the cook was fired in a logging camp where I was staying, for making a foul-tasting but potent liquor in such a jury-rigged still, and selling it to the hard-drinking lumberjacks. Let that man's fall dissuade you from any illicit use of this handy apparatus.

The field of herbal medicine is so huge and complex that we cannot hope to give it even a cursory survey in a book of this nature.

If we consider only the herbal medicine of the American Indians we find that they had, according to one authority,* "eighty-eight plants to use against colds, one hundred and thirteen plants to reduce fever, one hundred and one plants with which to treat wounds, forty-one plants to calm the nerves, sixty-eight plants to act as laxatives, and over a hundred from which to pick remedies for stomach-ache."

To this imposing list we must add hundreds of plants that have been brought in, often unintentionally, by the immigrants who have flocked to this country from all parts of the world, if we are to gain any idea of the present extent of nature's materia medica in America's fields and forests.

After giving such a tiny sample of herbal medicine we must now leave this alluring subject, but some day, I hope to return to it and do it more justice. The research in this field is fascinating. One moment one is reading the work of some medieval monk in quaint and obscure language, and the next moment one is trying to understand the equally obscure jargon of a current technical journal, delving into the latest scientific paper that throws light on this very old subject.

If a research team could be formed, consisting at a minimum of a medical doctor, a chemist, a pharmacist, an herbalist and a botanist, I feel sure they could make many valuable discoveries in this area, and I'm certain that the members of the research team would have a perfectly fascinating experience.

For the amateur, there are other thrills in this field. One of the greatest of these comes when, after long reading and study about an unfamiliar plant, you go out in the fields and byways and actually find it growing in its native habitat. When I first glimpse a long-sought plant, I sometimes seem to enter into the herb and feel its virtues and uses. I am one with its long history of healing man's ills and ministering to his comfort. And when I carry the plant home and transmute it into some grateful remedy it has a soul-healing power far beyond anything it might do for my body, and it brings a satisfaction no purchased product could ever provide.

* From *Plants That Heal* by Millicent E. Selsam. Copyright © 1959 by Millicent E. Selsam. Courtesy of William Morrow and Company, Inc.

The Proof of
the Pudding

I HAVE a friend, Steve, who, together with his wife, shares the hobby of wild food gathering with my wife and me. The four of us usually arrange to take our vacations together, and we have foraged wild food from Pennsylvania to Hawaii. We have enjoyed many delicious meals prepared partly or mostly from wild food, and had played around with the idea of sometime spending a week or so living entirely off the country.

The opportunity to make this experiment came when a mutual friend offered the four of us the use of his cabin in central Pennsylvania for one week in early July. The cabin's owner was very dubious about our plans, for he felt sure that little or nothing that was edible grew wild in that neighborhood. His pessimism bothered me very little, for I have become accustomed to being assured by local residents that absolutely nothing edible grows in their locality, even when all about literally tons of wild food are growing on every acre. This shows how far even our country people have departed from the ancient wisdom of their food-gathering ancestors.

I was a little concerned, however, with the season and our unfamiliarity with the area. Early July has always seemed to me an in-between period, when the early spring foods were finished and the summer and fall things still immature. It has been my experience that the food-furnishing potentialities of an area gradually unfold only as one explores it thoroughly, and that successful foraging depends on intimate knowledge of the locality. However, there were grocery stores in the neighborhood where food could be purchased if the experiment failed, so nothing was to be lost by making the attempt.

As we planned to arrive at the cabin after nightfall, we took along enough food for breakfast and lunch the next day; after that we would be on our own. We had a pound of margarine, a loaf of bread, a half-pound of bacon, a dozen eggs and a small package of lunch meat. In the cabin we found a few pounds of flour, a jug of cooking oil, a big canister of sugar, a box of salt and a few spices and condiments. There was also a nearly empty jar of instant coffee, which we rinsed out the next morning to get four cups of a very feeble brew. We limited ourselves to an egg apiece for breakfast, for I had remembered how many recipes for preparing wild foods require eggs.

We made sandwiches of the lunch meat and the remainder of the bread and set off on our foraging endeavors. So we could search in more places, Steve and his wife went one direction, while my wife and I went another. Each party carried a knife, a folding shovel, two pails and a pocketful of plastic bags.

At first, my worst fears seemed confirmed. As we made our way down a little valley, I noticed that the various wild mustards and the dandelion, chicory, docks and sorrels were all too old and tough to eat. The open woods through which we walked was made up mainly of huge hickory and black walnut trees, and many of them were heavy with developing immature nuts, promising an abundance for next autumn but offering nothing we could eat now. Near the little stream grew whole thickets of hazelnuts, the leafy whorls which would later be nuts just showing on them. Over these thickets clambered the vines of the fox grape, covered with clusters of tiny green grapes. A persimmon tree was covered with hard, green and totally inedible fruit.

Then we came to where a dim unused road crossed the stream into an abandoned field. Along the old road grew thickets of sassafras. We dug a bundle of the roots, thinking that if we could not eat from the wild, we could at least drink sassafras tea. At the edge of the old field we found wild apples growing. They were green and hard, with the seeds barely developed, but it would be possible to make applesauce from them, and we were becoming so anxious to gather something edible that I climbed the tree and filled a plastic bag. While I was up in the tree, I saw a patch of orange-colored bloom across the field. We walked that way and came on a great cluster of day lilies. This was more like it! We filled a bag with unopened buds and another with the shriveled corollas of yesterday's blooms. The little entrenching shovel was again brought into action and we collected a quantity of the yellow tubers found under the day lily, carefully separating out the new, white sprouts and the interiors of the immature stalks to serve as a salad. Picking the tubers and salad stuffs was tedious work, so we stayed at the day-lily bed for more than an hour, then took our loot to the stream to wash and clean it further.

While I was bending over the stream washing the day-lily tubers, my wife asked if the berries hanging directly over my head were edible. I looked up and there within reach of my hand was a shadbush, or Juneberry, growing from the rocky stream bank with branches loaded with ripe fruit. Now that our eyes had been opened, we saw others and began filling a pail with this excellent fruit. We picked several quarts before exhausting the supply in the immediate neighborhood.

I was beginning to feel more secure. At least we would have fruit, vegetables and salad for dinner and I had often dined on poorer fare. We found water cress growing in the stream and wild garlic growing at the edge of the old field. These we used as relish for our sandwiches and also added some of each to the salad bag. After lunch we walked around the old field and found that the abundant milkweed that grew there was just beginning to bloom. We gathered a bag of the unopened buds to cook as another green vegetable. My worry about finding enough to eat was being replaced by a fear that we would be unable to do justice to the bounteous fare that nature was providing.

My wife was beginning to complain about being loaded down like an Indian squaw, so we headed toward the cabin. On the way we stopped at a couple of blooming elder bushes and collected a bag of elder blow with next morning's breakfast in mind. We also took a few heads of top bulbs from the wild onions that grew by the roadside to add the final touch to our salad.

On arriving back at the cabin we found that the other couple had returned before us, bearing an even greater load of edibles. They had found a marsh full of cattails and had exploited that plant as thoroughly as we had the day lilies. They had peeled immature stalks to get a bag of "Cossack asparagus" and had gathered a large supply of cattail bloom spikes. They had even dug a bundle of roots from which we were supposed to wash out flour, and gathered a bag of yellow cattail pollen so we could have Sunshine Flapjacks for breakfast.

Then they had walked to a dry hillside which some farmer had planted to evergreens for Christmas trees and had found, between the young conifers, an abundance of ripe dewberries of huge size. They had spent the remainder of the morning gathering a ten-quart pail full of these. Then, on their way home, they had discovered a mazzard cherry tree loaded with ripe fruit and had filled their other pail with sweet cherries.

From the dewberry hill they had seen, in the distance, a large pond or small lake, where they thought we might catch some fish. While our wives dealt with the huge mass of vegetable foods we had collected, Steve and I drove down to investigate this possibility. We found it was an artificial lake covering about twenty acres and belonging to a boat club. We asked the caretaker if we could fish and he said, "You can if you want to, but you won't catch nothin' but bluegills."

Bluegills suited us fine, so after going to a nearby calamus marsh and digging some mudworms for bait, we rigged our rods for bluegill fishing (see Chap. X). Mudworms certainly pleased those bluegills and we soon saw that this lake could furnish all the fish we could eat for the week we would be here, if we didn't tire of bluegills. In almost less time than it takes to tell it, we had landed sixteen little fish, all of a size, between six and one-half and seven inches long. I insisted we catch no more, for I had been elected to clean them.

Even here we added to our vegetable food. Where a little stream emptied into the lake there was a large bed of water cress, rising eight inches above the level of the water. A few handfuls of this filled a pail. Along the embankment that formed the side of the lake we dug a dozen or more large roots of dandelion to make some "Coffee." Down in the marsh where we had dug our bait, we collected a bag of the tender bases of calamus stalks to make ourselves some candy.

It was sundown before we got back to the cabin and almost nine o'clock before we had our first foraged meal prepared, but what a meal it was. There was a huge platter of battered and fried bluegill fillets, flanked by five different wild vegetables and a tremendous tossed salad, all washed down with cups of sassafras tea and held down by the bowls of cherries, Juneberries and dewberries which we ate for dessert.

After dinner, while Steve roasted the dandelion roots, I made a batch of jelly, using ripe dewberries and green apples. We all agreed that we had been a bit too greedy in our gathering that first day, and decided to take it a bit easier in the future. We very well could, for we had gathered far too much of everything and the cabin was still fairly bulging with unused food.

Next morning we had Elderberry Blow Fritters filled with jelly, and Dandelion Coffee for breakfast, finishing off with more bowls of Juneberries and cherries. Our wives were still a bit knocked-out from the previous day's labor, so Steve and I set out without them.

Since obtaining a sufficient quantity of food was obviously going to be no problem, we decided to concentrate on seeing how fine a quality of food we could dig up for the rest of the week. All of us were very fond of frog's legs and the season on these amphibians had opened only a few days before, so Steve and I prepared to seek this delicacy. We dressed in old sneakers and dungarees and started wading up the middle of a stream. Steve was armed with a slingshot with which he was deadly, and I had a .22 rifle. It took us an hour to wade a mile upstream, but by that time we had eight big bullfrogs.

At this point the stream widened out and became shallow for several hundred yards. As we were crossing this shallow part, I noticed that the bottom was fairly crawling with good-sized crayfish. We quickly cached our frogs and weapons, and started after these most delicate of crustaceans with no tackle but our hands and a pail. We captured about two dozen on the first pass, then sat down and waited for the water to clear of the mud we had stirred in passing. On the second time through, we caught almost as many as the first time. It was great fun; the occasional nips we got from the vicious claws of the crawdads only served to heighten the interest by increasing the hazards. In two hours we had about eighty crawdads and our pail was so full that we had to cover it with a plastic bag to keep them from escaping. What with frogs and crayfish, we had secured enough meat of the very finest quality for the next two days.

We took our haul back to the cabin. I skinned the frog's legs for dinner that night, and Steve knocked some holes in a covered, 5-gallon can, dumped the crayfish in it and set it in the stream, so the crustacean would be alive and fresh for next day's dinner.

We lunched on leftovers, vegetables, fish fillets and Elder Blow Fritters, then loafed for an hour or two before setting out again. That afternoon we discovered two more kinds of wild fruit. In the edge of the woods by an old field, we gathered two quarts of black raspberries, and in an old burned-off area at the top of a ridge we found the early dwarf blueberry already ripening its blue-black fruit.

From that afternoon until the end of the week we kept living higher and higher with less and less work, if I can call my favorite recreation "work." Purslane and wild leek were pressed into service to give body and flavor to our already sumptuous salads. Poke, both peeled green stalks cooked like asparagus and tender little seedlings cooked like spinach, were added to our already ample variety of vegetables, as well as the roots and seedstalks of burdock, with lamb's-quarters and amaranth cooked as greens. Using white, newly molted crayfish as bait, we caught some nice bass, where the man had said we would find only bluegills.

One night we had a terrific rainstorm. The next day the streams were swollen and muddy, making ideal conditions for catching catfish. All four of us went to the creek and set our poles and lines. The law allowed three lines per person with three hooks per line, so we soon had thirty-six hooks, baited with mudworms, waiting to snare any passing "cat." Our catch was not spectacular in either quantity or size, but we did land nine catfish altogether, and four of them weighed more than a pound apiece. Besides the fish, we also caught three snapping turtles. These were delicious made into a huge pot of soup, to which we added shriveled day-lily corollas a few minutes before removing from the fire.

We made Cattail Pollen Muffins crowded with plump blueberries, and hot biscuits of the flour we washed from the cattail roots, and ate them with jam made from black raspberries. For beverages, we drank Dandelion Coffee and at least six kinds of wild woodland teas. Calamus candy and various desserts we prepared from wild fruits furnished us with sweets. The only objection to our bill of fare came from Steve's wife, who complained that she had gained five pounds in that one week.

Even after replacing the supplies we had used from the cabin our total food bill for the week came to less than four dollars. Actually, we figured it cost us less than nothing to eat, for we took home enough wild fruit, vegetables, jellies, jams and fresh fish to more than cover the cost of the food we bought. We took home more than foods, too. Each of us took home the memory of one of the most pleasant vacations we had ever spent, even though, unlike most holidays, it had cost us less than if we had stayed at home. All of us will recall that week with pleasure for the rest of our lives. Having to gather our own food gave meaning to our nature walks and sport fishing. It is a source of deep satisfaction to all of us to have proved by actual experience that we can walk into the wilderness and not only live, but live well. Probably none of us will have the occasion to "go native" but it is a satisfying feeling to know that we could if we wanted to. Who needs a South Sea island?

Index

Aaron's Rod, *see* Mullein
Acorn Bread, 13
   Black, Steamed, 13
Acorn Glacé, 12-13
Acorn Griddle Cakes, 13
Acorn Grits, 12, 13
Acorn Meal, 12, 13
Acorn Muffins, 13
Acorns, 10-13
   candied, 12
   roasted, 10, 11, 12
Adam's Flannel, *see* Mullein
Ague Tree, *see* Sassafras
Amaranth, Green, 14-16
Amaranthus Meal, 16
American Linden, *see* Basswood
American Mandrake, *see* May
      Apples
Apple Butter, 18, 19
Apple Jelly, 18, 19
Apple Pie, 18
Apples
   Crab, 19-20, 231
   Wild, 17-18, 231
Arrowhead, 21-24, 231
Arrowleaf, *see* Arrowhead
Artichoke, Jerusalem, 25-27, 231
Artichoke Chiffon Pie, 27
Asparagus, Wild, 28-31

Aspic Salad, 110
Astrological botany, 274
Atropine, 277

Barbe de Capucin, 233, 234
Basswood, 208-9
Basswood Tea, 209
Beer
   Birch, 34
   Maple-Spruce, 124-25
   Persimmon, 168
Beet, Wild, *see* Green Amaranth
Belle Isle Cress, *see* Winter Cress
Berries, *see* names of berries
Birch, Sweet, 32-35
Birch Beer, 34
Birch Sirup, 34-35
Birch Tea, 33-34, 35
Black Birch, *see* Sweet Birch
Black Walnuts, *see* Walnuts
Blackberries, 36-38
Blackberry Cobbler, 37
Blackberry Cordial, 38
Blackberry Jam, 37
Blackberry Jelly, 36-37
Blackberry Juice, 37-38
Blackberry Pie, 37
Blackberry Wine, 38
Blackberry-leaf Tea, 210

Bladder Cherry, *see* Ground Cherries
Blanket Leaf, *see* Mullein
Blue Sailors, *see* Chicory
Blueberries, 39-45
    canned, 44
    dried, 41-42
    frozen, 44
Blueberry Cream Cheese Pie,
    Glazed, 45
Blueberry Fluff Pie, 42
Blueberry Fritters, 43
Blueberry Muffins, 43
Blueberry Pudding, Steamed, 44
Blueberry-Maple-Nut-Loaf, 44-45
Bluegill Fillets, Pickled, 254
Bluegills, 249-55
Bluegills Tempura, 253
Blushing Betty, 67
Bobcat meat, 243-44
Botany, astrological, 275
Brandy, 287
Bread
    Acorn, 13
        Black, Steamed, 13
        Persimmon-Hickory Nut, 166-67
Brownies, Hickory-Nut, 216-17
Burdock, 46-49
Burro meat, 243
Butternut, 213, 215, 231

Calamus, 51-54
Calamus Root, Candied, 52-53
Calamus Tea, 54
Candle Plant, *see* Mullein
Carp, 256-59
Cascara, 277
Catmint, 210
Catnip, 210
Catnip Tea, 210
Cattails, 35, 55-60, 231
Chanterelles, 145-46
Checkerberry, *see* Wintergreen
Cherries
    Bird (Pin), 65
    Brandied, 63
    Rum (Sweet Black), 62-63

Sour, 62
Sweet, 61-62
    Wild, 61-68, 280
Cherry Birch, *see* Sweet Birch
Cherry Bounce, 63
Cherry Jelly, 65-66
    Sour, 62
Cherry Liqueur, 63
Cherry Olives, 61-62
Cherry Pie, 66
Cherry Soup, 66-67
Cherry Wine, 67-68
Chewing Stick, *see* Sassafras
Chicken and Mushroom Soup, 148-49
Chicory, 35, 69-72, 233-34
Chicory Brew, 70, 72
Chicory Flowers, 287
Chinese Lantern Plant, 102
Chokecherry, 63, 65-67
Christmas Pudding, 167-68
Chutney, Elderberry, 92-93
Cinnamonwood, *see* Sassafras
Clam and Mushroom Soup, 149
Clover, 209, 280, 281
Cobbler, Blackberry, 37
Cocktail, Crayfish, 263
Conservation, 6-7
Conserve, Grape, 98
Cookies
    Hickory-Nut Date, 216
    Oatmeal-Hickory-Nut, 216
Cordial, Blackberry, 38
Cortisone, 277
Cough drops, 281
Cough syrup, 280-81
Crab Apples, 19-20, 231
    Spiced Hopa, 19-20
Crabs, fresh-water, *see* Crayfish
Cranberries, Wild, 73-76
Cranberry Glacé, 74
Cranberry and Horseradish Relish, 74-75
Cranberry Pie, 75
Cranberry Sauce, 74
    Jellied, 74
Crawdads, *see* Crayfish

Crawfish, *see* Crayfish
Crayfish, 260-64
Crayfish Cocktail, 263
Curare, 277

Dandelion Crown Salad, 80
Dandelion Greens, 78, 81
Dandelion Wine, 81-82
Dandelions, 35, 77-82, 178, 232
Day Lilies, Wild, 35, 83-86
Dewberries, 36-38
Dewberry Pie, 37
Digitalis, 277
Divinity, Maple Nut, 122-23
Dock, 233
"Doctrine of signatures," 274-75
Duck Potatoes, *see* Arrowhead
Dwarf Cape Gooseberry, *see*
        Ground Cherries

Edible fungi, *see* Mushrooms
Elder Blow, 93
Elder Blow Wine, 94-95
Elderberries, 87-95
    dried, 92
Elderberry Chutney, 92-93
Elderberry Jelly, 88, 90, 91
Elderberry Juice, 92
Elderberry Rob, 92
Ephedrine, 277

Fairy Spuds, *see* Spring Beauties
Feltwort, *see* Mullein
Fish Fritters, 253
Fishing, 249-55
Flannelleaf, *see* Mullein
Fritters
    Blueberry, 43
    Fish, 253
    Mushroom, 148
Frog's Legs, 265-67
Fudge, 214
    Brown Sugar, 214-15
Fungi, edible, *see* Mushrooms

Game, Wild, 242-48
Garden, Wild Winter, 231-34

Garget, *see* Poke
Garlic, Wild, *see* Onions, Wild
Ginger, Wild, 281-83
Glacé
    Acorn, 12-13
    Cranberry, 74
Gobo, *see* Burdock
Goldenrod, 211
Goosefoot, *see* Pigweeds
Graham Cracker Crust, 198
Grape Conserve, 98
Grape Jelly, 97-98
Grape Juice, 98-99
Grape Leaves, 100
Grape Pie, 98
Grape Wine, 99-100
Grapes, Wild, 96-101, 231
Great Burdock, *see* Burdock
Green Amaranth, 14-16
Griddle Cakes
    Acorn, 13
    Cattail Root, 35
    Elder Blow, 94
Grits, Acorn, 12, 13
Ground Cherries, 102-5
Ground Cherry Jam, 104
Ground Cherry Pie, 104-5
Ground Cherry Preserves, 104
Ground Hog, *see* Woodchuck
Ground Holly, *see* Wintergreen
Groundnuts, 106-8

Hazelnuts, 231
Herb Butter, 222
Herbs, *see* Medicinal Herbs; Pot-
    herbs
Hickory Nuts, 213, 215-18, 231
Hickory-Nut Brownies, 216-17
Hickory-Nut Date Cookies, 216
Hickory-Nut Pie, 217
Hog Apple, *see* May Apples
Holly, Ground, *see* Wintergreen
Honey, Wild, 235-41, 281
Honey Vinegar, 241
Honey Wine, 241
Honey-Sassafras Jelly, 192
Hopa Ornamental Crab Apples, 19

Horehound, 281
Huckleberries, 39-40
Huckleberry Pie, 42-43
Husk Tomato, *see* Ground Cherries
Hypomyces Lactifluorum, 145

Indian medicine, 276
Indian Potatoes, *see* Groundnuts
Inkberry, *see* Poke
Iris, Wild, *see* Calamus

Jam
    Blackberry, 37
    Ground Cherry, 104
    Japanese Knotweed, 112
    Strawberry, 198-99
    Wineberry, 185
Japanese Knotweed, 109-13
Japanese Knotweed Jam, 112
Japanese Knotweed Pie, 112-13
Jelly
    Apple, 18, 19
    Blackberry, 36-37
    Cherry, 65
        Sour, 62
    Elderberry, 88, 90, 91
    Grape, 97-98
    Mulberry, 136
    Raspberry, Black, 184
    Sassafras, 192
    Wineberry, 186
Jelly test, 90
Jerusalem Artichoke, 25-27, 231
Jewelweed, 284-85
Juice
    Blackberry, 37-38
    Elderberry, 92
    Grape, 98-99
    May Apple, 129
    Mulberry, 136
Juneberries, 114-16
Juneberry Muffins, 116
Juneberry Pie, 116

Knotweed, Japanese, 109-13

Lamb's-quarters, *see* Pigweeds
Leeks, Wild, 35, 159-60

Lemon, Wild, *see* May Apples
Lilies, Wild Day, 35, 83-86
Lime Tree, *see* Basswood
Linden, American, *see* Basswood
Liqueur
    Blackberry, 38
    Cherry, 63
Lobsters, fresh-water, *see* Crayfish
Locust, 89, 93

Mandrake, *see* May Apples
Mangoes, 5
Maple Nut Divinity, 122-23
Maple Sirup, 117-18, 120, 122, 123
Maple Sugar, 5, 117-18, 122
Maple-Spruce Beer, 24-25
Marmalade, May Apple, 129
Maryland Potted Marsh Rabbit, 247
May Apple Juice, 129
May Apple Marmalade, 129
May Apples, 126-29
Mazzard, *see* Cherries, Wild
Mead, 241
Meadow Garlic, *see* Onions, Wild
Meal
    Acorn, 12, 13
    Amaranthus, 16
Medicinal herbs, 272-88
    Calamus, 53
    May Apples, 126-29
Medicine, Indian, 276
Menus, 8
Milkweeds, 130-33
Molasses, Persimmon, 168
Morels, *see* Mushrooms, Sponge
Muffins
    Acorn, 13
    Blueberry, 43
    Elder Blow, 94
    Juneberry, 116
Mulberries, 134-38
    dried, 137-38
    red, 134-36
    white, 136-38
Mulberry Jelly, 136
Mulberry Juice, 136

Mulberry Pie, 136
Mullein, 280
Mushroom and Chicken Soup, 148-49
Mushroom and Clam Soup, 149
Mushroom Fritters, 148
Mushroom Salad, Raw, 149-50
Mushroom Sauce, 151
Mushroom Shish Kabob, 150
Mushrooms, 139-51
   Beefsteak, 143-44
   books on, 140-41
   en Casserole, 149
   Coral, 142
   Early Inky, 143
   Elm, 142-43
   Fairy Ring, 144
   Inky, 143
   Orange Milk, 144-45
   Oyster, 142-43
   Pasture (Meadow), 146
   Sautéed, 146-47
   Shaggy-Mane, 143
   Sponge, 142
   Stuffed, 150
   Sulphur, 144
   on Toast, 147-48
Muskrat, 245, 247
Mustard
   Prepared, 155
   Wild, 152-56
Mustard Greens, 152, 153-54
Myrtle Sedge, see Calamus

New Jersey Tea, 211
Nuts, see Butternut; Hickory Nuts; Walnuts

Oaks, 10-11
Oatmeal-Hickory-Nut Cookies, 216
Oil Crust, for pie, 112-13
Onion Soup
   Cream of, 158
   French, 159
Onions
   White Pickled, 160
   Wild, 157-60
Opossum, 245-47

Pancakes, see Griddle Cakes
Papaw Pie, 162-63
Papaws, 161-63, 231
Papayas, 5
Pastry: Graham Cracker, 198
   Oil, 112-13
Pear, Swamp Sugar, 114
Pecans, 123, 231
Penicillin, 277
Peppergrass, 178
Peppermint, 209
Persimmon Beer, 168
Persimmon Molasses, 168
Persimmon Tea, 169
Persimmon Vinegar, 168-69
Persimmon-Hickory Nut Bread, 166-67
Persimmon-Nut Chiffon Pie, 167
Persimmons, 164-69, 231
Pickles, Purslane, 180-81
Pie
   Apple, 18
   Artichoke Chiffon, 27
   Blackberry, 37
   Blueberry Cream Cheese, Glazed, 45
   Blueberry Fluff, 42
   Cherry, 66
   Cranberry, 75
   Dewberry, 37
   Elderberry, 92
   Grape, 98
   Ground Cherry, 104-5
   Hickory-Nut, 217
   Huckleberry, 42-43
   Japanese Knotweed, 112-13
   Juneberry, 116
   Mulberry, 136
   Papaw, 162
   Persimmon-Nut Chiffon, 167
   Strawberry, 197-98
   Strawberry Chiffon, 198
Piecrust: Graham Cracker, 198
   Oil pastry, 112-13
Pigeonberry, see Poke
Pigweeds, 170-73
Pine, White, 280

Poha, see Ground Cherries
Poison Ivy, 283-85
Poison Oak, 283
Poke, 174-77, 232
Porcupine, 243, 245
'Possum, *see* Opossum
Potatoes
    Duck, *see* Arrowhead
    Indian, *see* Groundnuts
Potherbs
    Black Mustard, 152
    Green Amaranth, 14
    Pigweed, 172
    Poke, 174-77
Praline Sauce, 123
Pralines, 123
Preserves
    Ground Cherry, 104
    Strawberry, 198, 199
Pudding
    Blueberry, Steamed, 44
    Christmas, 167-68
Puffballs, 141-42
Purslane, 178-82
Purslane Pickles, 180-81

Quinine, 277

Raccoon, 245-47
Raccoon Berry, *see* May Apples
Raccoon Pie, 246-47
Ragged Sailors, *see* Chicory
Raspberries, 183-85
Raspberry Jelly, Black, 184
Raspberry-leaf Tea, 210
Rauwolfia plant, 277
Red Clover, 209, 280, 281
Redroot, *see* Green Amaranth
Relish, Cranberry and Horseradish,
    74-75
Reserpine, 277
Rice, Wild, 5, 223-25
Rough-Weed, *see* Green Amaranth

Sage, 273
Sage Wine, 272-73
Sagittaria Salad, 24

Salad
    Aspic, 110
    Burdock, 49
    Chicory, 69-70
    Dandelion Crown, 80
    Mushroom, Raw, 149-50
    Sagittaria, 24
Sap
    Birch, 32-33, 34, 35
    Maple, 118-20, 123-25
    Sycamore, 118-119
Sassafras, 187-93
Sassafras Jelly, 192
Sassafras Tea, 124, 189-90, 191-92
Sauce
    Cranberry, 74
        Jellied, 74
    Mushroom, 151
    Praline, 123
Scurvy Grass, *see* Winter Cress
Seeds
    Amaranth, 16
    Lamb's-quarters, 172
    Sunflower, 204-7
Serviceberries, 114-15
Shadberries, *see* Juneberries
Shallot, Wild, *see* Onions, Wild
Shish Kabob, Vegetarian, 150
Shortcake, Strawberry, 197
"Signatures, doctrine of," 274-75
Sirup
    Birch, 34-35
    Cough, 280-81
    Maple, 117-18, 120, 122, 123
Snapper Soup, 268, 269-70, 272
Snapweed, *see* Jewelweed
Soup
    Cherry, 66-67
    Chicken and Mushroom, 148-49
    Clam and Mushroom, 149
    Onion
        Cream of, 158
        French, 159
    Snapper, 268, 269-70, 272
    Water Cress, 221
Spearmint, 209
Spicebush, 124

Spicebush Tea, 124
Spinach, Wild, *see* Pigweeds
Spinning outfit, 250-51
Spring Beauties, 201-3
Spring Cress, *see* Winter Cress
Stew, Terrapin, 268, 270-71
Strawberries, Wild, 194-200
Strawberry Chiffon Pie, 198
Strawberry Jam, 198-99
Strawberry Pie, 197-98
Strawberry Preserves, 198, 199
Strawberry Roll-Ups, Wild, 197
Strawberry Shortcake, 197
Strawberry Tomato, *see* Ground
    Cherries
Strawberry-leaf Tea, 210
Succory, *see* Chicory
Sugar, Maple, 5, 117-18, 122
Sumac, 89, 91
Sunflowers, Wild, 204-7
Swamp Sugar Pear, 114
Sweet Birch, 32-35
Sweet Flag, *see* Calamus
Sweet Goldenrod, 211
Sweet Goldenrod Tea, 211
Sweet Grass, *see* Calamus
Sweet Rush, *see* Calamus
Sycamore, 118-19
Syrup, *see* Sirup

Tea
    Basswood, 209
    Berry-leaf, 210
    Birch, 33-34, 35
    Calamus, 54
    Catnip, 210
    Clover-Blossom—Mint, 209-10
    Distilled, 287
    New Jersey, 211
    Persimmon, 169
    Sassafras, 124, 189-90, 191-92
    Spicebush, 124
    Sweet Goldenrod, 211
    Wintergreen, 212
Tea Tree, *see* Sassafras
Teaberry, *see* Wintergreen
Terrapin Stew, 268, 270-71

Terrapins, 268-71
Tobacco, Wild, *see* Mullein
Touch-Me-Not, *see* Jewelweed
Turtles, 268-71

Upland Cress, *see* Winter Cress

Velvet Dock, *see* Mullein
Vinegar
    Honey, 241
    Persimmon, 168-69

Walnuts, 213-15, 231, 274
    Pickled, 215
Wapatoo, *see* Arrowhead
Water Cress, 219-22
Water Cress Soup, 221
White Pine, 280
White Walnuts, *see* Butternut
Whitewood, *see* Basswood
Wild Beet, *see* Green Amaranth
Wild Game, 242-48
Wild Gobo, *see* Burdock
Wild Iris, *see* Calamus
Wild Lemon, *see* May Apples
Wild Rice, 5, 223-25
Wine
    Blackberry, 38
    Cherry, 67-68
    Dandelion, 81-82
    Elder Blow, 94-95
    Grape, 99-100
    Honey, 241
    Sage, 272-73
Wineberries, 185-86
Wineberry Jam, 185
Wineberry Jelly, 186
Winter Cress, 226-30, 234
Winter Garden, Wild, 231-34
Wintergreen, 34, 212
Wintergreen Tea, 212
Wisteria, 93
Witch Hazel, 286
Witloof, 233-34
Woodchuck, 245, 247-48
Woodchuck in Sour Cream, 248

Yellow Rocket, *see* Winter Cress